5th Workshop on Automated Knowledge Base Construction (AKBC 2016)

Held at the 2016 Conference of the North American Chapter of the Association for Computational Linguistics: Human Language Technologies (NAACL HLT 2016)

San Diego, California, USA
17 June 2016

ISBN: 978-1-5108-2517-8

Proceedings of the 5th Workshop on
Automated Knowledge Base Construction (AKBC)

**Proceedings of the 5th Workshop on
Automated Knowledge Base Construction (AKBC)
at the 2016 Conference of the
North American Chapter of the
Association for Computational Linguistics:
Human Language Technologies**

Proceedings of the Workshop

Introduction

Extracting knowledge from Web pages and integrating it into a coherent knowledge base (KB) is a task that spans the areas of natural language processing, information extraction, information integration, databases, search, and machine learning. Recent years have seen significant advances in knowledge base construction, in both academia and industry. Many popular offerings, including digital assistants (Siri, Cortana, and Google Now) as well as search interfaces (Yahoo!, Bing, and Google) leverage semantic understanding and structured knowledge bases to respond to users. A similarly abundant set of knowledge systems have been developed at top universities such as Stanford (DeepDive), Carnegie Mellon (NELL), the University of Washington (OpenIE), the University of Mannheim (DBpedia), and the Max Planck Institut Informatik (YAGO, WebChild) among others. Our workshop serves as a forum for researchers on knowledge base construction in both academia and industry.

Unlike many other workshops, our workshop puts less emphasis on conventional paper submissions and presentations, but focuses on visionary papers and discussions, and structures the program around high-profile keynotes that foster discussion. In addition, one of the workshop's unique characteristics is its nomadic nature; AKBC has co-located with conferences which serve diverse communities, attesting to the broad appeal of the topic. Following the standalone AKBC 2010, AKBC 2012 (HLT-NAACL), AKBC 2013 (CIKM), and AKBC 2014 (NIPS), have each featured a dozen invited talks, drawn 20-35 submissions, and attracted audiences of 75-100 from NLP, information extraction, and machine learning communities. Our speakers are similarly diverse, drawing from experts in knowledge base construction from academia, industry, and government agencies. AKBC has featured senior invited speakers from Google, Microsoft, Facebook, leading universities (MIT, Stanford, Univ. of Washington, CMU, Univ. of Massachusetts, and more), and DARPA. With this year's proposal, we would like to continue the tradition of bringing together researchers on the frontier of breakthrough research from different communities. By inviting established researchers for keynotes, and by focusing particularly on vision paper submissions, we aim to provide a vivid forum of discussion about the field of automated knowledge base construction.

Topics of Interest:

- machine learning on text; unsupervised, lightly- and distantly-supervised learning representation learning; distributional semantics; ontology construction
- human-computer collaboration in KB construction; automated population of wikis
- inference for graphical models and structured prediction; scalable approximate inference
- named entity extraction; relation extraction; (open) information extraction
- entity resolution; information integration; schema alignment; ontology alignment; monolingual alignment; alignment between KBs and text
- pattern analysis; semantic analysis of natural language; learning by reading
- databases; distributed information systems; probabilistic databases
- scalable computation; distributed computation
- queries on mixtures of structured and unstructured data; querying under uncertainty
- dynamic models; online adaptation of knowledge; temporal KBs; belief revision in KBs
- languages, toolkits and systems for automated KB construction;
- demonstrations of existing automatically-built KBs

Organizers:

Jay Pujara, University of Maryland, College Park, USA
Tim Rocktaschel, University College London, UK
Danqi Chen, Stanford University, USA
Sameer Singh, University of Washington, USA

Program Committee:

Alan Akbik (Technical University of Berlin)
Gabor Angeli (Stanford University)
Stephen Bach (Stanford University)
Niranjan Balasubramanian (Stony Brook University)
Guillaume Bouchard (University College London)
Eunsol Choi (University of Washington)
Bhavana Dalvi (Allen Institute for Artificial Intelligence)
Doug Downey (Northwestern University)
Luis Galárraga (Télécom ParisTech University)
Matt Gardner (Carnegie Mellon University)
Annalisa Gentile (University of Sheffield)
Adam Grycner (Max-Planck-Institut für Informatik)
Roman Klinger (University of Stuttgart)
Sebastian Krause (German Research Centre for Artificial Intelligence)
Jayant Krishnamurthy (Carnegie Mellon University)
Omer Levy (Bar-Ilan University)
Victoria Lin (University of Washington)
Xiao Ling (University of Washington)
Daniel Lowd (Oregon State University)
Ndapa Nakashole (Carnegie Mellon University)
Jason Naradowsky (University College London)
Arvind Neelakantan (University of Massachusetts Amherst)
Hoifung Poon (Microsoft Research)
Pontus Stenetorp (University College London)
Partha Pratim Talukdar (Indian Institute of Science)
Niket Tandon (Max-Planck-Institut für Informatik)
Philippe Thomas (German Research Centre for Artificial Intelligence)
Larysa Visengeriyeva (Technische Universität Berlin)
Andreas Vlachos (University of Sheffield)
Bishan Yang (Carnegie Mellon University)

Table of Contents

Using Graphs of Classifiers to Impose Constraints on Semi-supervised Relation Extraction
Lidong Bing, William Cohen, Bhuwan Dhingra and Richard Wang 1

Discovering Entity Knowledge Bases on the Web
Andrew Chisholm, Will Radford and Ben Hachey 7

IKE - An Interactive Tool for Knowledge Extraction
Bhavana Dalvi, Sumithra Bhakthavatsalam, Chris Clark, Peter Clark, Oren Etzioni, Anthony Fader
and Dirk Groeneveld 12

Incorporating Selectional Preferences in Multi-hop Relation Extraction
Rajarshi Das, Arvind Neelakantan, David Belanger and Andrew McCallum 18

Knowledge Base Population for Organization Mentions in Email
Ning Gao, Mark Dredze and Douglas Oard 24

Enriching Wikidata with Frame Semantics
Hatem Mousselly Sergieh and Iryna Gurevych 29

Demonyms and Compound Relational Nouns in Nominal Open IE
Harinder Pal and Mausam - 35

But What Do We Actually Know?
Simon Razniewski, Fabian Suchanek and Werner Nutt 40

Learning Knowledge Base Inference with Neural Theorem Provers
Tim Rocktäschel and Sebastian Riedel 45

The Physics of Text: Ontological Realism in Information Extraction
Stuart Russell, Ole Torp Lassen, Justin Uang and Wei Wang 51

Know2Look: Commonsense Knowledge for Visual Search
Sreyasi Nag Chowdhury, Niket Tandon and Gerhard Weikum 57

Row-less Universal Schema
Patrick Verga and Andrew McCallum 63

An Attentive Neural Architecture for Fine-grained Entity Type Classification
Sonse Shimaoka, Pontus Stenetorp, Kentaro Inui and Sebastian Riedel 69

Regularizing Relation Representations by First-order Implications
Thomas Demeester, Tim Rocktäschel and Sebastian Riedel 75

Applying Universal Schemas for Domain Specific Ontology Expansion
Paul Groth, Sujit Pal, Darin McBeath, Brad Allen and Ron Daniel 81

Design of Word Association Games using Dialog Systems for Acquisition of Word Association Knowledge
Yuichiro Machida, Daisuke Kawahara, Sadao Kurohashi and Manabu Sassano 86

Call for Discussion: Building a New Standard Dataset for Relation Extraction Tasks
Teresa Martin, Fiete Botschen, Ajay Nagesh and Andrew McCallum 92

A Comparison of Weak Supervision methods for Knowledge Base Construction
Ameet Soni, Dileep Viswanathan, Niranjan Pachaiyappan and Sriraam Natarajan 97

A Factorization Machine Framework for Testing Bigram Embeddings in Knowledgebase Completion
Johannes Welbl, Guillaume Bouchard and Sebastian Riedel 103

Conference Program

Friday, June 17, 2016

9:00–9:10   *Opening Remarks*
AKBC Organizers

9:10–9:40   *Joint Compositional Learning from Text and Knowledge Bases*
Kristina Toutanova

9:40–10:10   *The Allen AI Science Challenge: Results, Lessons, and Open Questions*
Oren Etzioni

10:10–11:00   Morning Poster Session and Coffee Break

Using Graphs of Classifiers to Impose Constraints on Semi-supervised Relation Extraction
Lidong Bing, William Cohen, Bhuwan Dhingra and Richard Wang

Discovering Entity Knowledge Bases on the Web
Andrew Chisholm, Will Radford and Ben Hachey

IKE - An Interactive Tool for Knowledge Extraction
Bhavana Dalvi, Sumithra Bhakthavatsalam, Chris Clark, Peter Clark, Oren Etzioni, Anthony Fader and Dirk Groeneveld

Incorporating Selectional Preferences in Multi-hop Relation Extraction
Rajarshi Das, Arvind Neelakantan, David Belanger and Andrew McCallum

Knowledge Base Population for Organization Mentions in Email
Ning Gao, Mark Dredze and Douglas Oard

Enriching Wikidata with Frame Semantics
Hatem Mousselly Sergieh and Iryna Gurevych

Demonyms and Compound Relational Nouns in Nominal Open IE
Harinder Pal and Mausam -

But What Do We Actually Know?
Simon Razniewski, Fabian Suchanek and Werner Nutt

Learning Knowledge Base Inference with Neural Theorem Provers
Tim Rocktäschel and Sebastian Riedel

Friday, June 17, 2016 (continued)

11:00–11:30   *Andrew McCallum's Mysterious Production of Facts (Talk TBA)*
Andrew McCallum

11:30–12:00   *Look Ma, No Neurons: Using Explicit Inference Rules to Complete a KB*
William Cohen

12:00–13:20   Lunch Break and Morning Posters

13:20–13:50   Contributed Talks 1

13:20–13:35   *The Physics of Text: Ontological Realism in Information Extraction*
Stuart Russell, Ole Torp Lassen, Justin Uang and Wei Wang

13:35–13:50   *Know2Look: Commonsense Knowledge for Visual Search*
Sreyasi Nag Chowdhury, Niket Tandon and Gerhard Weikum

13:50–14:15   *Meaningful Discourses (Talk TBA)*
Christopher Manning

14:15–14:40   *Common Sense and Language*
Benjamin Van Durme

14:40–15:10   Contributed Talks 2

14:40–14:55   *Row-less Universal Schema*
Patrick Verga and Andrew McCallum

14:55–15:10   *An Attentive Neural Architecture for Fine-grained Entity Type Classification*
Sonse Shimaoka, Pontus Stenetorp, Kentaro Inui and Sebastian Riedel

15:10–16:00   Afternoon Poster Session and Coffee Break

Know2Look: Commonsense Knowledge for Visual Search
Sreyasi Nag Chowdhury, Niket Tandon and Gerhard Weikum

Regularizing Relation Representations by First-order Implications
Thomas Demeester, Tim Rocktäschel and Sebastian Riedel

Applying Universal Schemas for Domain Specific Ontology Expansion
Paul Groth, Sujit Pal, Darin McBeath, Brad Allen and Ron Daniel

Design of Word Association Games using Dialog Systems for Acquisition of Word Association Knowledge
Yuichiro Machida, Daisuke Kawahara, Sadao Kurohashi and Manabu Sassano

Call for Discussion: Building a New Standard Dataset for Relation Extraction Tasks
Teresa Martin, Fiete Botschen, Ajay Nagesh and Andrew McCallum

The Physics of Text: Ontological Realism in Information Extraction
Stuart Russell, Ole Torp Lassen, Justin Uang and Wei Wang

An Attentive Neural Architecture for Fine-grained Entity Type Classification
Sonse Shimaoka, Pontus Stenetorp, Kentaro Inui and Sebastian Riedel

A Comparison of Weak Supervision methods for Knowledge Base Construction
Ameet Soni, Dileep Viswanathan, Niranjan Pachaiyappan and Sriraam Natarajan

Row-less Universal Schema
Patrick Verga and Andrew McCallum

A Factorization Machine Framework for Testing Bigram Embeddings in Knowledgebase Completion
Johannes Welbl, Guillaume Bouchard and Sebastian Riedel

Friday, June 17, 2016 (continued)

16:00–16:25   *Querying Unnormalized and Incomplete Knowledge Bases*
Percy Liang

16:25–16:50   *Memory Networks for Language Understanding: Successes and Challenges*
Antoine Bordes

16:50–17:30   *Afternoon Speaker Panel*
Christopher Manning, Benjamin Van Durme, Percy Liang, Antoine Bordes

17:30–17:45   *Closing Remarks*
AKBC Organizers

17:45–18:15   **Evening Poster Session**

Using Graphs of Classifiers to Impose Constraints on Semi-supervised Relation Extraction

Lidong Bing and **William W. Cohen** and **Bhuwan Dhingra**
School of Computer Science
Carnegie Mellon Univeristy
{lbing, wcohen, bdhingra}@cs.cmu.edu

Richard C. Wang
US Development Center
Baidu USA
richardwang@baidu.com

Abstract

We propose a general approach to modeling semi-supervised learning constraints on unlabeled data. Both traditional supervised classification tasks and many natural semi-supervised learning heuristics can be approximated by specifying the desired outcome of walks through a graph of classifiers. We demonstrate the modeling capability of this approach in the task of relation extraction, and experimental results show that the modeled constraints achieve better performance as expected.

1 Introduction

Semi-supervised learning (SSL) methods often operate by introducing "soft constraints" on how a learned classifier will behave at points, or clusters of points, associated with unlabeled instances. For example, logistic regression with entropy regularization (Grandvalet and Bengio, 2004) and transductive SVMs (Joachims, 1999) constrain the classifier to make confident predictions at unlabeled points, and many graph-based SSL approaches require that the instances associated with the endpoints of an edge have similar labels (Zhu et al., 2003; Talukdar and Crammer, 2009). Other weakly-supervised methods also can be viewed as imposing constraints predictions made by a classifier: for instance, in distantly-supervised information extraction, constraints sometimes are imposed which requires that the classifier, when applied to the set S of mentions of an entity pair that is a member of relation r, classify at least one mention in S as a positive instance of r (Hoff-mann et al., 2011). Different constraints (and different assumptions about the loss function for the learner) lead to different SSL algorithms.

In this paper, we propose a general approach to modeling such constraints. In particular, we show that many types of constraints can be modeled by *specifying the desired behavior of random walks through a graph of classifiers*. In the graph, nodes correspond to relational conditions on small subsets of the data, and edges are annotated by feature vectors. Feature weights, combined with the feature vector at each edge and a non-linear postprocessing step, define a weighting of edges in the graph, and hence a transition function for a random walk. We will argue that traditional supervised classification tasks, as well as many natural SSL heuristics, can be approximated by specifying the desired outcome of walks through this graph.

Below we will make this notion precise. We will also define a succinct declarative language for specifying these models, and introduce a corresponding graphical "plate" language for the models. We then present results obtained by optimizing performance on an appropriate ensemble of graphs for the task of relation extraction.

2 Specifying SSL Tasks

2.1 An Example: Intuition

We begin with an simple example. The left-hand side of Figure 1 illustrates how a traditional supervised classification can be expressed as programs in ProPPR (Wang et al., 2013), a probabilistic first-order language. In ProPPR, following the convention used on logic programming, capital letters are

1

Proceedings of AKBC 2016, pages 1–6,
San Diego, California, June 12-17, 2016. ©2016 Association for Computational Linguistics

predict(X,Y) ←
   pickLabel(Y) ∧
   classify(X,Y).
classify(X,Y) ← true
   { *f(W,Y): hasFeature(X,W)* }.

mutexFailure(X) ←
   pickMutex(Y1,Y2) ∧
   classify(X,Y1) ∧
   classify(X,Y2).

Figure 1: Declarative specifications of the models for supervised learning, on the left, and for a mutual-exclusivity constraint, on the right.

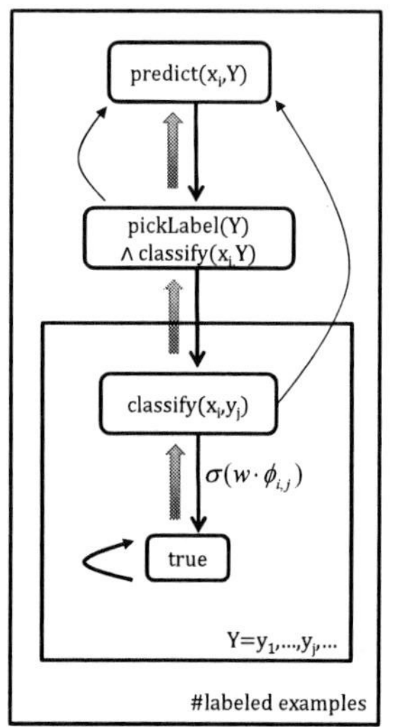

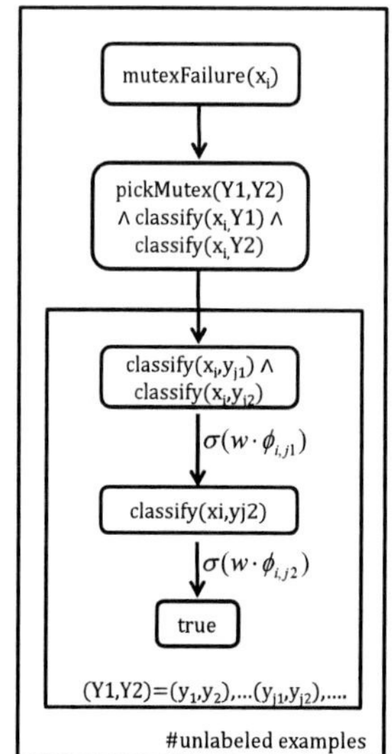

for each labeled example x_i,y_i:
- *predict(x_i,y_i) scores high*
- *predict(x_i,y_j) for y_j≠y_i scores low*

for each unlabeled example x_i:
- *mutexFailure(x_i) scores low*

Figure 2: Plate diagrams for supervised learning, on the left, and a mutual-exclusivity constraint, on the right.

implicitly variables, and are universally quantified when they appear in the "head" of a rule, and rules can also be annotated with a set of *features*, which then weighted to define a strength for the rule. The symbol *true* is a goal that always succeeds, and we omit, for brevity, the problem specific definition of *pickLabel(Y)*, which would consist of rules for each possible label y_i (relation types), i.e. *pickLabel(y_1)* ← *true*, . . . , *pickLabel(y_K)* ← *true*.

ProPPR programs, like Prolog programs, are associated with a backward-chaining proof process, and like Prolog programs, can be read either as logical constraints, or as a non-deterministic program, which is invoked when a query is submitted. If the queries processed by the program are all of the form *predict(x_i,Y)* where x_i is a constant, the theory on the left-hand side of Figure 1 can be interpreted as saying: (1) To prove the goal of the form *predict(x_i,Y)*—i.e., to predict a

label Y for the instance x_i—non-deterministically pick a possible class label y_j, and then prove the goal *classify(x_i,y_i)*; (2) proofs for every the goal *classify(x_i,y_j)* immediately succeed, with a strength based on a weighted combination of the features in the set $\{f(w, y_j) : hasFeature(x_i, w)\}$. This set is encoded in the usual way as a sparse vector ϕ_{x_i,y_j}, with one dimension for every object of the form $f(w, y_j)$ where y_j is a class label and w is a vocabulary word. For example, if the vocabulary contains the word *hope* and *sports* is a possible label, then one feature in ϕ_{x_i,y_j} might be active exactly when document x_i contains the word *hope* and $y_j = sports$. The set of proofs associated with this theory are described by the plate diagram on the left-hand side of Figure 2. Although the nodes are *not* associated with logical variables, the repetition suggested by the plates has the same meaning as in graphical models, and the heavy blue upward-pointing arrows denote logical implication.

In ProPPR[1] it is possible to train weights to maximize or minimize the score of a particular query response: i.e., one can say that for the query *predict(x_i, Y)* responses where $Y = y_{j*}$ are "positive" and responses where $Y = y_{j'}$ for $j' \neq j*$ are "negative". The training data needed for the supervised learning case is indicated in the bottom of the left-hand of the plate diagram. Learning is performed by stochastic gradient descent (Wang et al., 2013).

2.2 Unlabeled Data and Low-density Boundaries

We finally turn to the right-hand sides of Figures 1 and 2. These can be viewed as a sort of consistency test to be applied to an *unlabeled* example x_i. In ordinary classification tasks, any two distinct classes y_j and $y_{j'}$ should be mutually exclusive. The theory on the right-hand side of Figure 1

---

[1]ProPPR's semantics are defined by a slightly different graph, which contains the same set of nodes as the proof graph, but is weighted, and has a different edge set—namely, the downward-pointing black arrows, which run opposite to the implication edges. For this example, these edges describe a forest, with one tree for each labeled example x_i. The forest is further augmented with a self-loop on each *true* node, and a "reset" edge that returns to the root for each non-*true* node. To simplify, the reset and self-loop edges are only shown in the first plate diagram.

asserts that a "mutual exclusion failure" (mutex-Failure) occurs if x_i can be classified into two distinct classes. (Again there is a problem specific definition of *pickMutex(Y1,Y2)*, which would consist of trivial rules for each possible distinct label pair y_j, and $y_{j'}$.) The corresponding plate diagram is shown in Figure 2. To (softly) enforce this constraint, we need only introduce negative examples for each unlabeled example x_i, specifying that proofs for the goal *mutexFailure(x_i)* should have a low scores.

Conceptually, this constraint encodes a common bias of SSL systems, namely, that the decision boundaries should be drawn in low-probability regions of the space. In this case, if a decision boundary is close to an unlabeled example, then more than one *classify* goal with succeed with a high score.

2.3 Other SSL constraints

The framework describes above is flexible enough to handle many types of constraints. Here we are primarily interested in constraints associated with relation extraction. Before introducing these constraints, we first describe our task, relation extraction for entity-centric corpora.

Each document in an entity-centric corpus describes aspects of a particular entity (called *subject or title entity*), e.g. each Wikipedia article is such a document. Relation extraction from a entity-centric document is reduced to predicting the relation between the subject entity and an entity mention in the document. For example, for a drug article, if the target relation is sideEffects, we need to predict for each candidate (extracted from a single sentence) whether it is a side effect of this drug. If no such relation holds, we predict the special label "Other". Besides the entropy regularization constraint, i.e., mutexFailure introduced above, there are several other constraints that could be helpful for this task.

Sentence constraint. For each sentence, we constrain that only one mention (here a mention can also refer to a coordinate-term list such as "vomiting, headache and nausea") should be labeled as a particular relation:

sentFailure(X1,X2) ← pickRealLabel(Y1)∧
pickRealLabel(Y2)∧classify(X1,Y1)∧classify(X2,Y2),

where pickRealLabel(Y) picks a label other than "Other", X1 and X2 are a pair of mentions extracted from a single sentence. This constraint penalizes extracting multiple relation objects from a single sentence.

Document constraint. If an entity string appears as multiple mentions in one document, they should have the same relation label (relative to the subject entity), or some of them have "Other" label:

docFailure(X1,X2) ← pickMutex(Y1,Y2)∧
pickRealLabel(Y1)∧pickRealLabel(Y2)∧
classify(X1,Y1)∧classify(X2,Y2).

Section title constraint. In some entity-centric corpora, the content of a document is organized into different sections. This constraint basically says if two mentions appear in the same section (currently determined simply by matching section titles) of two documents, they should have the same relation label, relative to their own document subjects:

titleFailure(X1,X2) ← pickMutex(Y1,Y2)∧
pickRealLabel(Y1)∧pickRealLabel(Y2)∧
classify(X1,Y1)∧classify(X2,Y2).

3 Experiments

3.1 Settings

Corpora. Our drug corpus, DailyMed, is downloaded from dailymed.nlm.nih.gov which contains 28,590 XML documents, each of which describes a drug that can be legally prescribed in the United States. Our disease corpus, WikiDisease, is extracted from a Wikipedia dump of May 2015 and it contains 8,596 disease articles. We extract usedToTreat, conditionsThisMayPrevent, and sideEffects relations for the drug domain; treatments, symptoms, riskFactors, causes, and preventionFactors relations for the disease domain.

Preprocessing and features. We use the GDep parser (Sagae and Tsujii, 2007), a dependency parser trained on the GENIA Treebank, to parse the corpora. We use a simple POS-based chunker to extract NP mentions, and also extract a list for each coordinating conjunction that modifies a nominal (a list is regarded as a compound mention). We use the same feature generator for both mentions and lists. Shallow features include: tokens in the NPs, and character prefixes/suffixes of these tokens; tokens from the sentence containing the NP; and tokens and bigrams from a window around the NPs. From the dependency parsing, we also find the verb which is the closest ancestor of the head of the NP, all modifiers of this verb, and the path to this verb. For a list, the dependency features are computed relative to the head of the list.

Evaluation dataset. We manually labeled 10 pages from WikiDisease and 10 pages from DailyMed. The annotated text fragments are those NPs that are the second argument values of those 8 relations, with the title drug or disease entity of the corresponding document as the relation subject. In total, there are 436 triple facts for the disease domain and 320 triple facts for the drug domain. A pipeline's task is to extract values of the second arguments of relations from a given document.

3.2 Training Data with Distant Supervision

We extract triples from Freebase as supervision to distantly label training examples. If the subject of a triple matches with a drug or disease title entity in a corpus and its object value also appears in that document, it is extracted. In total, we get 2022, 2453, 905, 753, and 164 triples for 5 disease relations respectively, and 3112, 315, and 265 triples for 3 drug relations, respectively.

Each triple is used to label the document whose subject entity is the same as the triple subject. For instance, triple sideEffects(Aspirin,heartburn) will label a mention "heartburn" from the Aspirin article as an example of sideEffects relation. This raw data is very noisy (Bing et al., 2015; Bing et al., 2016), so we add a distillation step. We first distantly label these relations in two small structured corpora, namely, WebMD for drug and MayoClinic for disease.[2] They have well-defined section information, which can be matched with target relations. We only label usedToTreat and conditionsThisMayPrevent from the "Uses" section, and label sideEffects from "Side Effects" section of WebMD. Similarly, the disease relations are labeled from "Treatments and drugs","Symptoms", "Risk factors", "Causes", and "Prevention" sections of MayoClinic. After that we build a graph containing examples from both cor-

pora of a domain, and do label propagation in this graph with the section-labeled examples as seeds. We take top 2,000 examples from each WikiDisease relation and top 800 examples from each DailyMed relation as training data. We randomly pick 2,000 and 800 examples that are not distantly labeled by any relation as "Other" examples.

3.3 Algorithms Compared

Our SSL framework allows many constraints to be formulated, leading to several SSL methods: SSL_m uses only the mutex constraint; SSL_s, only the sentence constraint; SSL_d, only the document constraint; SSL_t, only the section title constraint. We also consider some combinations of these: SSL_sd; SSL_st; SSL_dt; and SSL_sdt. All the SSL pipelines employ the evaluation pages as unlabeled data for those constraints (i.e., they are used transductively).

As one baseline, we compare to a standard supervised learning pipeline, SL, which learns a classifier with no constraints using ProPPR. We also compare against three existing methods: *MultiR*, (Hoffmann et al., 2011) which models each relation mention separately and aggregates their labels using a deterministic OR; *Mintz++* from (Surdeanu et al., 2012), which improves on the original model from (Mintz et al., 2009) by training multiple classifiers, and allowing multiple labels per entity pair; and *MIML-RE* (Surdeanu et al., 2012) which has a similar structure to *MultiR*, but uses a classifier to aggregate the mention level predictions into an entity pair prediction. We used the publicly available code from the authors [3] for the experiments. Since these methods do not distinguish between structured and unstructured corpora, we used the union of these corpora in our experiments. We found that the performance of these methods varies significantly with the number of negative examples used during training, and hence we tuned these and other parameters, including the number of epochs (for both *MultiR* and *MIML-RE*) and the number of training folds for *MIML-RE*, directly on the evaluation data and report their best performance.

Finally we compare with our previous system, DIEBOLDS, (Bing et al., 2016) which uses docu-

---

[2]WebMD is collected from www.webmd.com, and each drug page has the same seven sections, such as Uses, Side Effects, Precautions, etc. WebMD contains 2,096 pages. MayoClinic is collected from www.mayoclinic.org. The sections of MayoClinic pages include Symptoms, Causes, Risk Factors, Treatments and Drugs, Prevention, etc. MayoClinic contains 1,117 pages.

[3]http://aiweb.cs.washington.edu/ai/raphaelh/mr/ and http://nlp.stanford.edu/software/mimlre.shtml

ment structure to construct a different label propagation graph. Briefly, DIEBOLDS first builds a bipartite graph from the merged structured corpus and target corpus, and then performs relation type propagation with the extracted lists (including singleton ones) and their items. One set of vertices correspond to relation mentions. The other set of vertexes are identifiers for the lists. Additional couplings use the document structure and BOW context features of pairs. Label propagation uses the subject-NP pairs distantly labeled with relation seeds as starting points, and then binary classifiers are trained with the top N mentioned as score by label propagation.

3.4 Results

The SL and SSL pipelines can classify both singleton and coordinate lists. After that, lists are broken into items, i.e. NPs, for evaluation. We evaluate the performance of different pipelines from IR perspective, with a title entity (i.e., document name) and a relation together as a query, and extracted NPs as retrieval results. The predicted probability by ProPPR serves as the ranking score inside each query. The results evaluated by precision, recall and F1 measure are given in Table 1. DIEBOLDS' results are extracted from (Bing et al., 2016), since the evaluation data is the same.

Among the individual constraints, SSL_s, SSL_d, and SSL_t are found to improve the performance over SL (which is a strong baseline, perhaps because of careful use of structured documents in our distant labeling procedure.) These SSL approaches lead to higher precision, showing that adding these constraints does reduce false positives. The sentence constraint is the most helpful for better precision: mentions from the same sentence share token features from sentence content, which often misleads the classifiers, and the sentence constraint is designed to penalize such cases. SSL_m is useful for improving recall, but its precision is much lower than SL. Unlike the other constraints, we note that SSL_m is a domain-independent heuristic: it simply encourages confident decision on unlabeled examples. This is a useful heuristic in many cases, and in particular encourages classifiers that lie in low-density areas of the example space; we conjectiure that this is inapproproate for this task because the data is noisy and the classes are not well-separated.

	Disease			Drug		
	P	R	F1	P	R	F1
DIEBOLDS	0.143	0.372	0.209	0.050	**0.435**	0.090
MultiR	0.198	0.333	0.249	0.156	0.138	0.146
Mintz++	0.192	0.353	0.249	0.177	0.178	0.178
MIML-RE	0.211	0.360	0.266	0.167	0.160	0.163
SL	0.247	0.353	0.290	0.288	0.368	0.323
SSL_m	0.191	**0.382**	0.255	0.207	0.418	0.277
SSL_s	0.284	0.317	0.299	0.294	0.367	0.326
SSL_d	0.257	0.350	0.296	0.293	0.366	0.325
SSL_t	0.257	0.362	0.301	0.292	0.364	0.324
SSL_sd	**0.294**	0.318	0.306	0.291	0.367	0.325
SSL_st	0.289	0.332	0.309	0.300	0.376	0.334
SSL_dt	0.264	0.369	0.308	0.299	0.384	0.336
SSL_sdt	0.292	0.335	**0.312**	**0.304**	0.378	**0.337**

Table 1: Average results from 3 runs.

Combining the individual constraints can further improve the results. SSL_sdt is the most effective pipeline. Compared with SL, it achieves 4.3% and 7% relative improvements for drug domain and disease domain, respectively. Compared with MultiR, Mintz++, and MIML-RE, the relative improvements are about 17% to 25% on the disease domain, and 89% to 131% on the drug domain. DIEBOLDS achieves the highest recall values, however, its precision is much lower.

4 Conclusions

We proposed a general approach to modeling SSL constraints. It can approximate traditional supervised learning and many natural SSL heuristics by specifying the desired outcome of walks through a graph of classifiers. An application case of this approach is given by modeling the task of relation extraction. There are a few open questions to explore: adding hyperparameters (e.g., different weights for different constraints); adding more control over the supervised loss versus the constraint-based loss; and testing the approach on more tasks.

Acknowledgments

This work was funded by grants from Baidu USA and Google.

References

Lidong Bing, Sneha Chaudhari, Richard Wang C, and William W Cohen. 2015. Improving distant supervision for information extraction using label propagation through lists. In *Proceedings of the 2015 Conference on Empirical Methods in Natural Language Processing*, pages 524–529, Lisbon, Portugal, September. Association for Computational Linguistics.

Lidong Bing, Mingyang Ling, Richard C. Wang, and William W. Cohen. 2016. Distant IE by bootstrapping using lists and document structure. In *The Thirtieth AAAI Conference on Artificial Intelligence*, AAAI '16.

Yves Grandvalet and Yoshua Bengio. 2004. Semi-supervised learning by entropy minimization. In *Advances in neural information processing systems*, pages 529–536.

Raphael Hoffmann, Congle Zhang, Xiao Ling, Luke Zettlemoyer, and Daniel S Weld. 2011. Knowledge-based weak supervision for information extraction of overlapping relations. In *Proceedings of the 49th Annual Meeting of the Association for Computational Linguistics: Human Language Technologies-Volume 1*, pages 541–550. Association for Computational Linguistics.

Thorsten Joachims. 1999. Transductive inference for text classification using support vector machines. In *Proceedings of the Sixteenth International Conference on Machine Learning*, ICML '99, pages 200–209, San Francisco, CA, USA. Morgan Kaufmann Publishers Inc.

Mike Mintz, Steven Bills, Rion Snow, and Dan Jurafsky. 2009. Distant supervision for relation extraction without labeled data. In *Proceedings of the Joint Conference of the 47th Annual Meeting of the ACL and the 4th International Joint Conference on Natural Language Processing of the AFNLP: Volume 2-Volume 2*, pages 1003–1011. Association for Computational Linguistics.

Mihai Surdeanu, Julie Tibshirani, Ramesh Nallapati, and Christopher D. Manning. 2012. Multi-instance multi-label learning for relation extraction. In *Proceedings of the 2012 Joint Conference on Empirical Methods in Natural Language Processing and Computational Natural Language Learning*, EMNLP-CoNLL '12, pages 455–465, Stroudsburg, PA, USA. Association for Computational Linguistics.

Partha Pratim Talukdar and Koby Crammer. 2009. New regularized algorithms for transductive learning. In *Machine Learning and Knowledge Discovery in Databases*, pages 442–457. Springer.

William Yang Wang, Kathryn Mazaitis, and William W Cohen. 2013. Programming with personalized pagerank: a locally groundable first-order probabilistic logic. In *Proceedings of the 22nd ACM international conference on Conference on information & knowledge management*, pages 2129–2138. ACM.

X. Zhu, Z. Ghahramani, and J. Lafferty. 2003. Semi-supervised learning using Gaussian fields and harmonic functions. In *Proceedings of ICML-03, the 20th International Conference on Machine Learning*.

Discovering Entity Knowledge Bases on the Web

Andrew Chisholm
Hugo Australia
Sydney, Australia
achisholm@hugo.ai

Will Radford
Hugo Australia
Sydney, Australia
wradford@hugo.ai

Ben Hachey
Hugo Australia
Sydney, Australia
bhachey@hugo.ai

Abstract

Recognition and disambiguation of named entities in text is a knowledge-intensive task. Systems are typically bound by the resources and coverage of a single target knowledge base (KB). In place of a fixed knowledge base, we attempt to infer a set of endpoints which reliably disambiguate entity mentions on the web. We propose a method for discovering web KBs and our preliminary results suggest that web KBs allow linking to entities that can be found on the web, but may not merit a major KB entry.

1 Introduction

Entity linking (EL) resolves textual mentions to the correct node in a knowledge base (KB). Linking systems typically rely on semantic resources like Wikipedia as endpoints for disambiguation. These sources provide context for entity modelling, but impose an upper bound on recall based on their domain of coverage. Wide domain KBs like Wikipedia constrain coverage based on notability, while narrow domain sources like IMDb[1] or MusicBrainz[2] give depth at the expense of breadth. While it is possible to merge resources from multiple KBs in some applications, an explicit reconciliation of distinct entity sets and KB schemata is often problematic.

We explore a relaxed definition of a KB – any URI which reliably disambiguates linked mentions on the web. This covers resources which both work as a KB by design (e.g. a Wikipedia article) and those

---

[1] http://www.imdb.com
[2] https://musicbrainz.org

CLASSES: URI PATTERNS
```
gtlaw.com/People
nytimes.com/topic/person
```
INSTANCES: ENTITY ENDPOINTS
```
gtlaw.com/People/Magdalena-Gad
nytimes.com/topic/person/madonna
```

Figure 1: Example of class and instance URIs.

which do so implicitly by disambiguating mentions. We focus on the latter case, by trying to identify and exploit *class-instance* URI patterns. Figure 1 shows these patterns extracted from a website URIs listing classes of entity and instances of them – the entity endpoints.

We start by reviewing existing views of KBs, then discussing the content editing and publishing behaviours that we seek to exploit. To actually exploit these resources, we must first infer their existence on the web. We refer to this task as Knowledge Base Discovery (KBD) and introduce a supervised classification setting for endpoint discovery leveraging information from inbound links and silver standard mention annotation. We evaluate performance for this task using crowdsourced judgements over a held out set of candidate URIs.

This paper introduces web KBs extracted from a collection of news articles and we plan to release evaluation data, code and crowdsourced annotation. While our initial extraction is not perfect, we propose that web KBs make for compelling endpoints against which to disambiguate mentions of less prominent entities. Furthermore, we believe that a mixture of domain-specific KBs can assist entity linking to traditional KBs.

7

Proceedings of AKBC 2016, pages 7–11,
San Diego, California, June 12-17, 2016. ©2016 Association for Computational Linguistics

2 Related Work

Entity linking and wikification have typically relied on Wikipedia (Cucerzan, 2007; Milne and Witten, 2008) or a subset (McNamee et al., 2009), or a larger structured resource such as Freebase (Zheng et al., 2012). Entries in the KB provide a point against which mentions that refer to that entity are clustered. In addition to this, the KBs provide extra information for an entity such as facts, text and other media. Hachenberg and Gottron (2012) address the reverse task of identifying *good links* that correspond to specific KB entities by searching for the entity name in a web search engine and refining the results.

Other tasks cluster mentions of the same entity, but without reference to a central KB, namely Cross Document Coreference (Bagga and Baldwin, 1998; Singh et al., 2011) and Web Person Search (Artiles et al., 2007). The task can be more challenging, as we are unable to exploit priors inferred from the KB or leverage information about an entity for clustering. While an EL KB and a set of coreference clusters are quite different, they both act as *aggregation* points for mentions of their respective entities.

Mining the content and structure to discover new entities is another important task. There is also substantial work in trying to identify instances of entity classes from text, exploiting language (Hearst, 1992) document structure (Wang and Cohen, 2007; Bing et al., 2016) and site structure (Yang et al., 2010). Clustering NIL entities (those that cannot be linked to the KB) has been a focus of the Text Analysis Conference (TAC) Knowledge Base Population shared tasks from 2011 (Ji et al., 2011). This work is important for growing KBs to include more entities about which we know less – the long tail. Other work shows that web links can produce models nearly as accurate as those built from richly structured KBs (Chisholm and Hachey, 2015), but does not include non-Wikipedia entities.

We examine whether we can successfully extract informal web KBs by exploiting the structure of individual URLs and the structure of the sites they describe. Like traditional linking KBs, they identify reference points against which mentions can be linked, but lack the information commonly expected in KBs.

3 Analysis of Linking Behaviour

We identify patterns of web linking behaviour producing endpoints for entity disambiguation.

Web News Some publishers maintain topic pages that aggregate structured and unstructured content on entities, e.g., `nytimes.com/topic/person/barack-obama` . These provide a landing page for search engine optimisation and enable some semantic analytics (e.g. "Do users click more on people than organisations?"). They also provide a link target to contextualise mentions in news articles and help prevent navigation away from the site. Notably, these may not include description of an entity, merely aggregate content.

Social Networks Social sites are a very rich source of entity information, e.g., `facebook.com/barackobama` . Our analysis identifies some of these endpoints. However, many links to social profiles have anchors that are not mentions of the target entity, e.g., "Find me on [Twitter]{ `twitter.com/BarackObama` }." Identifying these patterns is beyond the scope of the current work.

Organisation Directories Universites and law firms maintain directories of employee profiles, e.g., `gtlaw.com/People/Matthew-Galati` . These collect fewer inlinks than news site topic pages and social profile pages. They are nevertheless a promising source of information for entities that don't meet Wikipedia's notability requirements.

4 Knowledge Base Discovery (KBD)

We define an entity endpoint as any URI for which inlinks reliably identify and disambiguate named entity mentions. For example, we may observe that inlinks to `en.wikipedia.org/wiki/Barack_Obama` are typically mentions of the entity Barack Obama. Links targeting this URI in reference to some other entity are unlikely, so we should consider this an endpoint for the entity Barack Obama.

Web endpoints also yield disambiguated entity mentions. For every entity endpoint we discover, we may recover thousands of entity mentions via inlinks. While the effectiveness of inlink-driven entity disambiguation is known for a single KB setting, we extend this approach to leverage inlinks across a collection of automatically discovered web KBs. This process has the potential to both improve EL accuracy for well-covered entities and extend the coverage of EL systems by uncovering endpoints for previously unseen entities.

4.1 Endpoint Inference

We explore a simple supervised classifier for KBD. For a web anchor span linking to a URI u, we wish to model the probability that it both references an entity e and is a true named entity mention m.

$$P(e, m|u) = \frac{P(e, m, u)}{P(u)}$$
$$= P(e|m, u)P(m|u)$$

We approximate $P(e|m, u) \approx 1$ by assuming all mentions are entity references independent of their target URI. This allows for an estimation of our target distribution via a model which predicts the probability that links targeting u are a mention m.

$$P(e, m|u) \approx P(m|u)$$

In practice, we find this achieves good results.

4.2 Features

We represent endpoint patterns as a bag of binary features hashed to 500,000 dimensions to help manage model size. This section describes the two major categories of features used to represent instances.

Path Features We tokenize endpoint patterns by splitting on forward slash characters and include path component uni-gram and bi-grams as features. We find path tokens are good predictors of entity mentions and often generalize across KBs. For example, it is common to observe links to entity pages prefixed by terms like `profile` or `wiki`. Similarly, terms like `news` or date patterns `YYYY/MM/DD` in a URI can provide negative evidence.

Domain Features In many cases, patterns are not sufficient to identify a KB endpoint without prior knowledge. For example, `twitter` entities are only observed via a common `<domain>/<eid>` pattern. We allow the model to explicitly memorise likely KB URIs by including as features the conjunction of domain name with each bi-gram feature.

	Total	Aligned
$|Mentions|$	14.5	3.4
$|URIs|$	5.4	1.0
$|Anchors|$	4.4	0.6
$|Patterns|$	1.5	0.3

Table 1: Statistics of the corpus in millions. The first column includes all corpus links. The second column includes links whose anchor text aligns to an NER span.

While this subset of features cannot generalise to unseen domains, we are able to achieve high precision for known KBs observed in the seed corpus.

5 Experimental Setup

We validate the KBD approach described above on an internal corpus of links collected from 2,948,841 web news articles (Cadilhac et al., 2015). We leverage named entity recognition to identify likely entity references as link anchors that align to predicted mentions for person, location and organisation entity types. And we convert target URIs to endpoint patterns by normalising to lower case, removing protocol (e.g., http) and domain (e.g., sfgate.com), and removing entity identifiers (e.g., query=”Elon+Musk”).

Table 1 includes statistics of the full link corpus (Total) and the NER-aligned subset (Aligned). The full corpus includes a total of 14,462,659 links. 3,436,033 of these align to NER mentions, yielding 1,029,405 candidate entity endpoints across 309,182 URI patterns.

5.1 Estimating $P(m|u)$

We estimate $P(m|u)$ via logistic regression using a sample of (u, m) pairs that act as a silver standard. We consider all URI patterns with at least ten inlinks as possible training instances. We treat a URI pattern as a positive instance if a majority of inlinks from our corpus are aligned to mentions. If not, we treat it as a negative instance. To measure performance on unseen URI patterns, we group instances by domain name before partitioning. This produces a silver standard training set of 100,852 instances (10% positive), and a development test set of 10,404 (12% positive). Before training, we subsample positive instances to equal the number of negative instances.

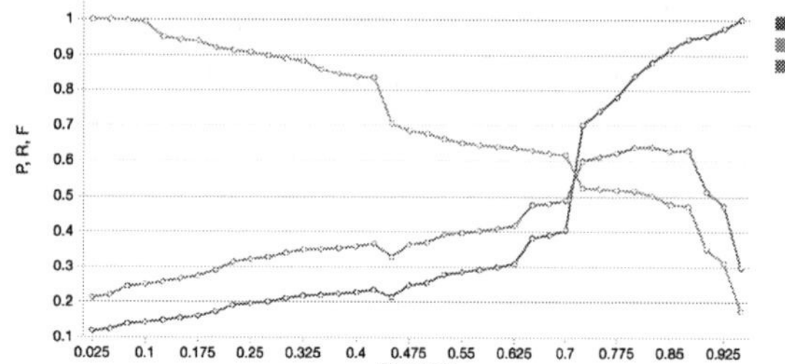

Figure 2: Precision-recall tradeoff across thresholds.

Endpoint	Entities
`linkedin.com/in`	3,246
`variety.com/t`	2,871
`data.cnbc.com/quotes`	2,958
`si.com/nfl/player`	1,426
`ign.com/stars`	933
`cyclingnews.com/riders`	899
`gtlaw.com/people`	257

Table 2: Sample of predicted URI patterns and entity counts.

5.2 Development Experiments

We select a threshold on held out instances from our development split. Figure 5.2 shows the precision-recall tradeoff across possible threshold values. We select a threshold of $P(m|u) >= 0.825$ here as this maximises F-score at 0.64 and is in the middle of the threshold range. Table 2 shows a sample of URI patterns predicted by this model and the number of corresponding entity endpoints discovered from the seed corpus. Encouragingly, apart from general news, we see two of the behaviour categories from Section 3: domain-specific news topic pages from Sports Illustrated and Cycling News, and professional profile pages like LinkedIn and legal web sites, which can inform disambiguation models for long-tail entities.

6 Evaluation

To evaluate how well our model for $P(m|u)$ estimates $P(e, m|u)$, we construct a corpus of human-annotated endpoint URIs. While it would be possible to randomly sample URIs, this would give us a highly imbalanced set with very few positive instances. We design a crowd task to collect pairwise identity judgements within clusters of candidate coreference pairs. To build clusters, we retrain our model over combined silver standard data

(train + test) and use it to collect endpoints from the complete seed corpus with classification confidence above our threshold. We use the anchor-URI graph to build candidate clusters from randomly selected seed URIs by enumerating inlink anchors and then collecting all target URIs linked to from these anchors. We repeat this a second time to create candidate clusters based on various names for the seed URI to help account for synonymy. Ambiguity means clusters also include endpoints corresponding to different underlying entities that share a name with the seed entity. Finally, we randomly select a pair of URIs from the cluster for evaluation.

We post 500 URI pairs to Crowdflower[3] and ask three workers to judge whether each endpoint is an entity page. We also ask whether they refer to the same underlying entity. The evaluation shows that 71.2% of the 1,000 endpoints are confirmed as entities. Of the 277 pairs that include two true endpoints, 70.8% are judged as coreferent providing reasonably balanced data for evaluating future endpoint reconciliation experiments.

Finally, we estimate the extent to which our approach can be used to extend knowledge beyond standard Wikipedia KBs. We sample 100 endpoints validated in the crowd annotation and search for a corresponding Wikipedia page. 20% of endpoints represent entities that are not in Wikipedia. This suggests that the approach does discover useful knowledge further down the tail of notability.

7 Conclusion

We described an approach for discovering knowledge bases on the web — endpoints that disambiguate entity mentions. An initial endpoint classifier trained on automatically created silver standard data was validated over a corpus of 2.9 million news articles. A crowd-sourced evaluation of 1,000 endpoints found that the classifier has precision of 71.2%. Acquiring new entities is a key aspect of populating KBs, and investigation of discovered endpoints finds that approximately 20% are not in Wikipedia. Rather than simply identifying a new NIL mentions, therefore, we identify new entities to add to the KB. We hope to refine this model and apply it to larger, more diverse web corpora.

---

[3] `http://www.crowdflower.com`

References

Javier Artiles, Julio Gonzalo, and Satoshi Sekine. 2007. The SemEval 2007 WePS Evaluation: Establishing a benchmark for the Web People Search task. In *SemEval*, pages 64–69.

Amit Bagga and Breck Baldwin. 1998. Entity-based cross-document coreferencing using the vector space model. In *COLING-ACL*, pages 79–85.

Lidong Bing, Mingyang Ling, Richard C. Wang, and William W. Cohen. 2016. Distant IE by bootstrapping using lists and document structure. In *AAAI*. to appear.

Anaïs Cadilhac, Andrew Chisholm, Ben Hachey, and Sadegh Kharazmi. 2015. Hugo: Entity-based news search and summarisation. In *CIKM Workshop on Exploiting Semantic Annotations in Information Retrieval*, pages 51–54.

Andrew Chisholm and Ben Hachey. 2015. Entity disambiguation with web links. *Transactions of the Association for Computational Linguistics*, 3:145–156.

Silviu Cucerzan. 2007. Large-scale named entity disambiguation based on Wikipedia data. In *EMNLP-CoNLL*, pages 708–716.

Christian Hachenberg and Thomas Gottron. 2012. Finding good URLs: Aligning entities in knowledge bases with public web document representations. In *ISWC Workshop on Linked Entities*, pages 17–28.

Marti A. Hearst. 1992. Automatic acquisition of hyponyms from large text corpora. In *COLING*, pages 539–545.

Heng Ji, Ralph Grishman, and Hoa Trang Dang. 2011. Overview of the TAC 2011 knowledge base population track. In *TAC*.

Paul McNamee, Heather Simpson, and Hoa Trang Dang. 2009. Overview of the TAC 2009 Knowledge Base Population Track. In *TAC*.

David Milne and Ian H. Witten. 2008. Learning to link with wikipedia. In *CIKM*, pages 509–518.

Sameer Singh, Amarnag Subramanya, Fernando Pereira, and Andrew McCallum. 2011. Large-scale cross-document coreference using distributed inference and hierarchical models. In *ACL*, pages 793–803.

Richard C. Wang and William W. Cohen. 2007. Language-independent set expansion of named entities using the web. In *ICDM*, pages 342–350.

Qing Yang, Peng Jiang, Chunxia Zhang, and Zhendong Niu. 2010. Reconstruct logical hierarchical sitemap for related entity finding. In *TREC*.

Zhicheng Zheng, Xiance Si, Fangtao Li, Edward Y. Chang, and Xiaoyan Zhu. 2012. Entity disambiguation with freebase. In *WI-IAT*, pages 82–89.

IKE - An Interactive Tool for Knowledge Extraction

**Bhavana Dalvi, Sumithra Bhakthavatsalam, Chris Clark,
Peter Clark, Oren Etzioni, Anthony Fader, Dirk Groeneveld**
Allen Institute for Artificial Intelligence
{bhavanad, sumithrab, chrisc, peterc, orene, dirkg}@allenai.org

Abstract

Recent work on information extraction has suggested that fast, interactive tools can be highly effective; however, creating a usable system is challenging, and few publically available tools exist. In this paper we present IKE, a new extraction tool that performs fast, interactive bootstrapping to develop high-quality extraction patterns for targeted relations. Central to IKE is the notion that an *extraction pattern* can be treated as a *search query* over a corpus. To operationalize this, IKE uses a novel query language that is expressive, easy to understand, and fast to execute - essential requirements for a practical system. It is also the first interactive extraction tool to seamlessly integrate symbolic (boolean) and distributional (similarity-based) methods for search. An initial evaluation suggests that relation tables can be populated substantially faster than by manual pattern authoring while retaining accuracy, and more reliably than fully automated tools, an important step towards practical KB construction. We are making IKE publically available (http://allenai.org/software/interactive-knowledge-extraction).

1 Introduction

Knowledge extraction from text remains a fundamental challenge for any system that works with structured data. Automatic extraction algorithms, e.g., (Angeli et al., 2015; Carlson et al., 2009; Nakashole et al., 2011; Hoffmann et al., 2011), have proved efficient and scalable, especially when leveraging existing search engine technologies, e.g., (Et-

zioni et al., 2004), but typically produce noisy results, e.g., the best F1 score for the KBP slot filling task was 0.28, as reported in (Angeli et al., 2015). Weakly supervised automatic bootstrapping methods (Carlson et al., 2010; Gupta and Manning, 2014) are more precise in the initial bootstrapping iterations, but digress in later iterations, a problem generally referred to as semantic drift.

More recently there has been work on more interactive methods, which can be seen as a "machine teaching" approach to KB construction (Amershi et al., 2014; Amershi et al., 2015; Li et al., 2012). For example, (Soderland et al., 2013) showed that users can be surprisingly effective at authoring and refining extraction rules for a slot filling task, and (Freedman et al., 2011) demonstrated that a combination of machine learning and user authoring produced high quality results. However, none of these approaches have evolved into publically available tools.

In this paper we present IKE, a usable, general-purpose tool for interactive extraction. Central to IKE is the notion that an *extraction pattern* can be treated as a *search query* over a corpus, building on earlier work by (Cafarella et al., 2005). It addresses the resulting requirements of expressiveness, comprehensibility, and speed with a novel query language based on chunking rather than parsing, and is the first tool to seamlessly integrate symbolic (boolean) and distributional (similarity-based) methods for search. It also includes a machine learning component for suggesting new queries to the user. A preliminary evaluation suggests that relation tables can be populated substantially faster with IKE than by manual pattern authoring (and more reliably than fully automated tools), while retaining accu-

12

Proceedings of AKBC 2016, pages 12–17,
San Diego, California, June 12-17, 2016. ©2016 Association for Computational Linguistics

racy, suggesting IKE has utility for KB construction.

Query	Interpretation
the dog	matches "the" followed by "dog"
NP grows	an NP followed by "grows"
(NP) grows	Capture the NP and place in column 1 (1 column table)
(NP) conducts (NP)	Capture the two NPs into columns 1 and 2 (2 column table)
(?<Energy> NP) is conducted by (?<Material> NP)	Capture the two NPs and place in columns named Energy and Material
the {cat,dog}	"the" followed by "cat" or "dog"
cats and {NN,NNS}	"cats and" followed by NN or NNS
JJ* dog	Zero or more JJ then "dog"
JJ+ dog	One or more JJ then "dog"
JJ[2-4] dog	2 to 4 JJ then "dog"
dog .[0-4] tail	"dog" followed by any 0 to 4 words followed by 'tail'
dog~50	Matches "dog" and the 50 words most distributionally similar to "dog"
. dog	Any word then "dog"
$colors	Any entry in the single-column "colors" table
$colors ~100	same plus 100 most similar words
$flower.color	Any in the "color" column of "flower" table

Table 1: IKE's Query Language, described by example.

2 Interactive Knowledge Extraction (IKE)

We first overview IKE and a sample workflow using it. IKE allows the user to create relation tables, and populate them by issuing pattern-based queries over a corpus. It also has a machine learning component that suggests high-quality broadenings or narrowings of the user's queries. Together, these allow the user to perform fast, interactive bootstrapping.

2.1 IKE's Query Language

A key part of IKE is treating an extraction pattern as a search query. To do this, the query language must be both comprehensible and fast to execute. To meet these requirements, IKE indexes and searches the corpus using a chunk-based rather than dependency-based representation of the text corpus. IKE's query language is presented by example in Table 1. The query language supports wildcards, window sizes, POS tags, chunk tags, and general regular

expression queries similar to TokenRegex (Chang and Manning, 2014) and Lucene, ElasticSearch's (Gormley and Tong, 2015) query language. Additionally, IKE supports distributional similarity based search (e.g. dog~50 would find 50 words similar to "dog"). "Capture groups", indicated by parentheses, instruct IKE to catch the matching element(s) as candidate entries in the table being populated. The user can also reference data in other already-constructed tables using the $ prefix.

The use of a chunk-based representation has several advantages over a dependency-based one (e.g., (Freedman et al., 2011; Gamallo et al., 2012; Hoffmann et al., 2015; Akbik et al., 2013)). First, both indexing and search are very fast (e.g., <1 sec to execute a query over 1.5M sentences), essential for an interactive system. Second, authoring queries does not require detailed knowledge of dependency structure, making the language more accessible. Finally, the system avoids parse errors, a considerable challenge for dependency-based systems. Corresponding challenges with chunk-based representations, e.g., defining constituent boundaries in terms of POS chunks, are partially alleviated by providing predefined, higher-level POS-based patterns, e.g., for verb phrases.

2.2 Machine Learning

IKE also has a ML-based Query Suggestor to propose improved queries to the user. This module performs a depth-limited beam search to explore the space of query variants, evaluated on the user-annotated examples collected so far. Variants are generated by broadening/narrowing a query.

Narrowing a query involves searching the space of restrictions on the current query, e.g., replacing a POS tag with a specific word, adding prefixes or suffixes to the query, adjusting distributional similarity based queries etc. Similarly, the broaden feature generalizes the given user query e.g. replacing a word by its POS tag. In both cases the candidate queries are ranked by the weighted sum of the number of positive n_p, negative n_n, and unlabeled n_u instances it matches, the weights being user-configurable (default 2, -1, -0.05 respectively). For example, for the query

($conducts.Material) VBZ ($conducts.Energy)

the top three suggested narrowings are:

($conducts.Material) conducts ($conducts.Energy)
($conducts.Material) absorbs ($conducts.Energy)
($conducts.Material) produces ($conducts.Energy)

all patterns that distinguish positive examples from negatives well.

2.3 Example Workflow

We now describe these features in more detail by way of an example. Consider the task of acquiring instances of the binary predicate **conducts**(*material,energy*), e.g., conducts("steel","electricity"). In IKE, relations are visualized as tables, so we treat this task as one of table population. A typical workflow is illustrated in Figure 1, which we now describe.

2.3.1 Define the types *material* and *energy*

First, the user defines the argument types *material* and *energy*. To define a type, IKE lets a user build a single column table, e.g., for type *material*, the user:

1. Creates a single column table called Material.
2. Manually adds several representative examples in the table, e.g., "iron", "wood", "steel".
3. Expands this set by searching for cosine-vector-similar phrases in the corpus, and marking valid and invalid members, e.g., the query

$Material ∼20

searches for the 20 phrases most similar to any existing member in the Material table, where similar is defined as the cosine between the phrase embeddings. Here we use 300 di-

mensional word2vec embeddings learned using (Mikolov et al., 2013)'s implementation of word2vec on a science document corpus.

4. Repeat step 3 until the table adequately characterizes the intended notion of *material*

The process is repeated for the type Energy. Note that here we are using only embedding-based features to populate a type. We could also use Hearst-style patterns (Hearst, 1992; Snow et al., 2004; Turney, 2006) to populate the type, e.g.,:

materials such as (NP)
materials such as $Material and (NP)

or a combination of patterns and word2vec expressions.

2.3.2 Create and Seed the conducts Table

The user next creates a two-column table **conducts**, and then uses a seed pattern to find initial pairs to populate it, e.g., the pattern

($Material) conducts ($Energy)

extracts pairs of materials and energies they conduct. The user selects valid pairs to initially populate the table. Invalid pairs (negative examples) are also recorded by IKE.

2.3.3 Bootstrapping to Expand the Table

The user can now bootstrap by invoking the ML-based Query Suggestor to find additional patterns (queries) expressing the target relation (Section 2.2). It does so by searching for narrowings or broadenings of the current query that cover a large number of positive pairs and few of the negative pairs in the table so far. The user then clicks on one of these patterns to select and execute it (with edits if desired) to find more instances of the relation, marks good/bad pairs, and expands the table (Figure 2). By repeating this process, the user rapidly populates the table.

2.4 Execution Speed

IKE uses BlackLab (Institute Dutch Lexicology, 2016) for indexing the corpus. This, combined with the chunk-based representation, results in fast query execution times (e.g., <1 second for a query over 1.5M sentences), an essential requirement for an interactive system (Table 2).

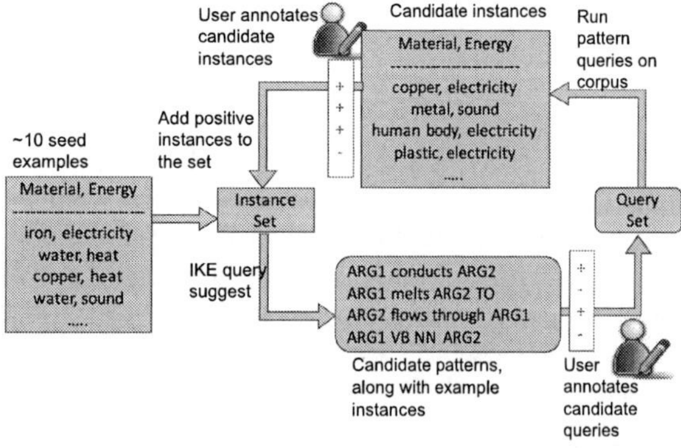

Figure 1: IKE interactive bootstrapping workflow

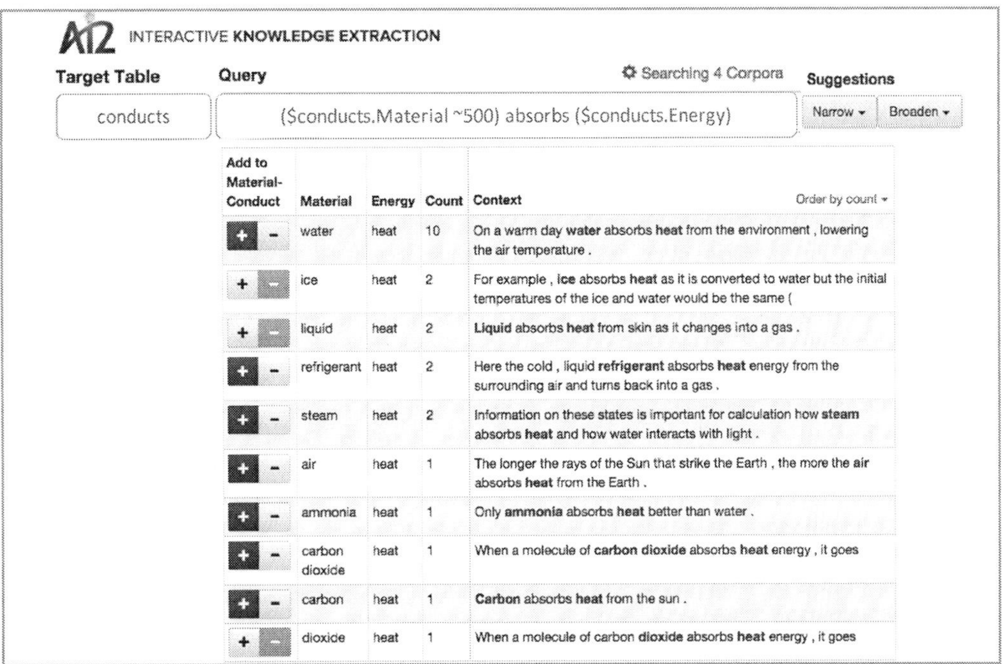

Figure 2: Search for examples of "X absorbs Y", where X is distributionally similar (∼500) to existing entries in the Material column of the **conducts** table. The user then annotates examples for inclusion in the table.

Corpus	# sentences	Avg. query-time (sec.)
Science textbook	1.2K	0.253
ck2.org texts	17K	0.286
SimpleWikipedia	1M	0.530
Web Subset (small)	1.5M	0.595
Web Subset (large)	20M	2.809

Table 2: Avg. query-times with different sized corpora.

3 Preliminary Evaluation

3.1 Experiments

Although IKE is still under development, we have conducted a preliminary evaluation, comparing it with two other methods for populating relation tables. Our interest is in how these different methods compare in terms of precision, yield and time:

- *Manual*: The user manually authors and refines patterns (without any automatic assistance) to populate a table.
- *Automatic*: The user provides an initial table with a few entries, and then lets the system bootstrap on its own, without any further interaction.
- *Interactive (IKE)*: Interactive bootstrapping, as described earlier.

The manual system was implemented in IKE by dis-abling the embedding-based set expansion and ML-based query suggestion features. The automatic approach was simulated in IKE by removing both user annotation steps in Figure 1, and instead adding all machine-learned patterns suggested by the Query Suggestor (Section 2.2) and instances that occur at least k times in the corpus (using $k = 2$). This is a simple baseline method of bootstrapping, compared with more sophisticated methods such as co-training (Collins and Singer, 1999; Neelakantan and Collins, 2014). For a fair comparison, we compared results after 3 bootstrapping iterations (for Automatic, IKE) and a similar amount of user time (∼30 mins, for Manual and IKE). The number of iterations were limited to 3 to keep the annotation time within reasonable limits.

3.2 Tasks and Datasets

We compared these methods to define and populate two target relations: **conducts**(*material,energy*), and **has-part**(*animal,bodypart*). All methods extract knowledge from the same corpora of science text, consisting of ∼1.5M sentences (largely) about elementary science drawn from science textbooks,

Simple Wikipedia, and the Web. For each relation, two (different) users familiar with IKE were asked to construct these tables. The numbers presented in Table 3 and Table 4 are averaged over these two users. Although this study is small, it provides helpful indicators about IKE's utility.

Method	Acquired Patterns		Extractions		Time
	No. of patterns	Average Precision	Number (total)	Yield (+ves)	in min.
Manual	7	25.5	106	27	30
Automatic	108	34.4	183	63	-
IKE	31	**52.7**	112	**59**	20

Table 3: **conducts**(*material,energy*) table after 3 iterations or ∼30 minutes user time. IKE helps the user discover substantially more patterns than the manual method (31 vs. 7), with better precision and in less time, resulting in the overall yield of 59 relation instances. Fully automatic bootstrapping produced a large number of lower precision (34.4%) patterns compared to IKE (52.7%) patterns.

Method	Acquired Patterns		Extractions		Time
	No. of patterns	Average Precision	Number (total)	Yield (+ves)	in min.
Manual	16	25.2	290	73	35
Automatic	228	3.5	1386	48	-
IKE	21	**22.5**	449	**101**	30

Table 4: **has-part**(*organism,bodypart*) table after 3 iterations or ∼30 minutes user time. Again, IKE produces the highest yield by helping the user discover 21 patterns with precision (22.5%) comparable to manual patterns (25.2%). Note that further use of IKE continues to expand the yield (e.g., after 3 more iterations of IKE the yield rises to **262** while maintaining average precision).

3.3 Results

Table 3 shows the results for building the **conducts**(*material,energy*) table. Most importantly, with IKE the user was able to discover substantially more patterns (31 vs. 7) with higher accuracy (52.7% vs. 25.5%) than the manual approach, resulting in a larger table (59 vs. 27 rows) in less time (20 vs. 30 mins). It also shows that fully automatic bootstrapping produced a large number of low quality (34.4% precision) rules, with an overall lower yield (63 rows).

Note that for both Manual and IKE, users have to decide how to spend their time budget, in particular between work on creating high-quality patterns vs. work on annotating examples found by those patterns. Thus the precision scores in the Tables reflect how the users chose to make this tradeoff, while the yield reflects their success at the overall goal, namely building a good table.

Table 4 shows similar results for constructing the **has-part**(*organism,bodypart*) table, IKE having the highest overall yield. Although this is a small case study, it suggests that IKE has value for rapid knowledge base construction.

4 Conclusion

We have presented IKE, a usable, general-purpose tool for interactive extraction. It has an expressive, easily comprehensible query language that integrates symbolic (boolean) and distributional (similarity-based) methods for search, and has a fast execution time. A preliminary evaluation suggests that IKE is effective for the task of knowledge-base construction compared to manual pattern authoring or using fully automated extraction tools. We are currently using this tool to expand the KB used by the Aristo system (Clark et al., 2016), and are making IKE publically available on our Web site at http://allenai.org/software/interactive-knowledge-extraction.

Acknowledgments

We are grateful to Paul Allen whose long-term vision continues to inspire our scientific endeavors. We would also like to thank Carissa Schoenick and Satwant Rana for their critical contributions to IKE.

References

[Akbik et al.2013] Alan Akbik, Oresti Konomi, and Michail Melnikov. 2013. Propminer: A workflow for interactive information extraction and exploration using dependency trees. In *ACL*.

[Amershi et al.2014] Saleema Amershi, Maya Cakmak, W. Bradley Knox, and Todd Kulesza. 2014. Power to the people: The role of humans in interactive machine learning. In *AI Magazine*.

[Amershi et al.2015] Saleema Amershi, Max Chickering, Steven M. Drucker, Bongshin Lee, Patrice Y. Simard, and Jina Suh. 2015. Modeltracker: Redesigning performance analysis tools for machine learning. In *CHI*.

[Angeli et al.2015] Gabor Angeli, Melvin Jose Johnson Premkumar, and Christopher D. Manning. 2015. Leveraging linguistic structure for open domain information extraction. In *ACL*.

[Cafarella et al.2005] Michael J. Cafarella, Doug Downey, Stephen Soderland, and Oren Etzioni. 2005. Knowitnow: Fast, scalable information extraction from the web. In *NAACL*.

[Carlson et al.2009] Andrew Carlson, Justin Betteridge, Estevam R Hruschka Jr, and Tom M Mitchell. 2009. Coupling semi-supervised learning of categories and relations. In *Proceedings of the NAACL HLT 2009 Workshop on Semi-supervised Learning for Natural Language Processing*, pages 1–9. Association for Computational Linguistics.

[Carlson et al.2010] Andrew Carlson, Justin Betteridge, Richard C Wang, Estevam R Hruschka Jr, and Tom M Mitchell. 2010. Coupled semi-supervised learning for information extraction. In *Proceedings of the third ACM international conference on Web search and data mining*, pages 101–110. ACM.

[Chang and Manning2014] Angel X Chang and Christopher D Manning. 2014. Tokensregex: Defining cascaded regular expressions over tokens. Technical Report CSTR 2014-02, Stanford University.

[Clark et al.2016] Peter Clark, Oren Etzioni, Tushar Khot, Ashish Sabharwal, Oyvind Tafjord, Peter Turney, and Daniel Khashabi. 2016. Combining retrieval, statistics, and inference to answer elementary science questions. In *Proc. IJCAI'16*.

[Collins and Singer1999] Michael John Collins and Yoram Singer. 1999. Unsupervised models for named entity classification. In *EMNLP&VLC'99*.

[Etzioni et al.2004] Oren Etzioni, Michael J. Cafarella, Doug Downey, Stanley Kok, Ana-Maria Popescu, Tal Shaked, Stephen Soderland, Daniel S. Weld, and Alexander Yates. 2004. Web-scale information extraction in knowitall: (preliminary results). In *WWW*.

[Freedman et al.2011] Marjorie Freedman, Lance A. Ramshaw, Elizabeth Boschee, Ryan Gabbard, Gary Kratkiewicz, Nicolas Ward, and Ralph M. Weischedel. 2011. Extreme extraction - machine reading in a week. In *EMNLP*.

[Gamallo et al.2012] Pablo Gamallo, Marcos Garcia, and Santiago Fernández-Lanza. 2012. Dependency-based open information extraction. In *Proceedings of the Joint Workshop on Unsupervised and Semi-Supervised Learning in NLP*, pages 10–18. Association for Computational Linguistics.

[Gormley and Tong2015] Clinton Gormley and Zachary Tong. 2015. *Elasticsearch: The Definitive Guide. "* O'Reilly Media, Inc.".

[Gupta and Manning2014] Sonal Gupta and Christopher D. Manning. 2014. Improved pattern learning for bootstrapped entity extraction. In *CONLL*.

[Hearst1992] Marti A. Hearst. 1992. Automatic acquisition of hyponyms from large text corpora. In *COLING*.

[Hoffmann et al.2011] Raphael Hoffmann, Congle Zhang, Xiao Ling, Luke Zettlemoyer, and Daniel S Weld. 2011. Knowledge-based weak supervision for information extraction of overlapping relations. In *Proceedings of the 49th Annual Meeting of the Association for Computational Linguistics: Human Language Technologies-Volume 1*, pages 541–550. Association for Computational Linguistics.

[Hoffmann et al.2015] Raphael Hoffmann, Luke S. Zettlemoyer, and Daniel S. Weld. 2015. Extreme extraction: Only one hour per relation. *CoRR*, abs/1506.06418.

[Institute Dutch Lexicology2016] INL Institute Dutch Lexicology. 2016. Blacklab: A corpus search engine. https://github.com/INL/BlackLab.

[Li et al.2012] Yunyao Li, Laura Chiticariu, Huahai Yang, Frederick Reiss, and Arnaldo Carreno-Fuentes. 2012. Wizie: A best practices guided development environment for information extraction. In *ACL*.

[Mikolov et al.2013] Tomas Mikolov, Ilya Sutskever, Kai Chen, Greg Corrado, and Jeffrey Dean. 2013. Distributed representations of words and phrases and their compositionality. In *NIPS*.

[Nakashole et al.2011] Ndapandula Nakashole, Martin Theobald, and Gerhard Weikum. 2011. Scalable knowledge harvesting with high precision and high recall. In *Proceedings of the fourth ACM international conference on Web search and data mining*, pages 227–236. ACM.

[Neelakantan and Collins2014] Arvind Neelakantan and Michael Collins. 2014. Learning dictionaries for named entity recognition using minimal supervision. In *EACL*.

[Snow et al.2004] Rion Snow, Daniel Jurafsky, and Andrew Y. Ng. 2004. Learning syntactic patterns for automatic hypernym discovery. In *NIPS*.

[Soderland et al.2013] Stephen Soderland, John Gilmer, Robert Bart, Oren Etzioni, and Daniel S. Weld. 2013. Open information extraction to kbp relations in 3 hours. In *TAC*.

[Turney2006] Peter D. Turney. 2006. Similarity of semantic relations. *COLING*.

Incorporating Selectional Preferences in Multi-hop Relation Extraction

Rajarshi Das, Arvind Neelakantan, David Belanger and Andrew McCallum
College of Information and Computer Sciences
University of Massachusetts Amherst
{rajarshi, arvind, belanger, mccallum}@cs.umass.edu

Abstract

Relation extraction is one of the core challenges in automated knowledge base construction. One line of approach for relation extraction is to perform multi-hop reasoning on the paths connecting an entity pair to infer new relations. While these methods have been successfully applied for knowledge base completion, they do not utilize the entity or the entity type information to make predictions. In this work, we incorporate *selectional preferences*, i.e., relations enforce constraints on the allowed entity types for the candidate entities, to multi-hop relation extraction by including entity type information. We achieve a 17.67% (relative) improvement in MAP score in a relation extraction task when compared to a method that does not use entity type information.

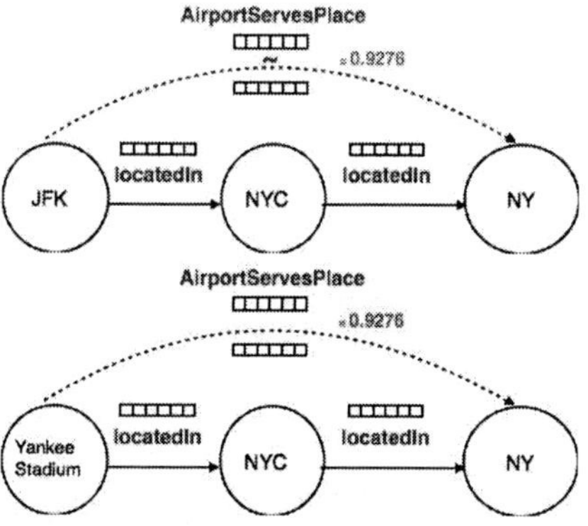

Figure 1: The two paths above consist of the same relations (`locatedIn → locatedIn`) and, hence, the model of Neelakantan (2015) will assign them the same score for the relation *AirportServesPlace* without considering the fact that *Yankee Stadium* is not an airport.

1 Introduction

Knowledge Bases (KB's) are structured knowledge sources widely used in applications like question answering (Kwiatkowski et al., 2013; Berant et al., 2013; Bordes et al., 2014) and search engines like *Google Search* and *Microsoft Bing*. This has led to the creation of large KB's like Freebase (Bollacker et al., 2008), YAGO (Suchanek et al., 2007) and NELL (Carlson et al., 2010). KB's contains millions of facts usually in the form of triples $(entity1, relation, entity2)$. However, KB's are woefully incomplete (Min et al., 2013), missing important facts, and hence limiting their usefulness in downstream tasks.

To overcome this difficulty, Knowledge Base Completion (KBC) methods aim to complete the KB using existing facts. For example, we can infer nationality of a person from their place of birth. A common approach in many KBC methods for relation extraction is reasoning on individual relations (single-hop reasoning) to predict new relations (Mintz et al., 2009; Bordes et al., 2013; Riedel et al., 2013; Socher et al., 2013). For example, predicting *Nationality(X, Y)* from *BornIn(X, Y)*. The performance of relation extraction methods have been greatly improved by incorporating *selectional preferences*, i.e., relations enforce constraints on the allowed entity types for the candidate entities, both in sentence level (Roth and Yih, 2007; Singh et

Proceedings of AKBC 2016, pages 18–23,
San Diego, California, June 12-17, 2016. ©2016 Association for Computational Linguistics

al., 2013) and KB relation extraction (Chang et al., 2014), and in learning entailment rules (Berant et al., 2011).

Another line of work in relation extraction performs reasoning on the paths (multi-hop reasoning on paths of length ≥ 1) connecting an entity pair (Lao et al., 2011; Lao et al., 2012; Gardner et al., 2013; Gardner et al., 2014; Neelakantan et al., 2015; Guu et al., 2015). For example, these models can infer the relation `PlaysInLeague(Tom Brady, NFL)` from the facts `PlaysForTeam(Tom Brady, New England Patriots)` and `PartOf(New England Patriots, NFL)`. All these methods utilize only the relations in the path and do not include any information about the entities.

In this work, we extend the method of Neelakantan (2015) by incorporating entity type information. Their method can generalize to paths unseen in training by composing embeddings of relations in the path non-linearly using a Recurrent Neural Network (RNN) (Werbos, 1990). While entity type information has been successfully incorporated into relation extraction methods that perform single hop reasoning, here, we include them for multi-hop relation extraction. For example, Figure 1 illustrates an example where reasoning without type information would score both the paths equally although the latter path should receive a lesser score since there is an entity type mismatch for the first entity. Our approach constructs vector representation of paths in the KB graph from representations of relations and entity types occurring in the path. We achieve a 17.67% improvement in Mean Average Precision (MAP) scores in a relation extraction task when compared to a method that does not use entity type information. Lastly, the *SHERLOCK* system (Schoenmackers et al., 2010) also discovers multi-hop clauses using typed predicates from web text, but, unlike our RNN approach it employs a Inductive Logic Programming method.

2 Model

This paper extends the Recurrent Neural Network model of Neelakantan (2015) by jointly reasoning over the relations and entity types occurring in the paths between an entity pair. Paths are represented

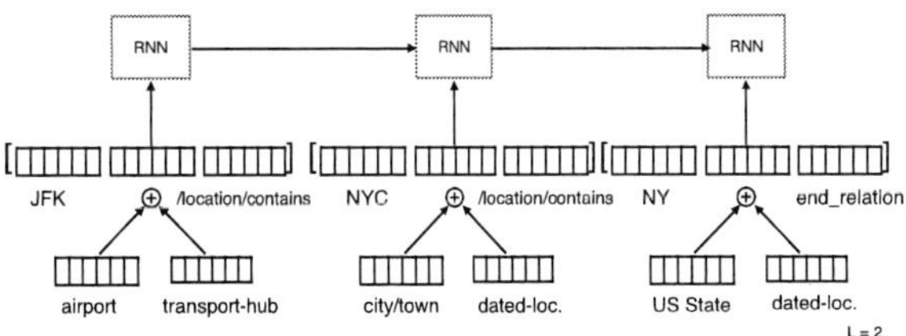

Figure 2: The encoder network for a path between an entity pair. The inputs to the network are embeddings of entities, entity types and relations. This architecture corresponds to equation 4 below. The network for other equations can be obtained by setting the appropriate input embeddings to zeros. Also note we have a dummy relation token `end_relation` for the last entity of the path. In the network above, at each time step, the entity embedding is concatenated with the sum of its type embeddings, followed by the embeddings of the relation type and are fed as input to the recurrent network

as dense vectors formed by composing embeddings of relations and entities occurring at each step. Figure 2 illustrates the encoder architecture for a path between an entity pair. The $[\cdot]$ in figure 2 denotes the concatenate operation. As will be described later, we also try representing the entity by its observed types.

The relation types considered in our work are either fixed symbolic types defined in the Freebase schema such as `/people/person/nationality` or a free text relation from Clueweb (Orr et al., 2013) such as `born in`. In Freebase, an entity is associated with several types. For example, the entity `Barack Obama` has types such as `President`, `Author` and `Award Winner`. In our work, we consider the top l types (sorted by corpus frequency) for an entity and we obtain a combined representation by summing the embeddings of types.

Let $v_r(\delta) \in \mathbb{R}^d$ denote the vector representation of relation type δ. Let $v_e(e) \in \mathbb{R}^m$ denote the vector representation of an entity e and $v_{et}(e) \in \mathbb{R}^n$ denote the combined representation of the types of e obtained by taking the sum of the representation of its top l types. Let π be a path between the entity pair $(e1, e2)$ containing the relation types $\delta_1, \delta_2, \ldots, \delta_N$.

In the following section, we first briefly describe

the model proposed by Neelakantan (2015) (RNN model henceforth) followed by our extensions to it.

2.1 RNN Model

The RNN model only considers the representations of relation type present in the path. More precisely, the vector representation $h_t \in \mathbb{R}^p$ of path $\delta_1, \delta_2, \ldots, \delta_t$ $(1 \leq t \leq N)$ is computed recursively as

$$h_t = f\left(W_{hh}h_{t-1} + W_{rh}v_r\left(\delta_t\right)\right) \qquad (1)$$

The vector representation of the entire path is h_N where N is the length of the path. Here $W_{h,h} \in \mathbb{R}^{p \times p}$ and $W_{rh} \in \mathbb{R}^{p \times d}$ are composition matrices between the previous step in the path and the relation vector at the current step respectively and f is a nonlinear activation function.

Extension with entity (and types)

The previous model can be extended to incorporate the embeddings of entities along with relations occurring at each step in the path. We consider learning a separate representation for every entity and representing an entity using its entity types.

- RNN + Entity: In this model, we add the embedding of the entity.

$$h_t = f\left(W_{hh}h_{t-1} + W_{rh}v_r\left(\delta_t\right) + W_{eh}v_e\left(e_t\right)\right) \qquad (2)$$

- RNN + Type: In this model, we add the embedding of the *entity* obtained from its types at each step.

$$h_t = f\left(W_{hh}h_{t-1} + W_{rh}v_r\left(\delta_t\right) + W_{th}v_{et}\left(e_t\right)\right) \qquad (3)$$

- RNN + Entity + Type: In this model, we use both the representations of the entity.

$$\begin{aligned} h_t = f(&W_{hh}h_{t-1} + W_{rh}v_r\left(\delta_t\right) \\ &+ W_{eh}v_e\left(e_t\right) + W_{th}v_{et}\left(e_t\right)) \end{aligned} \qquad (4)$$

Here e_t denotes the tth entity occurring in the path between an entity pair and $W_{eh} \in \mathbb{R}^{p \times m}, W_{th} \in \mathbb{R}^{p \times n}$ are new composition matrices due to the entity and its types respectively. In all of our experiments f is the sigmoid activation function.

2.2 Model Training

We train a separate RNN model for each target relation[1]. The parameters for each model are the embedding of the relations, entities and types, and the various composition matrices (as applicable) . They are trained to maximize the likelihood of the training data.The score of a path π w.r.t to the target relation δ is

$$score(\pi, \delta) = \sigma\left(v\left(\pi\right) \cdot v\left(\delta\right)\right) \qquad (5)$$

We then choose the path which has the highest score similar to (Weston et al., 2013; Neelakantan et al., 2014). Selecting just one path (out of typically hundreds to thousands of paths) between entity pairs might lead to our model ignoring informative paths, especially during the initial stages of training. To alleviate this issue we also experiment by selecting the top k paths that have the highest score for a given entity pair and relation with the resultant score being the average of the top k scores.

3 Experiments & Results

In all of our experiments, we set the dimension of the relations, entity and their type embeddings to be 50. For a fair comparison with our model, which has more number of parameters due to the entity and/or type embeddings, we experiment by varying the dimension of the relation embeddings between 50, 100 and 150 for the baseline model. We use Adam (Kingma and Ba, 2014) for optimization with the default hyperparameter settings. The models are trained for 15 epochs beyond which we observed overfitting on a held-out development set. We set $l = 7$ and $k = 5$ in our experiments. We experiment with 12 target relations.

3.1 Data

We run our experiments on the dataset released by Neelakantan el al. (2015) which is a subset of Freebase enriched with information from ClueWeb. The dataset comprises of entity pairs with a set of paths connecting them in the knowledge graph. The negative examples comprise of entity pairs for which the given query relation does not hold. However the paths had the entity information missing

---

[1]We are working on having a single model which can predict all relations as that would be more ideal than having a single specialized RNN for each relation

Stats	Full dataset	Current experiments
# test relations	46	12
# entity pairs	3.22M	839K
# entity pairs (train)	605K	161K
# entity pairs (test)	2M	533K
Avg. paths /relation	3.77M	3.43 M

Table 1: Statistics of the dataset

Model		MAP
Max	RNN (50)	0.5991
	RNN (100)	0.6020
	RNN (150)	0.6272
	RNN + Entity	0.5593
	RNN + Entity + Type	0.5995
	RNN + Types	**0.7084**
Top-K	RNN (50)	0.6241
	RNN (100)	0.6184
	RNN (150)	0.6312
	RNN + Entity	0.5968
	RNN + Entity + Type	0.6322
	RNN + Types	**0.7014**

Table 2: Mean Average Precision scores averaged over 12 relations. The number in the parentheses denotes the dimension of the embedding of the relations type in the baseline model.

from them and only contained the relation types occurring in them. For example, consider the path $SatyaNadella \xrightarrow{ceoAt} Microsoft \xrightarrow{locatedIn} Seattle \xrightarrow{cityIn} Washington$. The original dataset had the entities in-between such as $Microsoft$ and $Seattle$ missing from it.

We augment the dataset with the entities present in them. To gather the entities, we do a depth first traversal starting from the first entity of the entity pair and following the relation types until we reach the last entity of the pair. In cases of one-to-many relations we choose the next entity to be traversed at random. Due to the combinatorial search space we limit the total number of edges traversed beyond which we ignore the path. Therefore the number of paths between an entity pair would be less than in the original dataset. However, we are continuously augmenting the dataset and the latest version of the dataset can be downloaded from `http://iesl.cs.umass.edu/downloads/akbc16/`. Table 1 displays some statistics of the dataset gathered till now and also the subset that was used for running the current experiments.

3.2 Link Prediction

We compare our models with the baseline model on predicting whether an entity pair participates in a target relation. We rank the entity pairs in the test set based on their scores and calculate the Mean Average Precision (MAP) score for the ranking following previous work (Riedel et al., 2013; Neelakantan et al., 2015). Table 2 lists the MAP scores of both the models averaged over 12 freebase relation types.

Incorporating *selectional preferences* by adding entity types gives a significant boost in scores (17.67 % over the baseline model.). However, we see a drop in performance on adding just entities. This is primarily because during test time we encounter a lot of previously unseen entities and hence we do not have learned embeddings for them. We overcome this problem by representing the entity using its observed types in Freebase. In future work, we would consider using pre-trained entity embeddings and also by representing the entity additionally using context words (Yaghoobzadeh and Schütze, 2015).

Although considering top-k paths improves the performance of the baseline model, we observe that they provide almost similar scores with entity types. We run our experiments with $k = 5$ and we hope that the results would get better if we tune for k.

3.3 Predictive Paths

Table 3 shows maximum scoring paths for four entity pair and freebase relation triples chosen by the baseline and our model. We often find that the paths chosen by the baseline model have noisier textual relation, (like 'London'[2],'and at the') and have entities belonging to very different types than expected by the query relation. For example, in table 3, the path chosen by the baseline model for '/aviation/airport/serves' goes to a music education school, and a water body and for '/education/campus/institution', it goes to a country in which the institution is situated followed by a notable person in the country (unrelated to the query relation). It is quite clear that

---

[2]The freetext relation is different from the entity 'London' also occurring in the path

Relation : `/aviation/airport/serves` (Does the airport serve the location?)
Baseline Path: (0.5174) Sandy_Lake_Airport $\xrightarrow{\text{(/location/contains)}^{-1}}$ Ontario $\xrightarrow{\text{and at the}}$ Toronto_Royal_Conservatory_Of_Music $\xrightarrow{\text{(including the)}^{-1}}$ Canada $\xrightarrow{\text{(geography/lake/basin\_countries)}^{-1}}$ Big_Trout_Lake $\xrightarrow{\text{and to}}$ Sandy_Lake_First_Nation.
Our Model Path: (**0.9502**) Sandy_Lake_Airport $\xrightarrow{\text{(/location/contains)}^{-1}}$ Ontario $\xrightarrow{\text{(in northwestern)}^{-1}}$ Sandy_Lake_First_Nation.

Relation : `/aviation/airport/serves`
Baseline Score: (0.4348), Our Model Score: (**0.9731**) (Same path chosen by both models) St._Mary's_Airport $\xrightarrow{\text{(/location/contains)}^{-1}}$ Wade_Hampton_Census_Area $\xrightarrow{\text{/location/us\_county/hud\_county\_place}}$ St._Mary's

Relation : `/education/campus/institution` (Is the educational institution located in this campus?)
Baseline Path: (0.4869) Gray's Inn $\xrightarrow{\text{London}}$ England $\xrightarrow{\text{(/people/person/nationality)}^{-1}}$ Roger Fry $\xrightarrow{\text{/people/deceased\_person/place\_of\_death}}$ London $\xrightarrow{\text{/location/contains}}$ City_Law_School
Our Model Path: (**0.9676**) Gray's Inn $\xrightarrow{\text{(/location/contains)}^{-1}}$ London_Borough_of_Camden $\xrightarrow{\text{/location/contains}}$ City_Law_School

Relation : `/geography/river/mouth` (Does the river (tributary) flow into the other river?)
Baseline Path: (0.4578) Gard_River $\xrightarrow{\text{/geography/river/basin\_countries}}$ Romania $\xrightarrow{\text{(/geography/river/basin\_countries)}^{-1}}$ Jijia_River
Our Model Path: (**0.9231**) Gard_River $\xrightarrow{\text{(/location/contains)}^{-1}}$ Botosani_County $\xrightarrow{\text{/location/contains}}$ Jijia_River

Table 3: Predictive paths chosen by the baseline and our model for four entity pair and relation triples. The relations are edge labels and the entities occur in between them and at the ends. The freebase relations starts with '/', (`/location/contains`, for e.g.). Inverse relations are denoted by $^{-1}$ i.e. $r(x, y) \implies r^{-1}(y, x), \forall (x, y) \in r$. The scores are given in parentheses (higher is better). Sometimes, both models find the same path (second example in `/aviation/airport/serves`), but we often find that our model correctly scores it higher.

adding entity types helps us incorporate *selectional preference* and hence eliminate lot of noisy paths. We also find that sometimes both models finds the same max scoring path but our model assigns more confidence (higher scores) to them leading to better MAP scores.[3]

4 Conclusion

In this work, we incorporate *selectional preferences* to a multi-hop relation extraction method. We have released the dataset we collected for this project. We achieve a 17.67% relative improvement in MAP score in a relation extraction task when compared to a method that does not use entity type information.

[3]The reader can browse more examples at `http://people.cs.umass.edu/~rajarshi/paths.html`.

Acknowledgments

This work was supported in part by the Center for Intelligent Information Retrieval and in part by DARPA under agreement number FA8750-13-2-0020. The U.S. Govt. is authorized to reproduce and distribute reprints for Governmental purposes notwithstanding any copyright notation thereon, in part by DARPA contract number HR0011-15-2-0036, and in part by the NSF grant number IIS-1514053. Any opinions, findings and conclusions or recommendations expressed in this material are those of the authors and do not necessarily reflect those of the sponsor.

References

Jonathan Berant, Ido Dagan, and Jacob Goldberger. 2011. Global learning of typed entailment rules. In *NAACL*.

Jonathan Berant, Vivek Srikumar, Pei-Chun Chen, Abby Vander Linden, Brittany Harding, Brad Huang, and Christopher D. Manning. 2013. Semantic parsing on freebase from question-answer pairs. In *EMNLP*.

Kurt Bollacker, Colin Evans, Praveen Paritosh, Tim Sturge, and Jamie Taylor. 2008. Freebase: A collaboratively created graph database for structuring human knowledge. In *ICDM*.

Antoine Bordes, Nicolas Usunier, Alberto García-Durán, Jason Weston, and Oksana Yakhnenko. 2013. Translating embeddings for modeling multi-relational data. In *NIPS*.

Antoine Bordes, Sumit Chopra, and Jason Weston. 2014. Question answering with subgraph embeddings. In *EMNLP*.

Andrew Carlson, Justin Betteridge, Bryan Kisiel, Burr Settles, Estevam R. Hruschka, and Tom M. Mitchell. 2010. Toward an architecture for never-ending language learning. In *In AAAI*.

Kai-Wei Chang, Wen tau Yih, Bishan Yang, and Christopher Meek. 2014. Typed tensor decomposition of knowledge bases for relation extraction. In *EMNLP*.

Matt Gardner, Partha Pratim Talukdar, Bryan Kisiel, and Tom M. Mitchell. 2013. Improving learning and inference in a large knowledge-base using latent syntactic cues. In *EMNLP*.

Matt Gardner, Partha Talukdar, Jayant Krishnamurthy, and Tom Mitchell. 2014. Incorporating vector space similarity in random walk inference over knowledge bases. In *EMNLP*.

K. Guu, J. Miller, and P. Liang. 2015. Traversing knowledge graphs in vector space. In *EMNLP*.

Diederik P. Kingma and Jimmy Ba. 2014. Adam: A method for stochastic optimization. *CoRR*, abs/1412.6980.

Tom Kwiatkowski, Eunsol Choi, Yoav Artzi, and Luke. Zettlemoyer. 2013. Scaling semantic parsers with on-the-fly ontology matching. In *EMNLP*.

Ni Lao, Tom Mitchell, and William W. Cohen. 2011. Random walk inference and learning in a large scale knowledge base. In *EMNLP*, Stroudsburg, PA, USA.

Ni Lao, Amarnag Subramanya, Fernando Pereira, and William W. Cohen. 2012. Reading the web with learned syntactic-semantic inference rules. In *EMNLP*.

Bonan Min, Ralph Grishman, Li Wan, Chang Wang, and David Gondek. 2013. Distant supervision for relation extraction with an incomplete knowledge base. In *NAACL*.

Mike Mintz, Steven Bills, Rion Snow, and Dan Jurafsky. 2009. Distant supervision for relation extraction without labeled data. In *ACL*.

Arvind Neelakantan, Jeevan Shankar, Alexandre Passos, and Andrew McCallum. 2014. Efficient nonparametric estimation of multiple embeddings per word in vector space. In *EMNLP*, Doha, Qatar.

Arvind Neelakantan, Benjamin Roth, and Andrew McCallum. 2015. Compositional vector space models for knowledge base completion. In *ACL*, Beijing, China.

Dave Orr, Amar Subramanya, Evgeniy Gabrilovich, and Michael Ringgaard. 2013. 11 billion clues in 800 million documents: A web research corpus annotated with freebase concepts. http://googleresearch.blogspot.com/2013/07/11-billion-clues-in-800-million.html.

Sebastian Riedel, Limin Yao, Andrew McCallum, and Benjamin M. Marlin. 2013. Relation extraction with matrix factorization and universal schemas. In *NAACL*.

Dan Roth and Wen-tau Yih. 2007. Global inference for entity and relation identification via a linear programming formulation. In *In Introduction to SRL*.

Stefan Schoenmackers, Oren Etzioni, Daniel S. Weld, and Jesse Davis. 2010. Learning first-order horn clauses from web text. In *EMNLP*.

Sameer Singh, Sebastian Riedel, Brian Martin, Jiaping Zheng, and Andrew McCallum. 2013. Joint inference of entities, relations, and coreference. In *AKBC, CIKM*.

Richard Socher, Danqi Chen, Christopher D Manning, and Andrew Ng. 2013. Reasoning with neural tensor networks for knowledge base completion. In *NIPS*.

Fabian M. Suchanek, Gjergji Kasneci, and Gerhard Weikum. 2007. Yago: A core of semantic knowledge. In *WWW*.

P. Werbos. 1990. Backpropagation through time: what does it do and how to do it. In *Proceedings of IEEE*, volume 78.

Jason Weston, Ron Weiss, and Hector Yee. 2013. Nonlinear latent factorization by embedding multiple user interests. In *RecSys*.

Yadollah Yaghoobzadeh and Hinrich Schütze. 2015. Corpus-level fine-grained entity typing using contextual information. In *EMNLP, 2015*, pages 715–725.

Knowledge Base Population for Organization Mentions in Email

Ning Gao
University of Maryland, College Park
ninggao@umd.edu

Mark Dredze
Johns Hopkins University
mdredze@cs.jhu.edu

Douglas W. Oard
University of Maryland, College Park
oard@umd.edu

Abstract

A prior study found that on average there are 6.3 named mentions of organizations found in email messages from the Enron collection, only about half of which could be linked to known entities in Wikipedia (Gao et al., 2014). That suggests a need for collection-specific approaches to entity linking, similar to those have proven successful for person mentions. This paper describes a process for automatically constructing such a collection-specific knowledge base of organization entities for named mentions in Enron. A new public test collection for linking 130 mentions of organizations found in Enron email to either Wikipedia or to this new collection-specific knowledge base is also described. Together, Wikipedia entities plus the new collection-specific knowledge base cover 83% of the 130 organization mentions, a 14% (absolute) improvement over the 69% that could be linked to Wikipedia alone.

1 Introduction

The Text Analysis Conference Knowledge Base Population (TAC-KBP) track defines several knowledge base population tasks, including linking mentions to corresponding Knowledge Base (KB) entities (i.e., entity linking), extending the KB with newly discovered entities (i.e., NIL clustering), and discovering attribute values for both known and new entities (i.e., slot filling). When linking mentions of well known entities, general-coverage KBs such as those built from Wikipedia are useful. Prior work has, however, found that few people who are mentioned in the course of informal interactions (specifically, in Enron email) exist in such general-coverage KB's (Gao et al., 2014). That fact resulted in renewed interest in constructing collection-specific KBs, which had been investigated a decade earlier in other contexts (Elsayed and Oard, 2006). That approach proved productive, covering about 80% of all person named mentions found in the Enron collection (Elsayed et al., 2008). Several entity linking systems (some referred to in earlier work as "identity resolution") have been proposed for resolving named mentions of people in email messages to a collection-specific person KB (Minkov et al., 2006; Elsayed et al., 2008; Xu and Oard, 2012; Diehl et al., 2006). The next natural question to explore is whether similar techniques might be used to create collection-specific organization (ORG) KBs, since that same earlier study reported that only about half (53%) of ORG mentions in the Enron collection could be found in Wikipedia (Gao et al., 2014). That is our focus in this paper.

Collection-specific person KBs for email collections (Elsayed and Oard, 2006) are built by taking the set of email addresses found as senders or recipients in the collection as candidate entities for which names are then mined (e.g., from headers, salutations, signatures, or the address itself), finally clustering candidate entities that seem to refer to the same person into a single entity. We can draw on the same insight to create an ORG KB by observing that the domain names found in those email addresses provide a set of candidate ORG entities. From there, however, the approach necessarily diverges because collection-internal evidence for the

24

Proceedings of AKBC 2016, pages 24–28,
San Diego, California, June 12-17, 2016. ©2016 Association for Computational Linguistics

organization name associated with each of those entities is limited. It is, however, possible to also turn to external sources (e.g., Web search) for clues, since many organizations would be expected to have a Web presence. Another challenge is that some domain names (e.g., hotmail.com) are generic and thus not useful for resolving ORG mentions. To explore these questions, we have built a collection-specific KB from the domain names in the Enron collection. As we report below, organization names and additional information could be found for three-quarters (75%) of the non-generic domain names in the KB as attributes by using a fully automated process, nearly all of which are correct.

Building such a KB is just a first step; the next question is whether the organizations in that KB were actually mentioned often in the collection. To answer this question, we have built a new test collection containing 130 organization mentions, each of which we have tried to link manually (as ground truth) to Wikipedia and to our new collection-specific KB. Our results indicate that the Wikipedia coverage is somewhat higher than previously reported (69% from our manual linking, which is better than the previously reported 53%), and that the proper referent for an additional 14% of organization mentions can be found only in our new collection-specific organization KB. In total, 83% of all organization mentions can be linked to entities in one, the other, or both KB's.

There are two main contributions in this paper. First, we propose a completely automatic process to populate a collection-specific organization KB from email collection. Additional information extracted from four sources are inserted into the KB as attributes for 75% of the ORG entities. Second, we extend an existing entity linking evaluation collection by linking the organization named mentions detected from sampled Enron email messages to both Wikipedia and our new domain-specific KB. The results show that 60% of the named mentions could be linked to the entities in the collection-specific KB, 14% of which are novel entities compared with Wikipedia. Note that the proposed collection-specific KB is not only an additional linking source for organization named mentions, but also provides connections between the organization and person entities (e.g., a link could be created between the person entity "Kenneth Lay" and organization entity "Enron" through the email address "kenneth.lay@enron.com"), which benefits both knowledge base population and entity linking.

The remainder of the paper is organized as follows: Section 2 outlines our process for generating entities from the domain names found in email addresses. Section 3 then describes how we use four specific sources to identify information about the organizations associated with those domain names, providing accuracy and coverage statistics for each source. We then describe our new entity linking test collection in Section 4. Finally, Section 5 concludes the paper with a few remarks about future work.

2 Extracting Candidate Organization Entities

In the CMU Enron email collection (Klimt and Yang, 2004), there are 23,265 unique domain names extracted from the 158,097 unique email addresses in the collection as candidate ORG entities. 22,195 of these domain names have two levels (e.g., davis-bros.com) or three levels (e.g., dmi.maxinc.com). The remaining 1,070 domains have between 4 and 6 levels (e.g., dshs.state.texas.us). 39.5% of these unique domains are associated with at least two different email addresses. The most frequently used domain, "enron.com," is associated with 37,687 different email addresses in the collection, which indicates that "enron" might be the affiliation of as many as 37,687 person entities.

Three steps are applied to regularize the domains and merge identical ORG entities: (1) Domains are lower cased; (2) Domain segments that are not representing affiliations (i.e., main, alert, admin, student, exchange, list) are removed from the domain (e.g., alert.enron.com is recorded as enron.com in the KB); (3) Domains are merged by stripping the last element, which is the top level domain (e.g., enron.com and enron.net both become enron). This results in 23,008 entities in the collection-specific ORG KB with their associated domain variants and email addresses.

Table 1 shows the top 5 domains with the largest number of unique email addresses in the Enron corpus. The collection contains two types of domains: domains specific to the organization of the sender

Organization Domains		Email Service Providers	
Domain	Addresses	Domain	Addresses
enron	37,687	aol	9,065
haas.berkeley	727	hotmail	6,718
dynegy	633	yahoo	3,919
worldnet	609	msn	1,543
duke-energy	574	earthlink	1043

Table 1: The most frequently used email domains in the Enron corpus and the number of associated unique email addresses. We divide domains into organization domains, which are unique to a specific organization, and email service providers, which are shared by many organizations.

Source	Domains	Addresses	Accuracy
Google	68.4%	83%	20/20
Wikipedia	27.6%	64%	15/20
Signature	0.9%	26.3%	20/20
Body	3.4%	29.2%	17/20
Overall	75.1%	87.7%	

Table 2: Success rate of extracting organization information from different sources.

(e.g., enron, haas.berkeley, dynegy) (**Organization Domains**), and large email service providers (e.g., aol, hotmail) (**Email Service Providers**).

3 Extracting Organization Information

Table 2 shows the results of using four different sources (i.e., Google, Wikipedia, Signature and Body of email message) to extract additional information for the organizations. **Domains** and **Addresses** are the percentages of ORG entities and corresponding unique email addresses that can be associated with additional information through one of these sources. **Accuracy** shows the accuracy for the extracted information by manually judging the correctness on 20 randomly sampled non-generic domains (i.e., those that are not email service providers). The methodologies and results are described as following.

Google The domain for each ORG entity is submitted to Google as a search query. If the URL of the top returned webpage contains the domain, the webpage is considered as the organization's website. For example, searching for *bluegate* returns the site `http://www.bluegate.com/` with page title *BLUEGATE - Medical Grade Network*. Both the

URL and title of the matched webpage are stored as additional information for the ORG entity. Corresponding webpages are found for 68.4% of the ORG entities covering with 83% of the unique email addresses in Enron email collection. To measure the reliability of the Google source, 20 ORG entities with identified webpages were evaluated by the first author; all webpages were judged to be correct.

Wikipedia We extract the URL listed in the *Website* and *External Links* fields of Wikipedia Infoboxes and compare them to the domains for ORG entities. The Wikipedia entity with the longest domain segment match is used as the additional Wikipedia link for the ORG entities. For example, the *website* (`www.haas.berkeley.edu`) of the Wikipedia entity *Haas School of Business* has the longest domain segment match with the ORG entity with domain (haas.berkeley). Therefore, the titles and websites of Wikipedia entities are attached to the corresponding ORG entity in the KB. This method identified matches for 27.6% of the ORG entities covering 64% of the email addresses. Manual judgments on 20 matched ORG entities show that 15 of 20 of the entities are matched to the correct Wikipedia entities. When there is more than one segment in the domain of an ORG entity, it usually represents the hierarchy of the organization (e.g., *store.yahoo* represents *Yahoo Store* in *Yahoo!*). When the Wikipedia entity with longest domain segment match is only a partial match, there were misalignments (the 5 errors in the evaluation set) between the ORG in the KB and the ORG entity in Wikipedia. For example, the Wikipedia entity with longest domain segment match is *Yahoo!* (with *Website* `www.yahoo.com`) which is incorrect for the domain *store.yahoo*.

Signature Email signatures often contain the affiliation of the sender. We use the approach of Carvalho and Cohen (2004) to detect the signatures in email messages. Phrases with capital initials in the signature are recognized as potential organization names if there is a 5-gram string match between the domain of the sender's email address and the phrase. For example, *Harvard* and *Harvard Business School Publishing* are all valid organization names for domain *hbsp.harvard*. The frequency of the observed organization name / domain pairs are stored for each

ORG entity. Through the source of signature, we identify names for 0.9% of the ORG entities associated with 26.3% of the email addresses, in which 23.8% of the email addresses are registered under "enron" domain. Manual judgments on 20 randomly sampled Non-NIL ORG entities show that all 20 of the extracted organization names are correct.

Body   Similar to using the signature, organization names can appear in the body of the email. By using the source of email message body, 3.4% of the ORG entities are attached with additional organization information covering 29.2% of the email addresses. Manual judgments on 20 randomly sampled Non-NIL ORG entities show that 13 of the the extracted organization names contain valid information.

Analysis of the KB   Overall, Google is the best source for finding additional information for ORG entities. Wikipedia, Body and Signature provide coverage for an additional 6.7% of the entities. For example, the first returned Google search page for domain "infoseek" is "go.com" since the search engine "infoseek" was acquired by The Walt Disney Company and merged with the "go.com" network. Since we only examine the first returned result from Google, we miss this match. However, from Wikipedia we can find this historical information from the page of *Infoseek*. Another example is the domain of "ms1.lga2.nytimes". The first Google returned result is a page containing an email address "siteadm@ms1.lga2.nytimes.com", which doesn't provide domain information. However, the Body and Signature contain the strings "The New York Times Company" and "The New York Times".

In total, we identified information for 75.1% of the unique ORG entities covering 87.7% of the email addresses. 60.5% of the domains are associated with only one email address. If considering only the domains with at least two email addresses, additional information can be extracted for 77.8% of the entities covering 89% of the email addresses.

4   Entity Linking Test Collection

We now turn to an evaluation of the impact of our KB augmentation on the task of entity linking. Gao et al. (2014) created a collection of annotated email messages with links to a KB derived from Wikipedia. The collection contained 152 named organization mentions, of which 53% could be resolved to Wikipedia. We extended this work by also linking these mentions to our collection-specific organization KB.

We found that 22 mentions (which in the earlier work had been automatically detected) were not actually organizations. For example, "Rio Bravo IV Project" refers to a project rather than an organization. We therefore removed these 22 invalid mentions. For the 130 valid ORG mentions, 60 (46.1%) of them could be resolved to both Wikipedia and the collection-specific KB (e.g., "Pacific Gas and Electric Company" is an entity in Wikipedia and "pge" exists in the collection-specific KB). 30 mentions (23.1%) could only be resolved to Wikipedia (e.g., "Jacksonville Jaguars" are an American football team), while 18 mentions (13.8%) could only be resolved to an entity in the collection-specific KB (e.g., "PIRA" refers to PIRA Energy Group, with domain name "pira" after stripping the top-level domain). 22 of the mentions (16.9%) could not be linked to either KB ("SonoSite").

5   Conclusion

We have described a method for automatically populating organization information in a KB based on an email corpus. We gather information from Web sources (Google and Wikipedia) as well as the email collection (body and signature). Our methods identify organization information for 75% of the email domains, covering 87.7% of the unique email addresses in the collection. We show the value of the resulting collection by determining the coverage it provides to an email entity linking task.

Our methods were unable to provide information for one quarter of the entities. We believe additional coverage could be achieved through better processing of domains, such as identifying those that are originators of spam. We also plan to consider additional sources of information. Additionally, our work on organizations could be applied to other publicly available email collections (LDC, 2015), integrated with research into creating person KBs, and evaluated using an end-to-end entity linking system with both Wikipedia and a collection specific KB.

Acknowledgement

We would like to thank Dr. James Mayfield, Dr. Paul McNamee, Dr. Tim Finin, and Dr. Dawn Lawrie from Human Language Technology Center of Excellence (HLTCOE) at the Johns Hopkins University for their assistance and comments that greatly improved this proposed work.

References

Vitor R Carvalho and William W Cohen. 2004. Learning to extract signature and reply lines from email. In *CEAS*.

Christopher P Diehl, Lise Getoor, and Galileo Namata. 2006. Name reference resolution in organizational email archives. In *SIAM International Conference on Data Minng*, pages 70–91.

Tamer Elsayed and Douglas W Oard. 2006. Modeling identity in archival collections of email: A preliminary study. In *CEAS*, pages 95–103.

Tamer Elsayed, Douglas W Oard, and Galileo Namata. 2008. Resolving personal names in email using context expansion. In *ACL*, pages 941–949.

Ning Gao, Douglas W Oard, and Mark Dredze. 2014. A test collection for email entity linking. In *NIPS Workshop on Automated Knowledge Base Construction*.

Bryan Klimt and Yiming Yang. 2004. The Enron corpus: A new dataset for email classification research. In *Machine learning: ECML 2004*, pages 217–226.

LDC. 2015. Avocado research email collection, https://catalog.ldc.upenn.edu/LDC2015T03.

Einat Minkov, William W Cohen, and Andrew Y Ng. 2006. Contextual search and name disambiguation in email using graphs. In *SIGIR*, pages 27–34. ACM.

Tan Xu and Douglas W Oard. 2012. Exploring example-based person search in email. In *SIGIR*, pages 1067–1068. ACM.

Enriching Wikidata with Frame Semantics

Hatem Mousselly-Sergieh[1]
Iryna Gurevych[1,2]
[1]UKP Lab, Technische Universität Darmstadt
[2]UKP Lab, German Institute for Educational Research
`https://www.ukp.tu-darmstadt.de`

Abstract

Wikidata is a large-scale, multilingual and freely available knowledge base. It contains more than 14 million facts, however, it is still missing linguistic information. In this paper, we aim to bridge this gap by aligning Wikidata with FrameNet lexicon. We propose an approach based on word embedding to identify a mapping between Wikidata relations, called properties, and FrameNet frames and to annotate the arguments of each relation with the semantic roles of the matching frames. Early empirical results show the advantage of our approach compared to other baseline methods.

1 Introduction

Wikidata (hereafter WD) (Vrandečić and Krötzsch, 2014) is a large-scale, multilingual and freely available knowledge base containing more than 14 million facts. WD entities are directly linked to the corresponding Wikipedia articles. To increase the usability of WD for NLP tasks, we aim at enriching WD with linguistic information by aligning it to the famous lexicon FrameNet (Fillmore et al., 2003).

Several works considered aligning knowledge bases, e.g., Wikipedia with expert-resources like FrameNet and WordNet (Fellbaum, 1998) (refer to (Tonelli et al., 2013; Navigli and Ponzetto, 2012)). However, the focus of these works was on word-sense alignment. That means linking words having the same meaning among different resources. In contrast to previous efforts, we aim to perform the alignment on the relation level. Specifically, we aim to find a mapping between WD facts, e.g. *educated at(Person, University)* and similar structures in expert lexical resources. FrameNet (FN) provides such structure in terms of semantic frames. Briefly,

a frame is an abstract description of a situation, e.g. the frame *Education_teaching* and the participants in it, e.g. *Student*, *Teacher* and *Course*.

There are several advantages for such kind of alignment: FN is an essential resource for semantic role labeling (SRL) systems which are usually trained on the annotated corpus that is provided by FN. A crucial problem with such systems is that they are biased towards the domain of that corpus. By linking FN and WD, we could (semi) automatically create another frame-annotated corpus using the links between WD entities and the corresponding Wikipedia articles as well as the alignment between FN and WD. Consequently, the annotated Wikipedia corpus which covers a wide range of domains can be used to improve the performance of SRL systems. As for the knowledge base, in addition to the direct result of enriching WD with linguistic information, the alignments can be used to refine the property structure of WD by inducing new general/specific properties. For instance, the property *killed by* refers to someone (victim) killed by somebody else (killer). However, the property does not distinguish between different kinds of killing, such as execution. In FN such information is already captured through the frames *Execution* and *Killing*, where the former frame inherits from the latter. By aligning *killed by* to both frames, the property *killed by* can refined by introducing a new sub-property: *executed by*.

Our contributions are: (1) a method for extracting semantic representations for WD properties and their arguments, (2) an approach for frame-property as well as role-argument alignment[1] and (3) an experimental evaluation.

The rest of the paper is organized as follows: in

---

[1]FN-WD alignments: `https://goo.gl/FdhOkO`

Proceedings of AKBC 2016, pages 29–34,
San Diego, California, June 12-17, 2016. ©2016 Association for Computational Linguistics

the next Section, a short description of FrmeNet is provided while in Section 3 a method for extracting semantic representation for WD properties and their arguments is presented. Section 4 presents the alignment approach while the results of the experimental evaluation are presented in Section 5. Section 6 discusses related works and a conclusion is provided in Section 7.

2   FrameNet

The main entry in FN is the semantic **Frame** which is a description of a type of event or relation and the participants in it. Each frame consists of a set of semantic roles, called **Frame Elements (FEs)**, which correspond to the participants of the event. Additionally, each frame is associated with a collection of words called **lexical units (LUs)** that evoke that frame. FrameNet provides a corpus of example sentences, in which certain words, named **fillers**, are identified as frame **evoking elements (FEEs)** and annotated with a semantic frame.

3   WD Property Semantic Representation

WD distinguishes between two types of entries: **item** which corresponds to a Wikipedia article and **property** that defines a relation between an item/property and a value, e.g. *educated at(Barack Obama, Columbia University)*. We analyzed the WD data model in order to extract semantic representations for properties and their arguments as a pre-step towards aligning WD with FN. First, we use the notation $p(ARG1, ARG2)$ to refer to a property p and its left-side and right-side arguments, respectively. For each property, i.e., the element p, we extract the following information from the data model: 1) the label of the property and 2) the aliases which are alternative names or loosely speaking synonyms of that property. For example, the following set of semantic representations can generated for the property *educated at* (Figure 1): {educated at, alumni of, college attended, university attended, studied at,...}

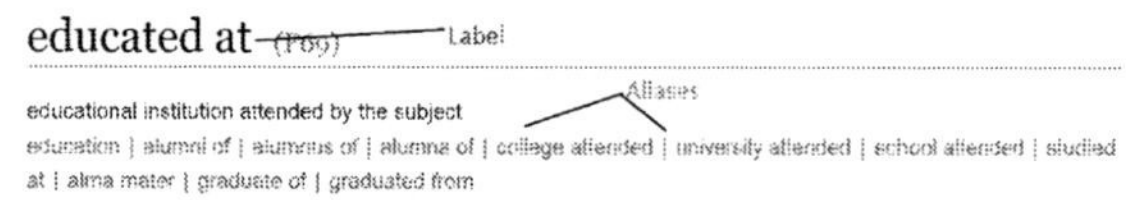

Figure 1: WD page for the property *educated at*

As for the arguments, we distinguish between two types of semantic representations: **semantic types** and **instances** which we will refer to as "fillers" in the following discussion. For a given argument, we leverage the structural property *instance of* to obtain the father concept of that argument. Furthermore, we exploits other structural relationships between WD properties, namely *subproperty of, inverse of* and *see also* to infer further semantic types about the arguments. Accordingly, the semantic types of the arguments of the related properties are propagated to the arguments of the source property. Take a look at the following instance of the property *father*: *father(George Washington,Augustine Washington)*. Instances of *ARG1* and *ARG2* of this property, i.e., *George Washington* and *Augustine Washington* are linked via *instance of* to the item *human* in WD. Accordingly, we deduce that *ARG1* and *ARG2* are of type *human*. Furthermore, the property *father* is defined as *subproperty* of *relative*. In a similar manner, we extract the semantic types of the property *relative* and use them as descriptors for the arguments of *father*. The same procedure is applied to the properties *see also* and *inverse of* where in the latter case the semantic types are propagated in the reverse order.

For each property in WD, a set of instances can be obtained from the knowledge base. For example, the property *educated at* connects the WD item *Barack Obama* (instance of *ARG1*) to the WD item *Columbia University* (instance of *ARG2*). In analogy to FN, we use the term *fillers* to refer to instances of property arguments. WD provides a large number of such fillers and we use them as further descriptors for property arguments.

4   Towards FrameNet-Wikidata Alignment

Although WD and FN have different objectives, they show considerable overlap in their semantics. Consider the definitions of the frame *Education_teaching* and the property *educated at*:

- **Education_teaching**: *This frame contains words referring to teaching and the participants in teaching. A <u>Student</u> comes to learn either about a <u>Subject</u>; a <u>Skill</u>; a <u>Precept</u>; or a <u>Fact</u> as a result of instruction by a <u>Teacher</u>.*

- **student of**: *person who has taught this person.*

Although the definitions have different granularity, their overlap is obvious. Moreover, the arguments $ARG1$ and $ARG2$ of *student of* (with the semantic types *student* and *teacher*, respectively), represent direct correspondences to the FEs *Student* and *Teacher*, respectively. However, the conceptual differences implies that the alignment between frames and properties is rather many-to-many than one-to-one. Additionally, properties are more specific than frames in the sense that they describe a single fact rather than a situation. Hence, a partial alignment between property arguments and FEs is natural.

4.1 Property-Frame Alignment

First, we aim to align WD properties with FN frames. For this purpose, we create for each property a context based on its label and aliases (refer to Section 3). Similarly, we create a context for each frame based on its lexical units and frame label.

In contrast to the rich frame context (each frame is associated with 13 lexical units on average), property context is rather poor. This is because a considerable part of WD properties has few to no aliases. Therefore, we expand the property context with additional words based the technique of word embedding (Mikolov et al., 2013b). Word embedding is a technique for representing words as vectors of real numbers in a low-dimensional space. It has gained much attention recently and has been successfully applied to a wide range of semantic tasks (Faruqui and Dyer, 2014). (Levy and Goldberg, 2014) presented a word embedding approach in which the context of a given word is created based on the dependency graph of that word over large collection of sentences. According to this approach, words with similar functionality, such as co-hyponyms lay close to each other in the embedding space. This type of embedding is good candidate for our case because we assume that words of similar functionality would evoke the same frame. Therefore, we use the pre-calculated word vectors provided by (Levy and Goldberg, 2014) to expand the context of WD properties. First, we identify for each label and alias (if available) a set of words that are close to them in the dependency-embedding space. Next, we combine the embedding vectors by summing them to obtain a single embedding vector for each property context. We also experimented with different combination methods, e.g. averaging, multiplication and subtraction, however, the sum led to the best results.

Similarly, we create for each frame context an embedding vector by looking up the corresponding words in the same embedding space and summing the identified embedding vectors.

Finally, the property-frame alignments are determined based on the cosine similarity between the final embedding vectors of the two contexts. Figure 2 illustrates the described alignment procedure.

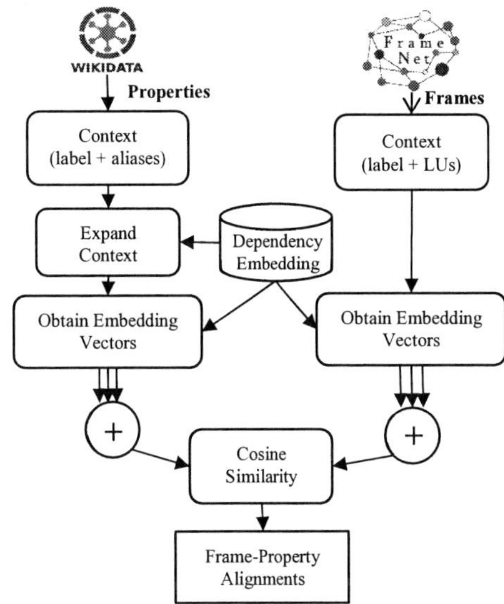

Figure 2: Property-Frame alignment workflow

4.2 Argument-FE Alignment

After identifying property-frame correspondences, property arguments are mapped to FEs as follows (Figure 3):

1) Creating Argument/FE Context:
Regarding property arguments, we apply the procedure described in Section 3 to create two contexts for each argument: *semantic type* and *filler* contexts. Similarly, we create for each FE two contexts: 1) semantic type context which consists of the label and the semantic type of that FE as defined in FN and 2) filler context which contains the headwords of the fillers of that FE which were obtained from the FN annotated corpus according to (Bauer et al., 2012).

2) Generating Word Embedding Vectors:
Next, the embedding vector for each word in the argument/FE context are retrieved from a word embedding space that was trained on the Google News

dataset as provided by the word2vec framework (Mikolov et al., 2013a). We chose this embedding space due to its high coverage of three million words and phrases. Indeed, phrases are crucial in our case, especially, since the majority of argument fillers correspond to named entities. Subsequently, the embedding vectors are summed to produced one final vector per context, i.e., one for the semantic type context and one for the filler context.

3) Calculating Argument-FE Similarities:
In this step, the pairwise similarity between each argument a and FE e of a matched frame-property pair is calculated. The similarity is based on a combination of two scores, i.e., the cosine similarities between the semantic type contexts and the filler contexts of a and e, respectively:

$$Sim(a, e) = \alpha S(V_a, V_e) + (1 - \alpha)S(W_a, W_e) \quad (1)$$

V_a/W_a, V_e/W_e are the combined embedding vectors of the semantic type/filler contexts of a and e, respectively, S is the cosine similarity and $\alpha \in [0, 1]$ is a weighting parameter that is used to tune the effect of the semantic type/filler contexts on the final similarity. Setting α to 0.5 leads to a equal effect of both contexts, $\alpha = 1$ ignores the filler contexts while $\alpha = 0$ eliminates the semantic type contexts from the similarity calculation.

The similarity scores are then used to determine the final alignments. Here, we ensure that the final alignments satisfy two constraints: 1) each argument is aligned to at most one FE and 2) each FE is aligned to at most one argument.

5 Evaluation

We created a gold standard from a sample of 130 WD properties. For each property, two annotators were provided with a list of 7 candidate frames on average and had to answer the question whether a property-frame pair is a match or not based on the corresponding definitions and an example per property/frame. The inter-annotator agreement according to Cohen's κ was 0.65. After removing the disparagement pairs, the gold standard contained 785 property-frame pairs with 279 positive and 506 negative alignments, respectively. For the proportion of positive alignments the same annotators also aligned the arguments and FEs. The final set contains 411 argument-FE alignments.

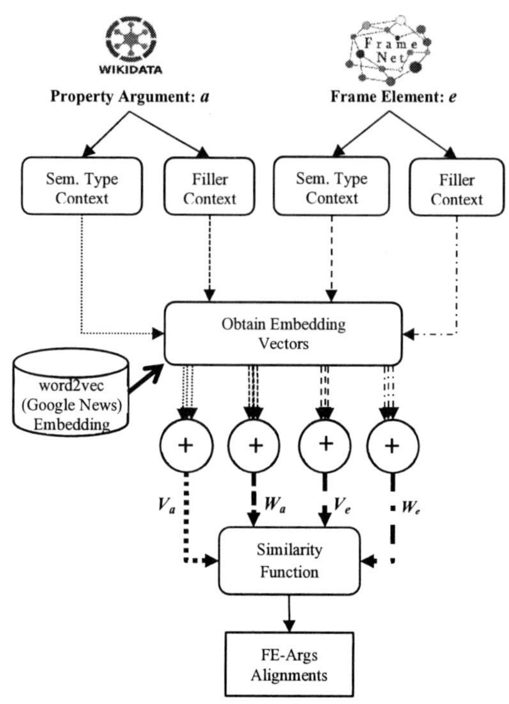

Figure 3: Argument-FE alignment workflow

5.1 Results: Property-Frame Alignment

The alignment approach was applied on FN version 1.5 which contains 1,019 frames and WD dump of 28/9/2015 which contains 1,745 properties. After filtering properties that describes identifiers (e.g. the property *GND identifier*) or structural relationships (e.g. *subproperty of, facet of*), we were able to align 638 properties (37% of the total WD properties) to a total of 380 unique frames (37% of the total frames).

We compared the performance of our method to other baselines. In the first baseline (BL1) the alignment is determined based on the lexical overlap between the frame and property contexts without expansion. The second baseline (BL2) expands the property context with words from the most frequent WordNet synsets instead of using the embedding space. Next, the embedding vectors of the expanded property context and frame context are summed and the cosine similarity is applied on the final context vectors.

For each property the top two matching frames were identified and precision, recall and f1-measure were reported (Table 1). The results show that enriching the context of the property with further words either from WordNet or using a given embedding space leads to better results compared to BL1. Moreover, expanding the property context using dependency-based embeddings (our method) outperforms WordNet based expansion (BL2).

Method	P	R	F1
BL 1	0.45	0.44	0.45
BL 2	0.65	0.68	0.66
Our Method	**0.70**	**0.72**	**0.73**

Table 1: Performance of frame-property alignment

5.2 Results: Argument-FE Alignment:

This task was evaluated by measuring the accuracy of the matching as the proportion of correctly aligned property arguments and taking the average. We experimented with different values of α (Equation 1). The experiments showed that the filler context has higher influence on the accuracy than the semantic type context (best results are obtained with $\alpha = 0.35$). Accordingly, we can conclude that the semantic types are less discriminative than the fillers. For example, the two arguments of the property *killed by* share the semantic types *human* and *person*, thus, it is impossible to determine which argument represents the victim and which one represents the killer. However, by using the fillers a better distinction can be made.

We also compared our approach to other baselines which use the filler as well as the semantic type contexts as input, however, without applying the described word embedding approach. We investigated three similarity measures: the lexical overlap, Jaccard similarity and the cosine similarity between the context vectors. Our approach outperforms the baselines (Table 2) and the results confirms the advantage of using word embedding for this task.

	ARG 1 Accuracy	ARG 2 Accuracy	AVG Accuracy
Overlap	0.55	0.56	0.56
Cosine	0.51	0.62	0.57
Jaccard	0.53	0.63	0.58
Our Method	**0.70**	**0.68**	**0.69**

Table 2: The accuracy of argument-FE alignments

6 Related Work

The problem of aligning expert lexical resources in order to increase their coverage was the topic of several research efforts (Shi and Mihalcea, 2005; Chow and Webster, 2007; Johansson and Nugues, 2007; De Cao et al., 2008; Lacalle et al., 2014). Another line of research considered aligning community-created resources like Wikipedia and Wiktionary to lexical resources like FrameNet. (Tonelli and Giuliano, 2009; Tonelli et al., 2013) presented an approach for extending FN by linking its LUs to Wikipedia articles using supervised WSD. (Hartmann and Gurevych, 2013) presented an approach for linking FN with Wiktionary in order to build a FrameNet-like resource for German. While our work consider the alignment on the relation level, the mentioned efforts focus on extending the coverage of FN by inducing new LUs using word-sense alignment techniques. In fact, the problem of aligning FN frames with knowledge base relations is new. An initial attempt with a similar goal as ours was presented by sar-graph (Krause et al., 2015). *sar-graph* is a graph that connects different contractions of a given relation. The nodes correspond to words or arguments of that relation and are labeled with lexical, syntactic and semantic information. The authors presented initial ideas for linking sar-graphs with FN using valency and phrase patterns and claimed that such a connection would allow linking FN frames with sar-graph relations. Compared to our work, where a concrete solution is presented, the mapping between sar-graph relations and FN is still in its early stage.

7 Conclusion and Future Work

We presented an approach for aligning WD with FN which addresses two tasks: frame-property mapping as well as mapping property arguments to FEs of the matching frames. We presented a simple but effective alignment approach based on the technique of word embedding. In future work, we will evaluate the advantage of the created alignments in the context of semantic role labeling.

References

Daniel Bauer, Hagen Frstenau, and Owen Rambow. 2012. The dependency-parsed framenet corpus. In Nicoletta Calzolari (Conference Chair), Khalid Choukri, Thierry Declerck, Mehmet Uur Doan, Bente Maegaard, Joseph Mariani, Asuncion Moreno, Jan Odijk, and Stelios Piperidis, editors, *Proceedings of the Eight International Conference on Language Resources and Evaluation (LREC'12)*, Istanbul, Turkey, may. European Language Resources Association (ELRA).

Ian C Chow and Jonathan J Webster. 2007. Integration of linguistic resources for verb classification: Framenet frame, wordnet verb and suggested upper merged ontology. In *Computational Linguistics and Intelligent Text Processing*, pages 1–11. Springer.

Diego De Cao, Danilo Croce, Marco Pennacchiotti, and Roberto Basili. 2008. Combining word sense and usage for modeling frame semantics. In *Proceedings of the 2008 Conference on Semantics in Text Processing*, pages 85–101. Association for Computational Linguistics.

Manaal Faruqui and Chris Dyer. 2014. Community evaluation and exchange of word vectors at wordvectors.org. In *Proceedings of the 52nd Annual Meeting of the Association for Computational Linguistics: System Demonstrations*, Baltimore, USA, June. Association for Computational Linguistics.

Christiane Fellbaum, editor. 1998. *WordNet: an electronic lexical database*. MIT Press.

Charles J Fillmore, Christopher R Johnson, and Miriam RL Petruck. 2003. Background to framenet. *International journal of lexicography*, 16(3):235–250.

Silvana Hartmann and Iryna Gurevych. 2013. Framenet on the way to babel: Creating a bilingual framenet using wiktionary as interlingual connection. In *Proceedings of the 51st Annual Meeting of the Association for Computational Linguistics (ACL 2013)*, volume 1, pages 1363–1373, Stroudsburg, PA, USA, August. Association for Computational Linguistics.

Richard Johansson and Pierre Nugues. 2007. Using wordnet to extend framenet coverage. In *Building Frame Semantics Resources for Scandinavian and Baltic Languages*, pages 27–30. Department of Computer Science, Lund University.

Sebastian Krause, Leonhard Hennig, Aleksandra Gabryszak, Feiyu Xu, and Hans Uszkoreit. 2015. Sar-graphs: A linked linguistic knowledge resource connecting facts with language. In *Fourth Workshop on Linked Data in Linguistics: Resources and Applications (LDL-2015) at ACL-IJCNLP 2015*. ACL.

Maddalen Lopez De Lacalle, Egoitz Laparra, and German Rigau. 2014. Predicate matrix: extending sem-link through wordnet mappings. In Nicoletta Calzolari (Conference Chair), Khalid Choukri, Thierry Declerck, Hrafn Loftsson, Bente Maegaard, Joseph Mariani, Asuncion Moreno, Jan Odijk, and Stelios Piperidis, editors, *Proceedings of the Ninth International Conference on Language Resources and Evaluation (LREC'14)*, Reykjavik, Iceland, may. European Language Resources Association (ELRA).

Omer Levy and Yoav Goldberg. 2014. Dependency-based word embeddings. In *Proceedings of the 52nd Annual Meeting of the Association for Computational Linguistics*, volume 2, pages 302–308.

Tomas Mikolov, Kai Chen, Greg Corrado, and Jeffrey Dean. 2013a. Efficient estimation of word representations in vector space. *arXiv preprint arXiv:1301.3781*.

Tomas Mikolov, Ilya Sutskever, Kai Chen, Greg S Corrado, and Jeff Dean. 2013b. Distributed representations of words and phrases and their compositionality. In *Advances in neural information processing systems*, pages 3111–3119.

Roberto Navigli and Simone Paolo Ponzetto. 2012. Babelnet: The automatic construction, evaluation and application of a wide-coverage multilingual semantic network. *Artif. Intell.*, 193:217–250, December.

Lei Shi and Rada Mihalcea. 2005. Putting pieces together: Combining framenet, verbnet and wordnet for robust semantic parsing. In *Computational linguistics and intelligent text processing*, pages 100–111. Springer.

Sara Tonelli and Claudio Giuliano. 2009. Wikipedia as frame information repository. In *Proceedings of the 2009 Conference on Empirical Methods in Natural Language Processing: Volume 1 - Volume 1*, EMNLP '09, pages 276–285, Stroudsburg, PA, USA. Association for Computational Linguistics.

Sara Tonelli, Claudio Giuliano, and Kateryna Tymoshenko. 2013. Wikipedia-based wsd for multilingual frame annotation. *Artificial Intelligence*, 194:203–221.

Denny Vrandečić and Markus Krötzsch. 2014. Wikidata: A free collaborative knowledgebase. *Commun. ACM*, 57(10):78–85, September.

Demonyms and Compound Relational Nouns in Nominal Open IE

Harinder Pal
Indian Institute of Technology
New Delhi, India
sethi.harinder@gmail.com

Mausam
Indian Institute of Technology
New Delhi, India
mausam@cse.iitd.ac.in

Abstract

Extracting open relational tuples that are mediated by nouns (instead of verbs) is important since titles and entity attributes are often expressed nominally. While appositives and possessives are easy to handle, a difficult and important class of nominal extractions requires interpreting compound noun phrases (e.g., "Google CEO Larry Page"). We substantially improve the quality of Open IE from compound noun phrases by focusing on phenomena like demonyms and compound relational nouns. We release RELNOUN 2.2, which obtains 3.5 times yield with over 15 point improvement in precision compared to RELNOUN 1.1, a publicly available nominal Open IE system.

1   Introduction

Open Information Extraction (Etzioni et al., 2008) systems output relational tuples from text without a pre-specified relational vocabulary by identifying relation phrases present in text. Early work on Open IE (Etzioni et al., 2011) focused on verb-mediated relations that could be expressed using a handful of patterns and still covered substantial information in text. Subsequent research has focused on increasing recall – a noteworthy approach (OLLIE) uses bootstrapping for learning general language patterns (Mausam et al., 2012). Various extensions improve on the amount of linguistic knowledge in the systems – EXEMPLAR (de Sá Mesquita et al., 2013) improves the set of rules on top of dependency parses; Open IE 4.0[1] uses carefully designed rules over

semantic role labeling systems (Christensen et al., 2011); several works attempt clause identification or sentence restructuring, thus identifying sentence components and applying extraction rules on top of these components (Schmidek and Barbosa, 2014; Corro and Gemulla, 2013; Bast and Haussmann, 2013). Other approaches include use of lexico-syntactic qualia-based patterns (Xavier et al., 2015), simple sentence-specific inference (Bast and Haussmann, 2014), and a supervised approach using tree kernels (Xu et al., 2013).

While the focus on verbs continues to be common in these Open IE systems, some works have directed attention on noun-mediated relations such as OLLIE (Mausam et al., 2012), RENOUN (Yahya et al., 2014), and RELNOUN.[2] A common observation is that many relations (e.g, *capital of*, *economist at*) are more frequently expressed using nouns, instead of verbs. Common noun-mediated patterns include appositive constructions, possessive constructions, and compound noun phrases (see Table 1 for examples). While most patterns give some syntactic cues for the existence of a relation (such as a comma or a possessive 's), interpreting and extracting tuples from compound NPs is specifically challenging, since they are just a continuous sequence of nouns and adjectives (e.g., "Google CEO Larry Page").

This paper substantially improves the quality of extraction from compound noun phrases. Our work builds on the publicly available RELNOUN system (ver 1.1) and extends it to RELNOUN 2.2, which incorporates three additional sources of recall from compound noun phrases: (1) capitalized relational

---

[1] *https://github.com/knowitall/openie*

[2] *https://github.com/knowitall/chunkedextractor*

35

Proceedings of AKBC 2016, pages 35–39,
San Diego, California, June 12-17, 2016. ©2016 Association for Computational Linguistics

Extractor	Phrase	Extraction
Verb1	Francis Collins is the director of NIH	(Francis Collins; is the director of; NIH)
Verb2	the director of NIH is Francis Collins	(Francis Collins; is the director of; NIH)
Appositive1	Francis Collins, the director of NIH	(Francis Collins; [is] the director of; NIH)
Appositive2	the director of NIH, Francis Collins,	(Francis Collins; [is] the director of; NIH)
Appositive3	Francis Collins, the NIH director	(Francis Collins; [is] the director [of]; NIH)
AppositiveTitle	Francis Collins, the director,	(Francis Collins; [is]; the director)
CompoundNoun	*NIH director Francis Collins*	*(Francis Collins; [is] director [of]; NIH)*
Possessive	NIH's director Francis Collins	(Francis Collins; [is] director [of]; NIH)
PossessiveAppositive	NIH's director, Francis Collins	(Francis Collins; [is] director [of]; NIH)
AppositivePossessive	Francis Collins, NIH's director	(Francis Collins; [is] director [of]; NIH)
PossessiveVerb	NIH's director is Francis Collins	(Francis Collins; is director [of]; NIH)
VerbPossessive	Francis Collins is NIH's director	(Francis Collins; is director [of]; NIH)

Table 1: RELNOUN 1.1 extractors along with the example phrases and corresponding extractions

nouns, (2) demonyms, the adjectives used to identify residents of a location (e.g., 'Japanese' for 'Japan'), and (3) compound relational nouns (see Table 2 for examples). Compared to its predecessor, RELNOUN 2.2 triples the yield with over 15 point improvement in precision. Our code is freely downloadable.[2]

2 Background on Nominal Open IE

Probably the earliest work on Nominal Open IE is OLLIE, which is a pattern learning approach based on a bootstrapped training data using high precision verb-based extractions (Mausam et al., 2012). It identified that nominal IE can't be completely syntactic, and, at the least, a list of relational nouns (e.g, *mother, director, CEO, capital*) is needed for high precision extraction. OLLIE is superseded by REL-NOUN, which is a rule-based extractor incorporating most of the high precision learnings of OLLIE.

A third work on nominal Open IE is RENOUN (Yahya et al., 2014). RENOUN builds a comprehensive list of relational nouns using bootstrapping over query logs and text. It then uses seed patterns to extract data and then uses these as source of distant supervision for additional pattern learning. Unfortunately, neither their list of relational nouns, nor their final extractor are available. Moreover, it is hard to reproduce their list of nouns since most researchers don't have access to query logs. Hence, we build upon the publicly available RELNOUN system.

RELNOUN 1.x series is a set of POS and NP-Chunk patterns defined to extract a high precision subset of noun-mediated extractions (see Table 1). The input to RELNOUN is a set of relational nouns, which are extracted using bootstrapping – these in-

clude words which are common headnouns for X in "is a X of" patterns, as well as words which are within the 'Person' subclass in WordNet hierarchy (Miller, 1995).[3] We added a couple of missing patterns and made small modifications to the previous RELNOUN release (version 1.0.9) to increase its coverage and precision. The resulting system REL-NOUN 1.1, acts as the baseline for our work.

Our analysis of RELNOUN 1.1 revealed significant missed recall when extracting from compound noun phrases such as "*Mechelen Mayor Bart Somers*", "*Chinese president Hu Jintao*", or "*United States health minister Levitt*". The desired extractions are (Bart Somers, [is] Mayor [of], Mechelen), (Hu Jintao, [is] president [of], China), and (Levitt, [is] health minister [of], United States). We attribute this to three important missing phenomena in RELNOUN 1.1 when extracting from compound noun phrases – capitalized relational nouns ('Mayor'), demonyms ('Chinese'), and compound relational nouns ('health minister'). Note that here a compound *relational noun* occurs within a larger compound noun phrase. RELNOUN 2.2 improves the analysis for all these three categories.

3 RELNOUN 2.2

RELNOUN 1.1 does not extract from phrases containing capitalized (NNP) relational nouns (e.g., "Mechelen Mayor Bart Somers") even though, at times, that is grammatically correct whereas uncapitalized nouns are not.[4] The main reason for this

---

[3]RELNOUN was not published as a research paper. Some of the system details are based upon personal communication with the main engineer, Michael Schmitz.

[4]http://blog.esllibrary.com/2012/11/01/when-do-we-

Phrase	RELNOUN 1.1	RELNOUN 2.2
"United States President Obama"		(Obama, [is] President [of], United States)
"Seattle historian Feliks"	(Feliks, [is] historian [of], Seattle)	(Feliks, [is] historian [from], Seattle)
"Japanese foreign minister Kishida"		(Kishida, [is] foreign minister [of], Japan)
"GM Deputy Chairman Lutz"		(Lutz, [is] Deputy Chairman [of], GM)

Table 2: Comparison of RELNOUN 1.1 and RELNOUN 2.2 on some phrases

choice is that allowing extractions from compound noun phrases with capitalized relational nouns can lead to a large number of false positives. On further analysis we observe three major categories of errors:

1. Organization names: Erroneous tuples are extracted when the compound NP is the name of an organization. For example, it extracts (Association, [is] Banker [of], New York) from the phrase *"New York Banker Association"*.

2. Demonyms: A common error is when the title is preceded by a demonym. For e.g., it extracts (Angela Merkel; [is] Chancellor [of]; German) from *"German Chancellor Angela Merkel"*.

3. Compound Relational Nouns: The relational noun with a pre-modifier often confuses the extractor. For example, *"Prime Minister Modi"* yields (Modi, [is] Minister [of], Prime).

The first set of errors is easy to fix. We create a list of 160 organization words and filter out any extractions where arg1 has an organization word. The list is created by extracting the most frequent last words from the list of organizations on Wikipedia. They include words like 'Committee', 'Limited', 'Group', and 'Association'. This ORG filtering improves the precision slightly, with almost no impact to recall.

The next two subsections detail our approaches for incorporating knowledge about demonyms and compound relational nouns in RELNOUN.

3.1 Demonyms

Demonyms are words derived from the name of a location and are used to identify residents or natives of that location. Typical examples include 'Israeli', 'Japanese', and 'South African' for residents from Israel, Japan, and South Africa, respectively. We first parse a list of demonyms from Wikipedia to populate a table of (Location, Demonym) pairs.[5] We expand this table with information from additional

geographical websites[6] leading to a total of 2,143 base entries. The demonyms (and locations) can frequently take region-related pre-modifiers. When checking for demonyms, we allow them to be preceded by 'North', 'South', 'East', 'West', 'Northern', 'Southern', 'Eastern', 'Western', and 'Central'.

To extract relationships expressed via demonyms appropriately (e.g. *"German Chancellor Angela Merkel"*), we simply check whether arg2's head-noun is in our demonym table, and if it is then we replace it with its corresponding location from the table. Demonym replacements are also needed for compound NPs without capitalization, for example, *"German chancellor Angela Merkel"*. This requires another small extension to RELNOUN – allowing arg2 to be a JJ when it is in the demonym list (typically arg2s can only be an NNP).

In addition to compound NPs, the demonym replacement can be useful for other patterns from Table 1 also. For example, AppositivePossessive and PossessiveAppositive both benefit from this (for example, *"Angela Merkel, German Chancellor"* and *"German Chancellor, Angela Merkel"*).

Domicile vs. Title Classification: Demonyms are used to denote two common relationships. First, arg1 may be directly related to the location or the government of the location through the relational noun. For example, *"United States President Obama"* – Obama is the President of the country of (or govt. of) United States. A second usage simply suggests that the location is arg1's *domicile*, i.e., arg1 is a native of, lives in, or has another substantial connection with the location. For example, *"Canadian pitcher Andrew Albers"* only denotes a domicile – Albers is not a player *of* Canada! Ideally, we would like to extract (Andrew Albers, [is] player [*from*], Canada), instead of [of].

We manually create a small list of ten relational nouns, which represent heads and other high-posts

capitalize-president/ says *"Use a capital when the title directly precedes the name"*

[5] https://en.wikipedia.org/wiki/Demonym

[6] http://www.geography-site.co.uk, http://everything2.com, http://geography.about.com

System	Precision	Yield
OLLIE-NOUN	0.29	136
RELNOUN 1.1	0.53	60
+ NNP relational nouns	0.37	100
+ ORG filtering	0.39	100
+ demonyms	0.52	158
+ compound relational nouns	0.69	209

Table 3: Precision and Yield (#correct extractions) for each system on a dataset of 2000 random Newswire sentences.

of the govt. of a city, state and country (includes 'king', 'president', 'mayor', 'governor') and use only those for titles. All other relational nouns are assumed to be in the domicile sense. While not perfect, the resulting extractions are often accurate, for example, (Sepoy Kanshi, [is] soldier [from], India) is accurate even if he is also a soldier of India.

3.2 Compound Relational Nouns

We now extend RELNOUN to handle *compound relational nouns* such as 'health minister', 'foreign secretary', and 'vice president'. We first observe that for all extractors in Table 1, except CompoundNoun there are lexical indicators ('of', ',', or possessive marker) to segment a relational noun. However, because CompoundNoun pattern is simply a sequence of nouns, segmenting relational nouns is harder and it is a common source of errors.

Segmenting compound relational nouns is relatively easy if it is followed by a demonym, since the demonym can help segment the left boundary (e.g., *"Indian Prime Minister Modi"*). However, the real challenge is in non-demonym cases – disambiguating whether *"GM Vice Chairman Bob Lutz"* should result in (Bob Lutz, [is] Vice Chairman [of], GM) or (Bob Lutz, [is] Chairman [of], GM Vice).

We bootstrap a list of common relational noun prefixes over a large text corpus. We collect all words (from 1.1 million sentences of ClueWeb12 corpus) that precede relational nouns and are in the same NP chunk, are of appropriate POS (JJ, NN, NNP, etc), are not a known demonym and don't end in a possessive. We keep all such prefixes of frequency greater than 20, resulting in a list of 5,606 prefixes. We use these prefixes to segment the final relational nouns in compound NPs. Even though noisy, this list serves our purpose since common prefixes are already present, and it is used only for non-demonym CompoundNoun extractor.

4 Experiments

Our goal is to compare RELNOUN 1.1 with REL-NOUN 2.2. We randomly sample 2,000 sentences from Newswire and run both (and other intermediate systems) on them. We ask two annotators (students) to tag if the sentence asserted or implied an extraction. Our inter-annotator agreement is 0.97 and we retain the subset of extractions on which the annotators agree for further analysis. Note that while precision and yield (number of correct extractions) can be naturally computed by tagging extractions, estimating recall is challenging, as it requires annotators to tag all possible extractions from these sentences. Following previous work (Mausam et al., 2012), we report yield, since recall is proportional to yield and suffices for system comparisons.

Table 3 reports the results. We find that OLLIE's noun patterns have a good yield but poor precision, whereas RELNOUN 1.1 has a decent precision of 0.53, but the yield is much lower. Allowing NNP relational nouns in RELNOUN 1.1 has a 66% increase in yield, but precision takes a severe hit. ORG filtering only helps a little bit in improving precision. Handling of demonyms has a huge impact since not only does yield increase by another 58%, precision goes up 13 points too. Finally, incorporating compound relational nouns adds another 51 extractions with a significant (17 point) improvement in precision. Overall, RELNOUN 2.2 has a 3.5x increase in yield with a 16 point increase in precision, making it a substantial improvement on the existing REL-NOUN 1.1 system.

5 Conclusions

An important subtask of Open IE is Nominal Open IE, within which dealing with compound NPs is particularly challenging owing to complications arising due to organization names, demonyms and compound relational nouns. We release RELNOUN 2.2, a significant improvement over the publicly available RELNOUN 1.1 system, which deals with each of these challenges. The main approach for improvement uses a combination of rule-based systems and semantic lists, bootstrapped automatically from text corpus and also compiled manually over the Web. RELNOUN 2.2 has 3.5x more yield with a substantial increase of 16 precision points.

Acknowledgments

The work was supported by Google language understanding and knowledge discovery focused research grants and a Bloomberg grant. We thank Michael Schmitz, the author of the original RELNOUN system, for helping with details of the algorithm.

References

Hannah Bast and Elmar Haussmann. 2013. Open information extraction via contextual sentence decomposition. In *2013 IEEE Seventh International Conference on Semantic Computing, Irvine, CA, USA, September 16-18, 2013*, pages 154–159.

Hannah Bast and Elmar Haussmann. 2014. More informative open information extraction via simple inference. In *Advances in Information Retrieval - 36th European Conference on IR Research, ECIR 2014, Amsterdam, The Netherlands, April 13-16, 2014. Proceedings*, pages 585–590.

Janara Christensen, Mausam, Stephen Soderland, and Oren Etzioni. 2011. An analysis of open information extraction based on semantic role labeling. In *Proceedings of the 6th International Conference on Knowledge Capture (K-CAP 2011), June 26-29, 2011, Banff, Alberta, Canada*, pages 113–120.

Luciano Del Corro and Rainer Gemulla. 2013. Clausie: clause-based open information extraction. In *22nd International World Wide Web Conference, WWW '13, Rio de Janeiro, Brazil, May 13-17, 2013*, pages 355–366.

Filipe de Sá Mesquita, Jordan Schmidek, and Denilson Barbosa. 2013. Effectiveness and efficiency of open relation extraction. In *Proceedings of the 2013 Conference on Empirical Methods in Natural Language Processing, EMNLP 2013, 18-21 October 2013, Grand Hyatt Seattle, Seattle, Washington, USA, A meeting of SIGDAT, a Special Interest Group of the ACL*, pages 447–457.

Oren Etzioni, Michele Banko, Stephen Soderland, and Daniel S. Weld. 2008. Open information extraction from the web. *Commun. ACM*, 51(12):68–74.

Oren Etzioni, Anthony Fader, Janara Christensen, Stephen Soderland, and Mausam. 2011. Open information extraction: The second generation. In *IJCAI 2011, Proceedings of the 22nd International Joint Conference on Artificial Intelligence, Barcelona, Catalonia, Spain, July 16-22, 2011*, pages 3–10.

Mausam, Michael Schmitz, Stephen Soderland, Robert Bart, and Oren Etzioni. 2012. Open language learning for information extraction. In *Proceedings of the 2012 Joint Conference on Empirical Methods in Natural Language Processing and Computational Natural Language Learning, EMNLP-CoNLL 2012, July 12-14, 2012, Jeju Island, Korea*, pages 523–534.

George A. Miller. 1995. Wordnet: A lexical database for english. *Commun. ACM*, 38(11):39–41.

Jordan Schmidek and Denilson Barbosa. 2014. Improving open relation extraction via sentence restructuring. In *Proceedings of the Ninth International Conference on Language Resources and Evaluation (LREC-2014), Reykjavik, Iceland, May 26-31, 2014.*, pages 3720–3723.

Clarissa Castellã Xavier, Vera Lúcia Strube de Lima, and Marlo Souza. 2015. Open information extraction based on lexical semantics. *J. Braz. Comp. Soc.*, 21(1):4:1–4:14.

Ying Xu, Mi-Young Kim, Kevin Quinn, Randy Goebel, and Denilson Barbosa. 2013. Open information extraction with tree kernels. In *Human Language Technologies: Conference of the North American Chapter of the Association of Computational Linguistics, Proceedings, June 9-14, 2013, Westin Peachtree Plaza Hotel, Atlanta, Georgia, USA*, pages 868–877.

Mohamed Yahya, Steven Whang, Rahul Gupta, and Alon Y. Halevy. 2014. Renoun: Fact extraction for nominal attributes. In *Proceedings of the 2014 Conference on Empirical Methods in Natural Language Processing, EMNLP 2014, October 25-29, 2014, Doha, Qatar, A meeting of SIGDAT, a Special Interest Group of the ACL*, pages 325–335.

But What Do We Actually Know?

Simon Razniewski
Free University of Bozen-Bolzano
Italy
`razniewski@inf.unibz.it`

Fabian M. Suchanek
Télécom ParisTech
France
`suchanek@enst.fr`

Werner Nutt
Free University of Bozen-Bolzano
Italy
`nutt@inf.unibz.it`

Abstract

Knowledge bases such as Wikidata, DBpedia, YAGO, or the Google Knowledge Vault collect a vast number of facts about the world. But while quite some facts are known about the world, little is known about how much is unknown. For example, while the knowledge base may tell us that Barack Obama is the father of Malia Obama and Sasha Obama, it does not tell us whether these are all of his children. This is not just an epistemic challenge, but also a practical problem for data producers and consumers. We envision that KBs become annotated with information about their recall on specific topics. We show what such annotations could look like, how they could be obtained, and survey related work.

1 Motivation

General-purpose knowledge bases (KBs) such as Wikidata [21], the Google Knowledge Vault [4], NELL [10], or YAGO [19] aim to collect as much factual information about the world as possible. They store information about entities (such as Barack Obama, Hawaii, or NAACL), and information about relationships between these entities (such as the fact that Barack Obama was born in Hawaii, and that NAACL took place in San Diego). These pieces of information typically take the form of triples, as in ⟨*Barack Obama, wasBornIn, Hawaii*⟩. KBs find applications in question answering, automated translation, or information retrieval.

The quality of a KB can be measured along several dimensions. A prominent one is the size. To-

day's KBs can contain millions, if not billions of triples. Another criterion is precision, i.e., the proportion of triples that are correct. YAGO, e.g., was manually evaluated on a sample, and was shown to have a precision of 95%. In this paper, we propose to look at a third criterion for quality which, besides in some manual evaluations that have ground truth available, has been largely neglected so far: recall, i.e., the proportion of facts of the real world that are covered by the KB. For some topics, today's KBs show very good recall values. For example,

- 160 out of 199 Nobel laureates in Physics are in DBpedia;
- 2 out of 2 children of Obama are in Wikidata;
- 36 out of 48 movies by Tarantino are shown in the Google Knowledge Graph.

On some other topics, today's KBs are nearly completely incomplete:

- DBpedia contains currently only 6 out of 35 Dijkstra Prize winners.
- According to YAGO, the average number of children per person is 0.02.
- The Google Knowledge Graph contains a predicate called "Points of Interest" for countries. Since this predicate is subjective, it is not even clear how to measure its recall.

Previous research [18, 9] has shown that between 69% and 99% of instances in popular KBs lack at least one property that other entities in the same class have. This gives us a hint of how incomplete KBs really are.

The problem is not just that KBs do not contain missing triples, but also that they do not know how

Proceedings of AKBC 2016, pages 40–44,
San Diego, California, June 12-17, 2016. ©2016 Association for Computational Linguistics

many are missing, or whether some are missing at all. This is an issue from several perspectives:

- Philosophical perspective: We do not know what we actually know, and what we don't.
- Data collection perspective: KB contributors and engineers do not know where to focus their effort. If they knew that 39 Nobel laureates in Physics are missing, they could focus on tracing and adding the missing ones.
- KB debugging perspective: One does not know when too much data is added. If there is reason to believe that Obama has two children, but a KB contains three, this could be highlighted.
- Rule learning perspective: KBs are often used for rule induction in order to learn new patterns and facts about the real world. But in order to evaluate learned rules, negative information is needed, which is usually not contained in KBs, but could be inferred from completeness information. Distant supervision, a popular pattern-based technique for automated knowledge base construction, faces the same challenge [9, 15, 20].
- Data consumption perspective: Consumers do not know whether a query really retrieves all answers. Also, results of aggregate queries (such as the average number of children per person) and queries with negation cannot be trusted.

In this paper, we investigate the problem of recall for KBs, and outline possible approaches to solve it.

2 Vision

Vision. Our vision is that a KB should know for which topics it is complete, and for which topics it is not. Under appropriate interpretation of terms, this could be phrased as

KBs should know what they know.

Defining Completeness. In line with work in databases [11, 8, 13], we define completeness by help of a hypothetical *ideal KB* $\mathcal{K}^*$. The ideal KB contains all facts of the real world. We say that a KB $\mathcal{K}$ is *correct*, if $\mathcal{K} \subseteq \mathcal{K}^*$. We say that $\mathcal{K}$ is *complete* for a query Q, if $Q(\mathcal{K}) \supseteq Q(\mathcal{K}^*)$. For example, we could say that a KB $\mathcal{K}$ is complete for the children of Obama by saying

$\mathcal{K}$ is complete for
```
SELECT ?x WHERE {Obama hasChild ?x.}
```

This means that evaluating this query on $\mathcal{K}$ will return at least the two children that we would expect as an answer in the real world. Completeness is always bound to a particular query, because we do not expect that we can ever construct a KB $\mathcal{K} = \mathcal{K}^*$. A query can represent the completeness of simple triples about a subject (as in the example), but also for complex constellations, such as "This KB is complete for all rivers longer than 100km in Europe". We believe that completeness assertions are particularly interesting for *class expressions*. These are conjunctive queries with a single selection variable. The class expression for the long rivers of Europe would be:

```
SELECT ?r
WHERE { ?r type river .
        ?r hasLength ?l .
        ?l > 100 .
        ?r locatedIn Europe .}
```

The notion of completeness is closely linked to a number of other concepts, which we detail next.

Closed World Assumption. The *closed world assumption* (CWA) says that if a fact is not in the KB, then it does not hold in the real world. Typically, one restricts this assumption to a certain topic or domain (say, all US presidents). Under the CWA, the KB is always complete for all queries in the domain.

Open World Assumption. Commonly, KBs are not interpreted under the CWA, but under the *open-world assumption* (OWA): The facts that are not in the KB are unknown, and may or may not be true. Under the OWA, we cannot tell whether a KB is complete or not for a given query (unless we have access to $\mathcal{K}^*$).

Negative Information. Negative information (facts that do not hold) is crucial for the correctness of queries with aggregation or negation. While there exists theoretical work about negative information in knowledge bases, none of the state-of-the-art KBs contains negative information. Completeness and negative information are closely related: If we find in a KB that Sasha and Malia are children of Obama, and that the KB contains all children of Obama, we can deduce that anyone else is not a child of Obama. We thus know an infinite number of negative facts.

Recall. The *recall* of a KB $\mathcal{K}$ for a query Q is $|Q(\mathcal{K}) \cap Q(\mathcal{K}^*)| \times |Q(\mathcal{K}^*)|^{-1}$. The recall is 1 for a query, if the KB is complete for that query.

Cardinality. The *cardinality* of a query on a KB is the number of results. If we know the cardinality of a query on $\mathcal{K}^*$, and if we know that the KB is correct, we can compute the recall of the KB for that query, and vice versa.

Size. The larger a KB is, the more likely it is to be complete, everything else being equal.

Confidence. Completeness assertions can be crisp, but they could also be made with a certain confidence score. For example, we could be 80% certain to have all children of Obama.

3 Challenges

We see four main challenges that need to be mastered in order to arrive at knowledge about the knowledge of KBs:

3.1 Knowing What Can Be Known

A prerequisite for completeness assertions are unambiguous definitions. Some relations such as "sibling" or "place of birth" are well-defined, while others, such as "affiliation" or "hobby" are not. For example, while one of Einstein's hobbies was playing the violin, he might have had an unclear number of other "hobbies" (such as going for a walk, or eating chocolate). If a topic is not well-defined, completeness has little meaning as well. One might assume that KBs generally contain well-defined predicates, yet this is not always the case. As mentioned before, the Google Knowledge Graph contains an attribute *pointOfInterest*. While some attractions are clearly points of interest (such as the Colosseum in Rome), others are less clearly so (e.g. the pub that DiCaprio allegedly threw up at). In such cases, the concept of crisp completeness is meaningless. We note that some fuzzy concepts can be turned into crisp ones by binding them to particular verifiable properties. For example, it makes sense to consider completeness for "Points of interest recommended by Tripadvisor", because this is a well-defined verifiable set.

3.2 Languages for Describing Completeness

Various formal languages for completeness assertions have been proposed [11, 8, 13], while Erxleben et al. [5] have introduced no-values into Wikidata (e.g. Elisabeth I has no children), thus allowing specifying completeness if the object has no values, but not in the general case. All proposals so far deal only with boolean descriptions, mentioning whether data of some kind is present or not, but do not allow descriptions of confidences or recall.

3.3 Obtaining Completeness Information

Experts. There are two main paradigms for constructing KBs: manual construction by experts or the crowd, and automated extraction from Web sources. For *expert-created data*, it makes sense to give the task of recall estimation to the experts too (as is the case already for the no-values in Wikidata, and wider envisioned in the tool COOL-WD [3]). In this way, a comparable quality of data and recall information can be guaranteed. For *automatically extracted data*, it is highly desirable to find automatic ways to estimate the recall.

Partial Completeness Assumption. The *partial completeness assumption* (PCA) [7] has been proven to do well in providing negative information [7, 4]. It assumes that if a KB contains one pair of property and object for a given subject, then the KB contains all objects for that given subject and property. For instance, if a KB contains the fact that Sasha is a child of Obama, then it is assumed that the KB contains all children of Obama. Hence, anyone who is not known to be a child of Obama is not. The validity of the PCA has been evaluated manually [6] on YAGO. For relations with generally high functionality [17], the PCA holds nearly perfectly. For example, the PCA holds for 90% of the subjects of the *worksAt* relation. For others, the PCA is less suited. For *hasChild*, e.g., the precision of the PCA is only around 27%.

Pattern Matching. Phrases on the Web such as "has no children" or "X and Y are all his children" can be used to infer completeness. Similarly, phrases such as "The 199 Nobel laureates in Physics..." could be used to assert the cardinality and hence the recall for a class.

Growth Patterns over Time. The growth of data over time, and especially the end of such a growth, might indicate completeness. For instance, we can imagine that once a new congress is established, its members are added to a KB until eventually all are inside. The fact that the number then remains constant could indicate completeness.

Interrelation. The completeness of a certain class

expression could be learned from the completeness of other class expressions. For instance, it might be that if parents of a person are complete, then also the children are complete with a higher probability.

Popularity of Entities. It might be that completeness correlates with the number of facts about an entity. For example, if a personality has numerous and very detailed facts in YAGO, then it could be more likely that some basic facts such as his children are complete.

Class Membership. If an entity is a member of a class, we can compare the entity to other members of the class. If other members have attributes that the entity does not have, this could indicate incompleteness. If all class members have the same attributes and the same number of objects, then this could indicate completeness. For example, if all world championships have 32 participants, then also a current championship with 32 participants has a higher probability of being complete.

Similar Entities. If some of the entities are labeled as complete, we could estimate the completeness of other, similar entities. For example, if most football clubs have between 20 and 30 players, and they have been labeled as complete, then a club with 28 players likely has a good recall.

Crowd Sourcing. The crowd could be used to manually generate completeness annotations. A related idea is to use games with a purpose [1].

Estimating Cardinalities. *Mark and recapture* techniques have been developed in the domain of ecology in order to estimate the size of a population of animals. For this purpose, a sample of animals is captured, marked, and freed. After some time, another sample of animals is captured. The ratio of marked animals in this sample can help estimate the size of the population. This technique works also if samples are not independent, and has been used in the estimation of cardinalities of search results [16]. We believe that it might also be useful for estimating the size of a set of entities, based on the overlap between different websites or datasources dealing with the same topic. Based on the size estimate, and the number of entities already in the KB, one could then estimate the recall.

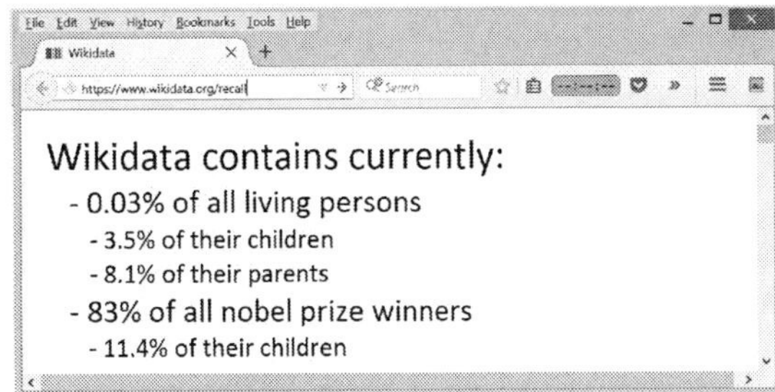

Figure 1: The ultimate vision.

3.4 Combining Completeness Information

Once information about the recall of KBs for individual classes exists, methods need to be found to present this information in a meaningful way. Several techniques can annotate query answers with completeness information [8, 13, 14], but only if the underlying database is annotated with such information, and only for crisp boolean completeness information. Techniques from the domain of query answering over probabilistic databases [2] could possibly be extended to handle non-crisp completeness assertions, while techniques from data profiling can help understand distributions and skew [12].

Also, one would need to apply these techniques to state-of-the-art KBs in order to finally know how much we currently know about the world (see Fig. 1). The community would then have to develop benchmarks for comparing the performance of completeness estimators, and for the completeness of KBs themselves, and would face the classic challenge of KB alignment, because information may be differently presented in different KBs.

4 Conclusion

In this paper, we have outlined our vision of knowledge bases (KBs) that know how complete they are. Their completeness assertions could be used to guide knowledge engineers in the extension and debugging of the KB, to provide negative examples for machine learning algorithms, and to qualify answers to user queries. We have surveyed the state of the art in the area, and concluded that we cannot yet automatically determine where KBs are complete. We have discussed the challenges in defining, determining, and combining completeness assertions, and have outlined possible paths to address them.

Acknowledgement

This work has been partially supported by the projects "TQTK - The Quest to Know", funded by the Free University of Bozen-Bolzano, and "MAGIC", funded by the Province of Bozen-Bolzano.

References

[1] L. v. Ahn. Games with a purpose. *Computer*, 39(6):92–94, June 2006.

[2] N. Dalvi and D. Suciu. Efficient query evaluation on probabilistic databases. *VLDB Journal*, 2007.

[3] F. Darari, S. Razniewski, R. Prasojo, and W. Nutt. Enabling fine-grained RDF data completeness assessment. *ICWE*, 2016.

[4] X. Dong, E. Gabrilovich, G. Heitz, W. Horn, N. Lao, K. Murphy, T. Strohmann, S. Sun, and W. Zhang. Knowledge vault: a web-scale approach to probabilistic knowledge fusion. In *SIGKDD*, 2014.

[5] F. Erxleben, M. Günther, M. Krötzsch, J. Mendez, and D. Vrandecic. Introducing wikidata to the linked data web. In *ISWC*, 2014.

[6] L. Galárraga, C. Teflioudi, K. Hose, and F. Suchanek. Fast Rule Mining in Ontological Knowledge Bases with AMIE+. *VLDB Journal*, 2015.

[7] L. Galárraga, C. Teflioudi, K. Hose, and F. M. Suchanek. AMIE: Association Rule Mining under Incomplete Evidence in Ontological Knowledge Bases . In *WWW*, 2013.

[8] A. Y. Levy. Obtaining complete answers from incomplete databases. In *VLDB*, 1996.

[9] B. Min, R. Grishman, L. Wan, C. Wang, and D. Gondek. Distant supervision for relation extraction with an incomplete knowledge base. In *HLT-NAACL*, pages 777–782, 2013.

[10] T. Mitchell, W. Cohen, E. Hruschka, P. Talukdar, J. Betteridge, A. Carlson, B. Dalvi, M. Gardner, B. Kisiel, J. Krishnamurthy, N. Lao, K. Mazaitis, T. Mohamed, N. Nakashole, E. Platanios, A. Ritter, M. Samadi, B. Settles, R. Wang, D. Wijaya, A. Gupta, X. Chen, A. Saparov, M. Greaves, and J. Welling. Never-ending learning. In *AAAI*, 2015.

[11] A. Motro. Integrity = Validity + Completeness. *TODS*, 1989.

[12] F. Naumann. Data profiling revisited. *SIGMOD Record*, 2014.

[13] S. Razniewski, F. Korn, W. Nutt, and D. Srivastava. Identifying the extent of completeness of query answers over partially complete databases. In *SIGMOD*, 2015.

[14] S. Razniewski and W. Nutt. Completeness of queries over incomplete databases. In *VLDB*, 2011.

[15] B. Roth, T. Barth, M. Wiegand, and D. Klakow. A survey of noise reduction methods for distant supervision. In *AKBC*, pages 73–78. ACM, 2013.

[16] P. Spoor, M. Airey, C. Bennett, J. Greensill, and R. Williams. Use of the capture-recapture technique to evaluate the completeness of systematic literature searches. *BMJ*, 1996.

[17] F. M. Suchanek, S. Abiteboul, and P. Senellart. PARIS: Probabilistic Alignment of Relations, Instances, and Schema . In *VLDB*, 2012.

[18] F. M. Suchanek, D. Gross-Amblard, and S. Abiteboul. Watermarking for Ontologies . In *ISWC*, 2011.

[19] F. M. Suchanek, G. Kasneci, and G. Weikum. Yago: a core of semantic knowledge. In *WWW*, 2007.

[20] S. Takamatsu, I. Sato, and H. Nakagawa. Reducing wrong labels in distant supervision for relation extraction. In *ACL*, pages 721–729. ACL, 2012.

[21] D. Vrandečić and M. Krötzsch. Wikidata: a free collaborative knowledgebase. *Communications of the ACM*, 2014.

Learning Knowledge Base Inference with Neural Theorem Provers

Tim Rocktäschel and **Sebastian Riedel**
University College London
London, UK
{t.rocktaschel,s.riedel}@cs.ucl.ac.uk

Abstract

In this paper we present a proof-of-concept implementation of *Neural Theorem Provers* (NTPs), end-to-end differentiable counterparts of discrete theorem provers that perform first-order inference on vector representations of symbols using function-free, possibly parameterized, rules. As such, NTPs follow a long tradition of neural-symbolic approaches to automated knowledge base inference, but differ in that they are differentiable with respect to representations of symbols in a knowledge base and can thus learn representations of predicates, constants, as well as rules of predefined structure. Furthermore, they still allow us to incorporate domain-knowledge provided as rules. The NTP presented here is realized via a differentiable version of the backward chaining algorithm. It operates on substitution representations and is able to learn complex logical dependencies from training facts of small knowledge bases.

1 Introduction

Current state-of-the-art methods for automated knowledge base (KB) construction learn distributed representations of fact triples (Nickel et al., 2012; Riedel et al., 2013; Socher et al., 2013; Chang et al., 2014; Neelakantan et al., 2015; Toutanova et al., 2015). An open question is how to enable first-order reasoning with commonsense knowledge (Nickel et al., 2015). We believe a promising direction towards this goal is the integration of deep neural networks with the capabilities of theorem provers. Neural networks can learn to generalize well when ob-

serving many input-output examples, but lack interpretability and straightforward ways of incorporating domain-specific knowledge. Theorem provers on the other hand provide effective ways to reason with logical knowledge. However, by operating on discrete symbols they do not make use of similarities between predicates or constants in training data (*e.g.*, LECTURERAT $\sim$ PROFESSORAT, ORANGE $\sim$ LEMON, etc).

Recent neural network architectures such as Neural Turing Machines (Graves et al., 2014, NTMs), Memory Networks (Weston et al., 2015b), Neural Stacks/Queues (Grefenstette et al., 2015; Joulin and Mikolov, 2015), Neural Programmer (Neelakantan et al., 2016), Neural Programmer-Interpreters (Reed and de Freitas, 2016) and Hierarchical Attentive Memory (Andrychowicz and Kurach, 2016) replace discrete functions and data structures by end-to-end differentiable counterparts. As such, they can learn complex behaviour from raw input-output examples via gradient-based optimization.

NTMs and their relatives are capable of learning programs and could in principle learn to emulate a theorem prover. However, they might not be the most efficient neural architecture for learning first-order reasoning from input-output examples. Akin to NTMs, which are end-to-end differentiable counterparts of Turing machines, we investigate *Neural Theorem Provers* (NTPs): end-to-end differentiable versions of automated theorem provers. A distinguishing property of NTPs is that they are differentiable with respect to symbol representations in a knowledge base. This enables us to learn representations of symbols in ground atoms (predicates and

Proceedings of AKBC 2016, pages 45–50,
San Diego, California, June 12-17, 2016. ©2016 Association for Computational Linguistics

constants) and parameters of first-order rules of pre-defined structure using backpropagation. Furthermore, NTPs can seamlessly reason with provided domain-specific rules. As NTPs operate on distributed representations of symbols, a single hand-crafted rule can be leveraged for many proofs of queries with similar symbol representations. Finally, NTPs allow for a high degree of interpretability by providing such proofs.

Our contributions are threefold: (i) we present the construction of an NTP based on differentiable backward chaining and unification, (ii) we show that when provided with rules this NTP can perform first-order inference in vector space like a discrete theorem prover would do on symbolic representations, and (iii) we demonstrate that NTPs can learn representations of symbols and first-order rules of predefined structure.

2   Related Work

Combining neural and symbolic approaches for relational learning and reasoning has let to many promising neural network architectures over the past decades (Garcez et al., 2012). Early proposals for neural-symbolic networks are limited to *propositional formulae* (*e.g.*, EBL-ANN (Shavlik and Towell, 1989), KBANN (Towell and Shavlik, 1994) and C-ILP (Garcez and Zaverucha, 1999)). Other neural-symbolic approaches focus on first-order inference, but do not allow one to learn vector representations of symbols from training facts of a KB (*e.g.*, SHRUTI (Shastri, 1992), Neural Prolog (Ding, 1995), CLIP++ (França et al., 2014) and Lifted Relational Neural Networks (Sourek et al., 2015)). Neural Reasoner (Peng et al., 2015) translates query representations in vector space without rule representations and can thus not incorporate domain-specific knowledge. Rocktäschel et al. (2014), Rocktäschel et al. (2015), Vendrov et al. (2016) and Hu et al. (2016) regularize distributed representations via domain-specific rules, but do not learn such rules from data and only support a restricted subset of first-order rules. The NTP proposed here builds upon differentiable backward chaining and is thus related to Unification Neural Networks (Komendantskaya, 2011; Hölldobler, 1990), but operates on vector representations of symbols instead of scalar

values. Yin et al. (2015) and Andreas et al. (2016) map queries to multiple differentiable modules that can be used to retrieve answers from a KB. Clark et al. (2014) extract common-sense knowledge from textbooks in form of rules to improve KB inference by soft-matching and non-recursive forward inference. Lee et al. (2016) propose a Tensor Product Representation to answer Facebook bAbI (Weston et al., 2015a) questions. Gu et al. (2015) traverse KBs in vector space to answer queries. Socher et al. (2012) and Bowman et al. (2015) demonstrate that recursive neural networks can learn to evaluate propositional logic expressions.

3   Differentiable Backward Chaining

Backward chaining is a common method for automated theorem proving, and we refer the reader to Russell and Norvig (1995) for details. Given a goal/query (*e.g.* GRANDPARENTOF(X, Y)), backward chaining finds substitutions of free variables with constants of facts in a KB (*e.g.* $\{X/\text{ABE}, Y/\text{BART}\}$). This is achieved by recursively iterating through rules that translate a goal into sub-goals which it attempts to prove, thereby exploring possible proofs. For example, the KB could contain the following rule that can be applied to find answers for the above goal: $\forall X, Y, Z : \text{PARENTOF}(X, Y) \land \text{PARENTOF}(Y, Z) \Rightarrow \text{GRANPARENTOF}(X, Z)$. For the rest of the paper we assume all free variables are universally quantified. Furthermore, we call the conjunction of atoms before the implication symbol the left-hand side (or body) of the rule and the atom after the implication the right-hand side (or head) of the rule.

The proof exploration in backward-chaining is divided into two functions called <u>Or</u> and <u>And</u>. The former attempts to prove a goal by unifying it with every rule's right-hand side in a KB, yielding intermediate substitutions. For rules where this succeeds, the left-hand side and substitution is passed to the <u>And</u> function. <u>And</u> then attempts to prove every atom in the body sequentially by first applying substitutions and subsequently calling <u>Or</u>. This is repeated recursively until unification fails, atoms are proven by unification with facts in the KB, or a certain proof-depth is exceeded.

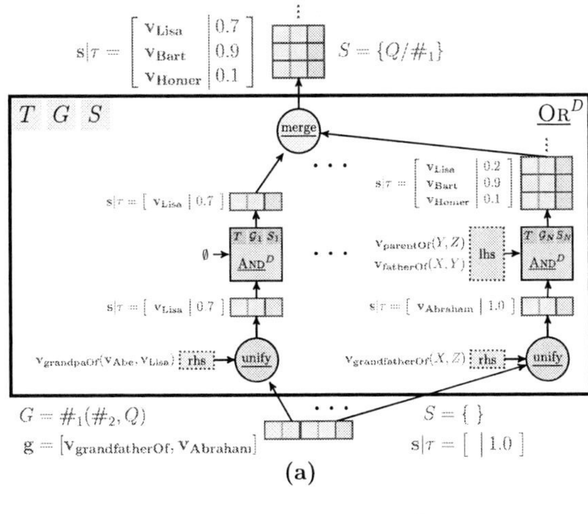

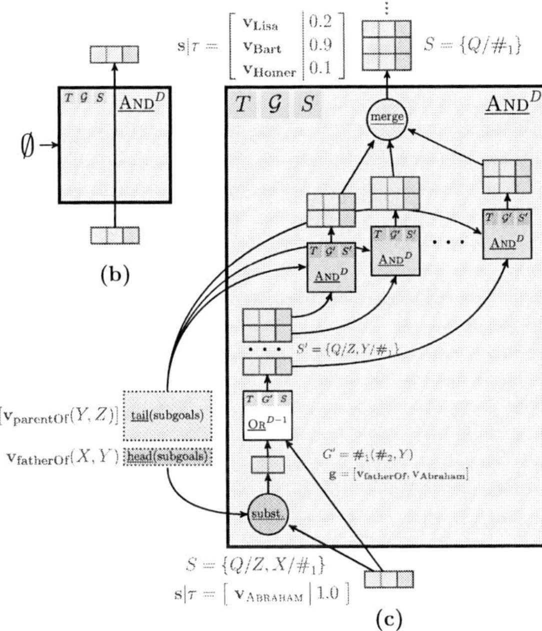

Figure 1: Overview of differentiable backward chaining.

Goal and Substitution Structures The key idea behind the proof-of-concept NTP presented here is to recursively construct a neural network by replacing operations on symbols in backward chaining with differentiable operations on distributed representations. To build such a network we separate goals and substitutions into *vector representations* of involved predicates and constants, and *structures* that define the connections of a neural network.

For instance, $G = \#_1(\#_2, X)$ is an example of a structure of an entire *class* of goals. This structure encodes that such goals encompass a vector repre-

sentation of a predicate symbol $\#_1$ and the first argument of the predicate $\#_2$. For example, the goal GRANDPAOF(ABE, X) can be specified by G and vector representations $\mathbf{g} = [\mathbf{v}_{\text{GRANDPAOF}}, \mathbf{v}_{\text{ABE}}]$. Furthermore, based on the structure G it is clear that proofs of that goal will be substitutions for X (*e.g.* $\mathbf{v}_{\text{BART}}$). Akin to goals, we divide substitutions into structures and representations, as well as a scalar score $\tau \in (0, 1)$ that measures the success of the substitution. For example, proofs of goals of the structure G as defined above will be substitutions with the structure $S = \{X/\#_1\}$ accompanied by substitution representations (*e.g.* $\mathbf{s} = [\mathbf{v}_{\text{BART}}]$).

With this divide we can now redefine operations in backward chaining as follows. Operations that concern variables and rules are mapping goal and substitution structures (G and S) to new structures that instantiate sub-networks. In contrast, operations on symbols of predicates and constants can be computed in vector space in a differentiable manner. The resulting recursively constructed NTP is end-to-end differentiable. An overview of the model architecture with an example is given in Figure 1 and discussed in detail below.

OR The entry point to the NTP is an OR network (Figure 1a) that for a given goal and substitution structure (G and S) instantiates a sub-network for each one of the N rules in a knowledge base T. The unification of the ith rule's right-hand side with a goal structure results in a new substitution structure S_i. When provided with a goal representation, a unification network is computing the unification success in vector space. For example, assume at some proof-depth D in the NTP we unify GRANDFATHEROF(ABRAHAM, Q) with GRANDPAOF(ABE, LISA). This will result in a new substitution structure $S'_i = \{Q/\#_1\}$, representation $\mathbf{s} = [\mathbf{v}_{\text{LISA}}]$ and success τ^D that is passed further in the network. In contrast to discrete unification that checks for symbol equality, we calculate a soft unification from the previous unification success of the outer network τ^{D+1} and the similarity of predicate and constant representations as follows:

$$\tau_{\text{predicate}} = \text{sigmoid}(\mathbf{v}_{\text{GRANDFATHEROF}}^T \mathbf{v}_{\text{GRANDPA}}) \quad (1)$$

$$\tau_{\text{arg}_1} = \text{sigmoid}(\mathbf{v}_{\text{ABRAHAM}}^T \mathbf{v}_{\text{ABE}}) \quad (2)$$

$$\tau^D = \min(\tau^{D+1}, \tau_{\text{predicate}}, \tau_{\text{arg}_1}) \quad (3)$$

AND The new substitution structure calculated by unification instantiates an AND network (Figure 1c) at depth D that attempts to sequentially prove the left-hand side atoms of the rule given the current substitutions. If the rule's left-hand side structure is empty (*e.g.* when the right-hand side represents a fact in the KB) the AND network simply passes the substitutions and their success through (Figure 1b). Otherwise, it applies the substitution on the first atom of the left-hand side, resulting in a new goal structure and representation, and instantiates an OR network with that structure and the previous substitution.

For example, assume we have unified the right-hand side of FATHEROF(X, Y) $\wedge$ PARENTOF(Y, Z) $\Rightarrow$ GRANDFATHEROF(X, Z) with the goal GRANDFATHEROF(ABRAHAM, Q). The result is a unification success τ^D as calculated in Eq. 3, as well as a new substitution structure $S = \{Q/Z, X/\#_1\}$ where $s = [\mathbf{v}_{\text{ABRAHAM}}]$ becomes the input to the AND network. This network will first apply the substitution to FATHEROF(X, Y), resulting in a new goal structure $G' = \#_1(\#_2, Y)$. This structure now instantiates another NTP (*i.e.* an OR module) of depth $D - 1$, which attempts to prove the input goal representation $\mathbf{g} = [\mathbf{v}_{\text{FATHEROF}}, \mathbf{v}_{\text{ABRAHAM}}]$.

For every proof, *i.e.*, every possible substitution of the structure $S' = \{Q/Z, Y/\#_1\}$, a new AND module is instantiated that attempts to recursively prove the remainder of the left-hand side (PARENTOF(Y, Z) in the example above). Finally, the successes of all identical substitutions (*i.e.* substitutions to the same variables or representations of constants) are merged by taking their max.

Note that given a KB, goal structure and depth, the network structure of the NTP is fully specified and many goals of the same structure can be used to perform training and inference with the NTP.

Trainable Rules NTPs are not only differentiable with respect to symbol representations in the KB, but also latent symbol representations in first-order rules of predefined structure. For instance, we could assume that for some predicates in a KB a transitive relationship holds. We can define a rule template $\#_1(X, Y) \wedge \#_1(Y, Z) \Rightarrow \#_2(X, Z)$ whose latent predicates $\mathbf{v}_{\#_1}, \mathbf{v}_{\#_2}$ are trainable parameters and op-

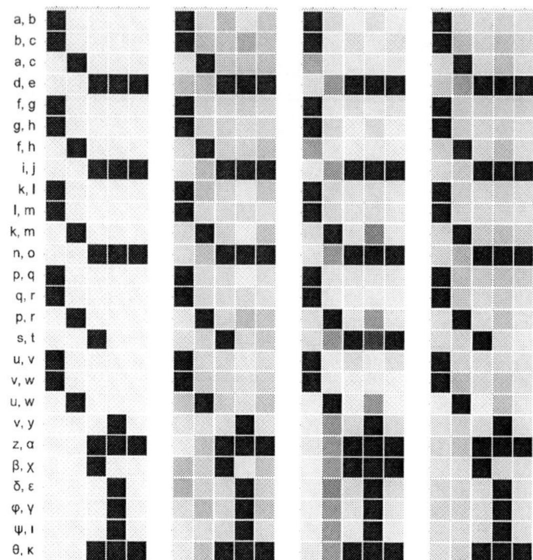

Figure 2: Predictions of different NTP modes on a toy KB where every column (within a subplot) represents a predicate and every row an entity-pair. Training facts (red) and test facts (blue) in the first subplot are consistent with two rules: $r_1(X, Y) \wedge r_1(Y, Z) \Rightarrow r_2(X, Z)$ and $r_3(X, Y) \wedge r_4(X, Y) \Rightarrow r_5(X, Y)$. The other three subplots show predictions between 0 (white) and 1 (black) of the different modes discussed in text.

timized in the same way as symbol representations.

4 Experiments and Results

We implemented an NTP with differentiable backward chaining in TensorFlow (Abadi et al., 2015). Symbol representations are initialized randomly and constrained to unit-length. During training we iterate over the set of known facts, and optimize negative log-likelihood of the proof success of every fact based on all other facts (and rules) using Adam (Kingma and Ba, 2015). Furthermore, for every training fact we sample an unobserved fact for the same predicate (but different entity-pair) and optimize its proof with a target success of zero.

Our NTP implementation is tested on toy KBs for different scenarios shown in the four different subplots in Figure 2. Every column (within a subplot) represents a predicate and every row an entity-pair. First, we run the NTP with given ground-truth rules without training symbol or rule representations, and test whether it can act as a discrete theorem prover. As expected, given rules the NTP can infer all test facts (2nd subplot in Figure 2). The third subplot shows predictions when we let the NTP try to reconstruct training facts only with the help of other facts by learning symbol representations (similar to other representation learning approaches for KB inference). Finally, a core benefit of the NTP is visible once we provide few reasonable rule templates[1] and optimize for rule representations that best explain observed facts (4th subplot). We found that this can work remarkably well, but also noticed that the quality of trained rules is varying with different random initialization of the rule's parameters. We need to investigate in future work how the robustness of rule learning in NTPs can be improved.

5 Conclusion and Future Work

We proposed neural theorem provers for knowledge base inference via differentiable backward chaining, which enables learning of symbol representations and parameters of rules of predefined structure.

Our current implementation has severe computational limitations and does not scale to larger KBs as it investigates all possible proof paths. However, there are many possibilities to improve upon the presented architecture. For instance, one can batch-unify all rules whose right-hand side have the same structure and employ existing architectures such as Memory Networks or hierarchical attention for this task. Furthermore, it is possible to partition and batch rules not only by their right-hand side but also left-hand side structure to instantiate a single AND module for every partition. To further speed-up the prover, we want to investigate processing batches of queries, as well as differentiable ways of maintaining only the N best instead of all possible substitution representations at every depth of the prover. In addition, we will work on more flexible versions of neural theorem provers, for instance, where unification, rule selection and application itself are trainable functions, or where facts in a KB and goals can be natural language sentences.

Acknowledgments

We thank Isabelle Augenstein, Dirk Weissenborn, Johannes Welbl and the reviewers for comments on drafts of this paper. This work was supported by Microsoft Research through its PhD Scholarship Programme and an Allen Distinguished Investigator Award.

References

[Abadi et al.2015] Martın Abadi, Ashish Agarwal, Paul Barham, Eugene Brevdo, Zhifeng Chen, Craig Citro, Greg S Corrado, Andy Davis, Jeffrey Dean, Matthieu Devin, et al. 2015. Tensorflow: Large-scale machine learning on heterogeneous systems.

[Andreas et al.2016] Jacob Andreas, Marcus Rohrbach, Trevor Darrell, and Dan Klein. 2016. Learning to compose neural networks for question answering. In *NAACL*.

[Andrychowicz and Kurach2016] Marcin Andrychowicz and Karol Kurach. 2016. Learning efficient algorithms with hierarchical attentive memory. *arXiv preprint arXiv:1602.03218*.

[Bowman et al.2015] Samuel R Bowman, Christopher Potts, and Christopher D Manning. 2015. Recursive neural networks can learn logical semantics. In *CVSC*.

[Chang et al.2014] Kai-Wei Chang, Wen-tau Yih, Bishan Yang, and Christopher Meek. 2014. Typed tensor decomposition of knowledge bases for relation extraction. In *EMNLP*.

[Clark et al.2014] Peter Clark, Niranjan Balasubramanian, Sumithra Bhakthavatsalam, Kevin Humphreys, Jesse Kinkead, Ashish Sabharwal, and Oyvind Tafjord. 2014. Automatic construction of inference-supporting knowledge bases. In *AKBC*.

[Ding1995] Liya Ding. 1995. Neural prolog-the concepts, construction and mechanism. In *3rd Int. Conference Fuzzy Logic, Neural Nets, and Soft Computing*.

[França et al.2014] Manoel VM França, Gerson Zaverucha, and Artur S dAvila Garcez. 2014. Fast relational learning using bottom clause propositionalization with artificial neural networks. *Machine learning*, 94(1):81–104.

[Garcez and Zaverucha1999] Artur S d'Avila Garcez and Gerson Zaverucha. 1999. The connectionist inductive learning and logic programming system. *Applied Intelligence*, 11(1):59–77.

[Garcez et al.2012] Artur S d'Avila Garcez, Krysia Broda, and Dov M Gabbay. 2012. *Neural-symbolic learning systems: foundations and applications*. Springer.

[Graves et al.2014] Alex Graves, Greg Wayne, and Ivo Danihelka. 2014. Neural turing machines. *arXiv preprint arXiv:1410.5401*.

---

[1]We use $\#_1(X,Y) \Rightarrow \#_2(X,Y)$, $\#_1(X,Y) \land \#_2(X,Y) \Rightarrow \#_3(X,Y)$ and $\#_1(X,Y) \land \#_1(Y,Z) \Rightarrow \#_2(X,Z)$.

[Grefenstette et al.2015] Edward Grefenstette, Karl Moritz Hermann, Mustafa Suleyman, and Phil Blunsom. 2015. Learning to transduce with unbounded memory. In *NIPS*.

[Gu et al.2015] Kelvin Gu, John Miller, and Percy Liang. 2015. Traversing knowledge graphs in vector space. In *EMNLP*.

[Hölldobler1990] S Hölldobler. 1990. A structured connectionist unification algorithm. In *AAAI*.

[Hu et al.2016] Zhiting Hu, Xuezhe Ma, Zhengzhong Liu, Eduard Hovy, and Eric Xing. 2016. Harnessing deep neural networks with logic rules. *arXiv preprint arXiv:1603.06318*.

[Joulin and Mikolov2015] Armand Joulin and Tomas Mikolov. 2015. Inferring algorithmic patterns with stack-augmented recurrent nets. In *NIPS*.

[Kingma and Ba2015] Diederik Kingma and Jimmy Ba. 2015. Adam: A method for stochastic optimization. *ICLR*.

[Komendantskaya2011] Ekaterina Komendantskaya. 2011. Unification neural networks: unification by error-correction learning. *Logic Journal of IGPL*, 19(6):821–847.

[Lee et al.2016] Moontae Lee, Xiaodong He, Wen-tau Yih, Jianfeng Gao, Li Deng, and Paul Smolensky. 2016. Reasoning in vector space: An exploratory study of question answering. In *ICLR*.

[Neelakantan et al.2015] Arvind Neelakantan, Benjamin Roth, and Andrew McCallum. 2015. Compositional vector space models for knowledge base completion. In *ACL*.

[Neelakantan et al.2016] Arvind Neelakantan, Quoc V Le, and Ilya Sutskever. 2016. Neural programmer: Inducing latent programs with gradient descent. In *ICLR*.

[Nickel et al.2012] Maximilian Nickel, Volker Tresp, and Hans-Peter Kriegel. 2012. Factorizing yago: scalable machine learning for linked data. In *WWW*.

[Nickel et al.2015] Maximilian Nickel, Kevin Murphy, Volker Tresp, and Evgeniy Gabrilovich. 2015. A review of relational machine learning for knowledge graphs: From multi-relational link prediction to automated knowledge graph construction. *IEEE*.

[Peng et al.2015] Baolin Peng, Zhengdong Lu, Hang Li, and Kam-Fai Wong. 2015. Towards neural network-based reasoning. In *RAM*.

[Reed and de Freitas2016] Scott Reed and Nando de Freitas. 2016. Neural programmer-interpreters. In *ICLR*.

[Riedel et al.2013] Sebastian Riedel, Limin Yao, Andrew McCallum, and Benjamin M Marlin. 2013. Relation extraction with matrix factorization and universal schemas. In *NAACL*.

[Rocktäschel et al.2014] Tim Rocktäschel, Matko Bosnjak, Sameer Singh, and Sebastian Riedel. 2014. Low-dimensional embeddings of logic. In *SP14*.

[Rocktäschel et al.2015] Tim Rocktäschel, Sameer Singh, and Sebastian Riedel. 2015. Injecting Logical Background Knowledge into Embeddings for Relation Extraction. In *NAACL*.

[Russell and Norvig1995] Stuart J Russell and Peter Norvig. 1995. *Artificial Intelligence: Modern Approach*. Prentice Hall, 3rd edition.

[Shastri1992] Lokendra Shastri. 1992. Neurally motivated constraints on the working memory capacity of a production system for parallel processing: Implications of a connectionist model based on temporal synchrony. In *Conference of the Cognitive Science Society*. Psychology Press.

[Shavlik and Towell1989] Jude W Shavlik and Geoffrey G Towell. 1989. An approach to combining explanation-based and neural learning algorithms. *Connection Science*, 1(3):231–253.

[Socher et al.2012] Richard Socher, Brody Huval, Christopher D Manning, and Andrew Y Ng. 2012. Semantic compositionality through recursive matrix-vector spaces. In *EMNLP*.

[Socher et al.2013] Richard Socher, Danqi Chen, Christopher D Manning, and Andrew Ng. 2013. Reasoning with neural tensor networks for knowledge base completion. In *NIPS*.

[Sourek et al.2015] Gustav Sourek, Vojtech Aschenbrenner, Filip Zelezny, and Ondrej Kuzelka. 2015. Lifted relational neural networks. *arXiv preprint arXiv:1508.05128*.

[Toutanova et al.2015] Kristina Toutanova, Danqi Chen, Patrick Pantel, Pallavi Choudhury, and Michael Gamon. 2015. Representing text for joint embedding of text and knowledge bases. In *EMNLP*.

[Towell and Shavlik1994] Geoffrey G Towell and Jude W Shavlik. 1994. Knowledge-based artificial neural networks. *Artificial intelligence*, 70(1):119–165.

[Vendrov et al.2016] Ivan Vendrov, Ryan Kiros, Sanja Fidler, and Raquel Urtasun. 2016. Order-embeddings of images and language. In *ICLR*.

[Weston et al.2015a] Jason Weston, Antoine Bordes, Sumit Chopra, and Tomas Mikolov. 2015a. Towards ai-complete question answering: A set of prerequisite toy tasks. *arXiv preprint arXiv:1502.05698*.

[Weston et al.2015b] Jason Weston, Sumit Chopra, and Antoine Bordes. 2015b. Memory networks. In *ICLR*.

[Yin et al.2015] Pengcheng Yin, Zhengdong Lu, Hang Li, and Ben Kao. 2015. Neural enquirer: Learning to query tables. *arXiv preprint arXiv:1512.00965*.

The Physics of Text: Ontological Realism in Information Extraction

Stuart Russell
UC Berkeley
russell@berkeley.edu

Ole Torp Lassen
Roskilde University
otl@propercontext.org

Justin Uang
Palantir Technologies
justin.uang@gmail.com

Wei Wang
UPMC, Paris
benwei.wang@outlook.com

Abstract

We propose an approach to extracting information from text based on the hypothesis that text sometimes describes the world. The hypothesis is embodied in a generative probability model that describes (1) possible worlds and the facts they might contain, (2) how an author chooses facts to express, and (3) how those facts are expressed in text. Given text, information extraction is done by computing a posterior over the worlds that might have generated it. As a by-product, this unsupervised learning process discovers new relations and their textual expressions, extracts new facts, disambiguates instances of polysemous expressions, and resolves entity references. The probability model also explains and improves on Brin's bootstrapping heuristic, which underlies many open information extraction systems. Preliminary results on a small corpus of New York Times text suggest that the approach is effective.

1 Introduction

The purpose of information extraction (IE) is to produce both general knowledge structures and specific facts that will support inference, problem solving, and question answering. The primary difficulties include (1) the huge variety and ambiguity of linguistic expressions of underlying content; (2) the problem of resolving multiple entity references within and across documents; (3) the complexity of the underlying information itself: its ontology, temporal and causal structure, provenance, etc. Section 2 describes the major approaches that have been taken and their shortcomings.

Recent developments in probabilistic modeling and inference make it possible to revisit a Bayesian approach to IE championed by Charniak and Goldman (1992), among others. The approach is based on what one might call *ontologically realistic* generative models: that is, probability models that describe, in a very general sense, both the ways that the real world might be and the ways that world might be described in text. [1] Such models explain why this text is on the page in the same way that physical theories explain laboratory measurements—that is, by reference to an underlying reality. Perhaps surprisingly, commonly used generative models of language make no such reference.

A simple, initial model (Section 3) posits a world of facts (binary relations between entities) that are expressed using arbitrary dependency paths connecting named-entity mentions. Using the machinery of a probabilistic programming language such as BLOG (Milch and Russell, 2010) (augmented with a new form of proposal distribution for split–merge MCMC (Wang and Russell, 2015)) and a small, preprocessed corpus of New York Times sentences, preliminary results (Section 4) indicate that the approach is surprisingly effective in discovering relations, lexicons, and facts in an unsupervised fashion. A key advantage of this vertically integrated generative approach, compared to more classical bottom-up pipelines with deterministic stages, is that no hard decisions are made and all available context is ap-

---

[1] The word "realistic" in this context refers to the philosophical position of *realism*, usually ascribed to the Scottish School of Common Sense, which asserts that there is a real world and it is the subject of scientific theories and factual discourse.

Proceedings of AKBC 2016, pages 51–56,
San Diego, California, June 12-17, 2016. ©2016 Association for Computational Linguistics

plied to reduce uncertainty at every level, resulting in much higher accuracy (Pasula et al., 2003; Singh et al., 2013). Parsing, entity resolution, event recognition, and extraction emerge from a single, vertically integrated inference process—no special algorithms are needed.

2 Background and related work

The classical approach to IE involves a multi-stage pipeline: text goes in one end; each level processes small sets of input elements to produce larger elements; the output is usually a partially filled "template" describing a complex event. Intermediate levels include complex words, semantic elements (noun phrases, verb phrases), and elementary facts with unresolved entity references. Each pipeline stage requires manually created rules, specific to a particular domain, to recognize patterns among elements; or, learned classifiers can be used, but they require supervised training. The pipeline architecture has two major drawbacks: (1) decisions made using only local information are often wrong, and (2) errors propagate upwards leading to low overall accuracy.

Brin (1998) proposed a more scalable and automated approach called *bootstrapping*. Given a seed fact for a relation, such as $Author(Charles Dickens, Great Expectations)$, bootstrapping aims to find all authorship facts and all textual patterns for expressing such facts. It alternates two steps:

1. Find sentences with known author–book pairs, e.g., "Charles Dickens wrote Great Expectations," and extract the pattern, "x **wrote** y."

2. Find sentences matching known patterns, e.g., "JK Rowling **wrote** Harry Potter," and extract the corresponding fact, $Author(JK Rowling, Harry Potter)$.

Bootstrapping is effective but not perfect: for example, it finds *correlated facts* such as "JK Rowling made millions from Harry Potter" and concludes (optimistically, perhaps) that "x **made millions from** y" describes authorship; moreover, because of *polysemy* in "wrote", it finds "JK Rowling wrote Neville Longbottom out of the movie" and concludes an incorrect fact,

$Author(JK Rowling, Neville Longbottom)$. Despite these issues, bootstrapping is the core of modern "open" IE systems, such as CMU's Never-Ending Language Learning (Mitchell et al., 2015). Section 3 describes an IE method grounded in probability theory that (1) generates bootstrapping inferences as a natural consequence, (2) explains why and when bootstrapping works, and (3) avoids the difficulties mentioned above.

As in other areas of NLP, recent work on IE has adopted statistical models for text. *Discriminative* models such as conditional random fields (CRFs) are trainable, bottom-up classifiers usable for the early stages of a pipeline approach; they require less manual labor than rule-based methods, although they do require supervised data. *Generative* models describe a stochastic process whose *output* is text; given some actual text, an inference algorithm can reconstruct the underlying hidden variables that would explain the observed text. Several other groups (see, e.g., Rink and Harabagiu (2011) or Yao *et al.* (2011) and many variants cited by Grycner et al. (2014)) are developing generative models for IE and relation discovery, but their models generate text from a descriptive model of text, rather than from a model of an underlying real world. That is, the hidden variables include the *dictionaries* describing the words that each relation uses to express itself and the *types* for each of its arguments, but not the *facts* that explain why the text is there. Thus, they cannot truly reconstruct such a world from text. The difficulty can be illustrated very simply: if one generates a very large sample of authorship sentences from such a model, one will find sentences claiming that every person has written every book. In real text, on the other hand, sentences are statistically coupled by an important latent variable, namely the real world. Thus, the statistics of corpora are completely different in the two cases. Because this difference is so important in understanding the model we propose, we return to it in more detail in Section 3.1.

3 An elementary generative model for declarative text

Here is a naive but ontologically realistic explanation for declarative text: the world contains facts; people choose to report some of those facts; they choose a way to report each fact; the text is the collection of sentences that results. More precisely, the model assumes only that the world contains

- some unknown number N of objects, $x_1, \ldots, x_N$;
- some unknown number K of binary relations, $R_1, \ldots, R_K$;
- a collection of facts $R_k(x_i, x_j)$; each of the N^2 potential facts for R_k holds with probability σ_k, which is an unknown *sparsity parameter* between 0 and 1.

Here, N and K use a broad prior such as a discrete log-normal; σ_k has a beta prior with a small mean. In this naive, declarative world, a theory of pragmatics predicts what will be reported (Gordon and Durme, 2013). The initial theory is trivial: when writing sentence s_t, the author chooses a fact $R_k(x_i, x_j)$ at random from the set of true facts and reports it.

Then the semantic–syntactic model describes the text of sentence s_t given fact $R_k(x_i, x_j)$:

- a "verb" v is sampled from the relation R_k's dictionary D_k, an unknown categorical distribution over dependency paths that is drawn from a Dirichlet prior;
- the arguments x_i, x_j are mentioned verbatim as named entities (later versions have generative models for named-entity mentions);
- the final sentence is given by $s_t = x_i \, v \, x_j$.

This model can be written in roughly 10 lines of BLOG code. When supplied with suitable text as evidence, it automatically produces an improved and more robust version of bootstrapping, handles polysemy, needs no seed facts, and discovers new relations and their common forms of expression without requiring hand-engineered features measuring similarity of dependency paths.

Given a probability model that exhibits bootstrapping behavior, one can ask *why it works*: why is bootstrapping a reasonable inference in many cases? The answer is *sparsity*: given just the sentences "Charles Dickens **wrote** Great Expectations" and "Charles Dickens **authored** Great Expectations," one can show by simple calculation that the posterior odds that **wrote** and **authored** refer to the same relation are approximately proportional to $1/\sigma_k$. Intuitively, if they are not the same relation, the second sentence requires the reader to believe that a new

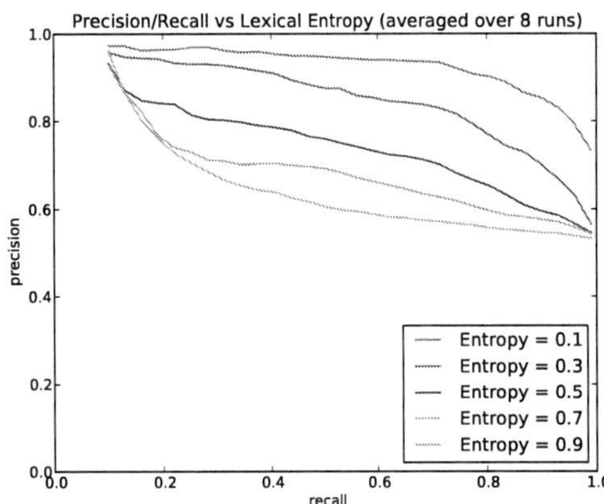

Figure 1: Measuring the ability of inference to extract accurate facts under polysemy: precision–recall curves for different levels of lexical entropy.

fact holds in the world, which is an unlikely coincidence if σ_k is small. And common sense suggests that nearly all relations are very sparse: for example, the relation matrix $Author(person, book)$ has a sparsity of approximately 1 in 7 billion. (In practice sparsity must be adjusted for the fact that authors are much more likely to be mentioned in text than the average human, so the effective sparsity is probably closer to 1 in ten thousand.) Inferences of this type are not only strong but also frequent, due to the "birthday paradox" phenomenon: given, say, a million facts for a relation expressible by two distinct patterns, a bootstrapping opportunity (when the two patterns are used with the same pair of arguments) occurs with overwhelming probability after about 2000 sentences. Each new bootstrapping opportunity of this kind connects two previously disjoint subgraphs of sentences; one expects that probabilistic analysis of graphs should become a key technique in the mathematics of information extraction.

One can also study properties of the mathematical model via simulation. For example, one can generate worlds whose relational dictionaries exhibit different levels of polysemy, generate text from those worlds, and measure the ability of inference to extract true facts. Let $d_{k,i}$ be the probability assigned by dictionary D_k to word (or dependency path) w_i, and define the *lexical entropy* of a collection of dictionaries $D_{k_1}, \ldots, D_{k_m}$ to be the frequency-weighted average over words w_i of the entropy of the categorical distribution $[d_{k_1,i}, \ldots, d_{k_m,i}]/Z$. Then identical dictionaries (yielding completely ambiguous text) have lexical entropy 1 and disjoint dictionaries (yielding unambiguous text) have lexical entropy 0. The results shown in Figure **??** show that with lexical entropy 0.9, i.e., almost identical dictionaries that generate text that is impenetrable to mere humans, it is possible to achieve 90% precision at 10% recall—i.e., to reliably identify relations in some cases. Thus, the approach should be highly robust to polysemy in practice.

Like the original bootstrapping algorithm, it is susceptible to correlated facts, because it assumes that each relation samples its facts independently. Independence fails with relations such as marriage and divorce, since the latter implies the former; when the data contain "A got married to B" and "A just divorced B", bootstrapping assumes that "x got married to y" and "x just divorced y" mean the same thing. This is unfortunate. A similar problem arises with pairs of relations where one is a more specific version of the other, for example "x is a professor at y" and "x is employed by y". A more sophisticated model of reality fixes this problem; e.g., one allows a relation R_k to be either *de novo* or *highly correlated* (according to some unknown, but not small, correlation factor $\rho_{k,l}$) with some other relation R_l.

3.1 Comparison to other generative models for relational text

In Section 2, we claimed that an ontologically realistic model is fundamentally distinct from other generative models for relational text that have appeared in the literature. Here we go into more detail on this point, using as an example the Rel-LDA model in Figure 1 of Yao et al. (2011). (We choose Rel-LDA because of its superficial similarity to our model, not because of any particular failings.) In Rel-LDA, the generative process is as follows:

- For each relation $r \in \{1, \ldots, R\}$, multinomials $p_{r,1}$, $p_{r,v}$, $p_{r,2}$ are drawn from Dirichlet priors, representing distributions over "words" for the first argument, "verb", and second argument, respectively.
- For each document, a multinomial q over R values is drawn from a Dirichlet prior, where $q(r)$ indicates the probability that any given sentence is generated by relation r.

- For each sentence, a relation indicator r is drawn from the multinomial, and "Words" for the first argument, verb, and second argument are drawn independently from $p_{r,1}$, $p_{r,v}$, $p_{r,2}$, respectively.

Subsequent elaborations of this model add features for the "verb" dependency path and types for the arguments. Given an actual document containing subject-verb-object sentence triples, inference with this model discovers the underlying relations by clustering the sentences.

The difference between this model and an ontologically realistic model is that Rel-LDA posits no underlying world. A trained Rel-LDA model describes what text for a given relation "looks like", but lacks the distinction between world and text and the statistical coupling that a latent world introduces. For example, a model trained on text that lists facts about books purchased on Amazon might learn that Stephen King is the most common first argument for the author relation. If we include a new sentence in the corpus, "Vladimir Vapnik wrote The Nature of Statistical Learning Theory", and then ask the model, "Who wrote The Nature of Statistical Learning Theory?", the answer will be "Stephen King".

Another important consequence of the absence of a latent world is that the Rel-LDA model does not assign high probability to bootstrapping inferences. We speculate that this leads to a learning process that requires many more sentences to reliably discover a set of relations and dictionaries, but we have yet to carry out this experiment. For now, we report only a very preliminary and anecdotal set of results with our model.

4 Preliminary experiments

The model was applied to a small subset (8500 sentences) of an NYT corpus (Yao et al., 2011). The subset was chosen heuristically to have a relatively small number of distinct entity mentions, so as to increase the number of bootstrapping opportunities. The sentences contain two named entities connected by a grammatical dependency path, matching our trivial grammatical model. The inference process discovers (1) roughly 200 relations that underlie the text; (2) the dictionaries describing how each relation is expressed by dependency paths; and (3) the facts belonging to each relation.

We ran smart–dumb/dumb–smart split–merge MCMC (Wang and Russell, 2015) for about 10 minutes and inspected the most likely sampled world. We found that relation 46, which we might call "subsidiary of", emerged with the following highly probable dependency paths in its dictionary:

```
[appos|->unit->prep->of->|pobj]
[appos|-> part->prep->of-> pobj]
[nn| <-unit->prep->of->[pobj]
[partmod|-> own->prep->by->[pobj]
[rcmod|-> own->prep->by-> |pobj]
[appos|-> subsidiary->prep->of-> |pobj]
[rcmod|-> part->prep->of-> |pobj]
[rcmod|-> unit->prep->of ->|pobj]
[poss|<- parent-> |appos]
[appos|-> division->prep->of-> |pobj]
[pobj|<- of<-prep<-office->appos
     ->part->prep->of-> |pobj]
[pobj|<- of<-prep<-unit->appos
     ->part->prep->of-> |pobj]
[nn|<- division->prep->of-> |pobj]
[appos|-> unit-> |nn]
[nsubjpass|<-own->prep->by-> |pobj]
[nn|<- office->prep->of-> |pobj]
```

We also found 60 facts such as $rel_{46}(BBDO\ Worldwide, Omnicom\ Group)$ and $rel_{46}(Fox, News\ Corporation)$. Manual verification of all facts for the most common 20 relations shows roughly 95% precision, with most errors arising from the limitations of the preprocessor and named entity extractor. Because of the strength and frequency of bootstrapping inferences, it seems likely (although this remains to be verified) that the relation discovery process is more accurate than in other approaches and requires less data. Extensions to the generative model to include entity attributes and a more complete semantic grammar (see Section 5) will automatically resolve entity references and avoid the need for pre-parsing or named-entity recognition.

4.1 A note on evaluation

The traditional method of evaluation for IE systems relies on the ability to inspect the extracted knowledge base for correctness. As probability models become more sophisticated, this approach will fail, because (1) the knowledge is represented using internal symbols referring to relations and entities the system discovers for itself, that may not correspond to standard concepts in English, and (2) the meaning of a given internal symbol varies across possible worlds in the inference process. Instead, as with humans, the query interface must, inevitably, be via language itself. For example, one can ask whether the subjects of sentences 14 ("Obama roasts WH press") and 22 ("President seeks second term") are the same entity, or ask for x such that "x is President of South Sudan" is true.

5 Conclusions and further work

An ontologically realistic generative probabilistic model has many advantages for information extraction. Initial experiments show that the approach can discover relations and extract facts in an unsupervised fashion, performing bootstrapping and disambiguation inferences without special heuristics.

Of course, the initial model is vastly oversimplified. We need to add types, generative models for entity mentions, the ability to extract general knowledge (Clark et al., 2014), and a standard upper ontology including mereology, time, actions, and events. (There is no point in forcing a learning algorithm to rediscover these concepts.) A more sophisticated model of reporting bias is needed (Gordon and Durme, 2013). There should be a "backoff hierarchy" of weaker and more general semantic–syntactic models to cope with uninterpretable text; as learning proceeds, new and more specific grammatical forms are added and probability mass moves down the hierarchy. Finally, our purely symbolic semantics can be augmented by a vector-space model of word meaning; this should result in faster generalization via sharing among dictionaries.

Obviously there is much new ground to explore before the proposed approach can handle unrestricted text. Engaging in this exploration seems preferable to trying to extract information about the world from models that deny the world's existence.

Acknowledgments

This research was funded by a Chaire Blaise Pascal awarded to the first author, administered by the Fondation de l'École Normale Supérieure, and by a Senior Chaire d'excellence of the Agence Nationale de la Recherche. The Laboratoire d'Informatique de Paris VI and its Director, Patrick Gallinari, generously hosted the project and its authors.

References

Sergey Brin. 1998. Extracting patterns and relations from the World-Wide Web. In *WebDB Workshop at EDBT-98*.

E. Charniak and R. Goldman. 1992. A Bayesian model of plan recognition. *Artificial Intelligence*, 64:53–79.

Peter Clark, Niranjan Balasubramanian, Sumithra Bhakthavatsalam, Kevin Humphreys, Jesse Kinkead, Ashish Sabharwal, and Oyvind Tafjord. 2014. Automatic construction of inference-supporting knowledge bases. In *AKBC-14*.

Jonathan Gordon and Benjamin Van Durme. 2013. Reporting bias and knowledge acquisition. In *AKBC-13*.

Adam Grycner, Gerhard Weikum, Jay Pujara, James Foulds, and Lise Getoor. 2014. A unified probabilistic approach for semantic clustering of relational phrases. In *AKBC-14*.

Brian Milch and Stuart Russell. 2010. Extending Bayesian networks to the open-universe case. In *Heuristics, Probability and Causality: A Tribute to Judea Pearl*. College Publications.

T. Mitchell, W. Cohen, et al. 2015. Never-ending learning. In *Proc. AAAI-15*.

H. Pasula, B. Marthi, B. Milch, S. J. Russell, and I. Shpitser. 2003. Identity uncertainty and citation matching. In *NIPS-02*.

B. Rink and S. Harabagiu. 2011. A generative model for unsupervised discovery of relations and argument classes from clinical texts. In *EMNLP-11*.

Sameer Singh, Sebastian Riedel, Brian Martin, Jiaping Zheng, and Andrew McCallum. 2013. Joint inference of entities, relations, and coreference. In *AKBC-13*.

Wei Wang and Stuart Russell. 2015. A smart-dumb/dumb-smart algorithm for efficient split-merge MCMC. In *UAI-15*.

L. Yao, A. Haghighi, S. Riedel, and A. McCallum. 2011. Structured relation discovery using generative models. In *EMNLP-11*.

Know2Look: Commonsense Knowledge for Visual Search

Sreyasi Nag Chowdhury   **Niket Tandon**   **Gerhard Weikum**

Max Planck Institute for Informatics
Saarbrücken, Germany
`sreyasi, ntandon, weikum@mpi-inf.mpg.de`

Abstract

With the rise in popularity of social media, images accompanied by contextual text form a huge section of the web. However, search and retrieval of documents are still largely dependent on solely textual cues. Although visual cues have started to gain focus, the imperfection in object/scene detection do not lead to significantly improved results. We hypothesize that the use of background commonsense knowledge on query terms can significantly aid in retrieval of documents with associated images. To this end we deploy three different modalities - text, visual cues, and commonsense knowledge pertaining to the query - as a recipe for efficient search and retrieval.

1   Introduction

Motivation: Image retrieval by querying visual contents has been on the agenda of the database, information retrieval, multimedia, and computer vision communities for decades (Liu et al., 2007; Datta et al., 2008). Search engines like Baidu, Bing or Google perform reasonably well on this task, but crucially rely on textual cues that accompany an image: tags, caption, URL string, adjacent text etc.

In recent years, deep learning has led to a boost in the quality of visual object recognition in images with fine-grained object labels (Simonyan and Zisserman, 2014; LeCun et al., 2015; Mordvintsev et al., 2015). Methods like LSDA (Hoffman et al., 2014) are trained on more than 15,000 classes of ImageNet (Deng et al., 2009) (which are mostly leaf-level synsets of WordNet (Miller, 1995)), and annotate newly seen images with class labels for bound-

(a) Good object detection

(b) Poor object detection

Figure 1: Example cases where visual object detection may or may not aid in search and retrieval.

ing boxes of objects. For the image in Figure 1a, for example, object labels *traffic light, car, person, bicycle* and *bus* have been recognized making it easily retrievable for queries with these concepts. However, these labels come with uncertainty. For the image in Figure 1b, there is much higher noise in its visual object labels; so querying by visual labels would not work here.

Opportunity and Challenge: These limitations of text-based search, on one hand, and visual-object search, on the other hand, suggest combining the cues from text and vision for more effective retrieval. Although each side of this combined feature space is incomplete and noisy, the hope is that the

Proceedings of AKBC 2016, pages 57–62,
San Diego, California, June 12-17, 2016. ©2016 Association for Computational Linguistics

Figure 2: Sample queries containing abstract concepts and expected results of image retrieval.

combination can improve retrieval quality.

Unfortunately, images that show more sophisticated scenes, or emotions evoked on the viewer are still out of reach. Figure 2 shows three examples, along with query formulations that would likely consider these sample images as relevant results. These answers would best be retrieved by queries with abstract words (e.g. "environment friendly") or activity words (e.g. "traffic") rather than words that directly correspond to visual objects (e.g. "car" or "bike"). So there is a vocabulary gap, or even concept mismatch, between what users want and express in queries and the visual and textual cues that come directly with an image. This is the key problem addressed in this paper.

Approach and Contribution: To bridge the concepts and vocabulary between user queries and image features, we propose an approach that harnesses commonsense knowledge (CSK). Recent advances in automatic knowledge acquisition have produced large collections of CSK: physical (e.g. color or shape) as well as abstract (e.g. abilities) properties of everyday objects (e.g. bike, bird, sofa, etc.) (Tandon et al., 2014), subclass and part-whole relations between objects (Tandon et al.,

2016), activities and their participants (Tandon et al., 2015), and more. This kind of knowledge allows us to establish relationships between our example queries and observable objects or activities in the image. For example, the following CSK triples establish relationships between *'backpack'*, *'tourist'* and *'travel map'*: `(backpacks, are carried by, tourists)`, `(tourists, use, travel maps)`. This allows for retrieval of images with generic queries like *"travel with backpack"*.

This idea is worked out into a *query expansion model* where we leverage a CSK knowledge base for automatically generating additional query words. Our model unifies three kinds of features: *textual features* from the page context of an image, *visual features* obtained from recognizing fine-grained object classes in an image, and *CSK features* in the form of additional properties of the concepts referred to by query words. The weighing of the different features is crucial for query-result ranking. To this end, we have devised a method based on statistical language models (Zhai, 2008).

The paper's contribution can be characterized as follows. We present the first model for incorporating CSK into image retrieval. We develop a full-fledged system architecture for this purpose, along with a query processor and an answer-ranking component. Our system *Know2Look*, uses commonsense *know*ledge to *look for* images relevant to a query by *looking at* the components of the images in greater detail. We further discuss experiments that compare our approach to state-of-the-art image search in various configurations. Our approach substantially improves the query result quality.

2 Related Work

Existing Commonsense Knowledge Bases: Traditionally commonsense knowledge bases were curated manually through experts (Lenat, 1995) or through crowd-sourcing (Singh et al., 2002). Modern methods of CSK acquisition are automatic, either from test corpora (Liu and Singh, 2004) or from the web (Tandon et al., 2014).

Vision and NLP: Research at the intersection of Natural Language Processing and Computer Vision is in limelight in the recent past. There have been work on automatic image annotations (Wang et al.,

2014), description generation (Vinyals et al., 2014; Ordonez et al., 2011; Mitchell et al., 2012), scene understanding (Farhadi et al., 2010), image retrieval through natural language queries (Malinowski and Fritz, 2014) etc.

Commonsense knowledge from text and vision: There have been attempts for learning CSK from real images (Chen et al., 2013) as well as from non-photo-realistic abstractions (Vedantam et al., 2015). Recent work have also leveraged CSK for visual verification of relational phrases (Sadeghi et al., 2015) and for non-visual tasks like fill-in-the-blanks by intelligent agents (Lin and Parikh, 2015). Learning commonsense from visual cues continue to be a challenge in itself. The CSK used in our work is motivated by research on CSK acquisition from the web (Tandon et al., 2014).

3 Multimodal document retrieval

Adjoining text of images may or may not explicitly annotate their visual contents. Search engines relying on only textual matches ignore information which may be solely available in the visual cues. Moreover, the intuition behind using CSK is that humans innately interpolate visual or textual information with associated latent knowledge for analysis and understanding. Hence we believe that leveraging CSK in addition to textual and visual information would take results closer to human users' preferences. In order to use such background knowledge, curating a CSK knowledge base is of primary importance. Since automatic acquisition of canonicalized CSK from the web can be costly, we conjecture that noisy subject-predicate-object (SPO) triples extracted through Open Information Extraction (Banko et al., 2007) may be used as CSK. We hypothesize that the combination of the noisy ingredients – CSK, object-classes, and textual descriptions – would create an ensemble effect providing for efficient search and retrieval. We describe the components of our architecture in the following sections.

3.1 Data, Knowledge and Features

We consider a document x from a collection X with two kinds of features:

- **Visual features** xv_j: labels of object classes recognized in the image, including their hypernyms (e.g., king cobra, cobra, snake).

- **Textual features** xx_j: words that occur in the text that accompanies the image, for example image caption.

We assume that the two kinds of features can be combined into a single feature vector $x = \langle x_1 \ldots x_M \rangle$ with hyper-parameters α_v and α_x to weigh visual vs. textual features.

CSK is denoted by a set Y of triples $y_k (k = 1..j)$ with components ys_k, yp_k, yo_k (s - subject, p - predicate, o - object). Each component consists of one or more words. This yields a feature vector $y_kj (j = 1..M)$ for the triple y_k.

3.2 Language Models for Ranking

We study a variety of query-likelihood language models (LM) for ranking documents x with regard to a given query q. We assume that a query is simply a set of keywords $q_i (i = 1..L)$. In the following we formulate equations for unigram LMs, which can be simply extended to bigram LMs by using word pairs instead of single ones.

Basic LM:

$$P_{basic}[q|x] = \prod_i P[q_i|x] \tag{1}$$

where we set the weight of word q_i in x as follows:

$$P[q_i|x] = \alpha_x P[q_i|xx_j]P[xx_j|x] + \alpha_v P[q_i|xv_j]P[xv_j|x] \tag{2}$$

Here, xx_j and xv_j are unigrams in the textual or visual components of a document; α_x and α_v are hyper-parameters to weigh the textual and visual features respectively.

Smoothed LM:

$$P_{smoothed}[q|x] = \alpha P_{basic}[q|x] + (1-\alpha)P[q|B] \tag{3}$$

where B is a background corpus model and $P[q|B] = \prod_i P[q_i|B]$. We use Flickr tags from the YFCC100M dataset (Thomee et al., 2015) along with their frequency of occurrences as a background corpus.

Commonsense-aware LM (a translation LM):

$$P_{CS}[q|x] = \prod_i \left[\frac{\sum_k P[q_i|y_k]P[y_k|x]}{|k|} \right] \tag{4}$$

The summation ranges over all y_k that can bridge the query vocabulary with the image-feature vocabulary; so both of the probabilities $P[q_i|y_k]$ and $P[y_k|x]$ must be non-zero. For example, when the query asks for "electric car" and an image has features "vehicle" (visual) and "energy saving" (textual), triples such as (car, is a type of, vehicle) and (electric engine, saves, energy) would have this property. That is, we consider only commonsense triples that overlap with both the query and the image features.

The probabilities $P[q_i|y_k]$ and $P[y_k|x]$ are estimated based on the word-wise overlap between q_i and y_k and y_k and x, respectively. They also consider the confidence of the words in y_k and x.

Mixture LM (the final ranking LM):
Since a document x can capture a query term or its commonsense expansion, we formulate a mixture model for the ranking of a document with respect to a query:

$$P[q|x] = \beta_{CS}P_{CS}[q|x] + (1 - \beta_{CS})P_{smoothed}[q|x] \tag{5}$$

where β_{CS} is a hyper-parameter weighing the commonsense features of the expanded query.

3.3 Feature Weights

By casting all features into word-level unigrams, we have a unified feature space with hyper-parameters (α_x, α_v, and β_{CS}). For this submission the hyper-parameters are manually chosen.

For weights of visual object class xv_j of document x, we consider the *confidence score* from LSDA (Hoffman et al., 2014). We extend these object classes with their hypernyms from WordNet which are set to the same confidence as their detected hyponyms. Although not in common parlance this kind of expansion can also be considered as CSK. We define the weight for a textual unigram xx_j as its informativeness – the inverse document frequency with respect to a background corpus (Flickr tags with frequencies).

The words in a CSK triple y_k have non-uniform weights proportional to their similarity with the query words, their *idf* with respect to a background corpus, and the salience of their position – boosting the weight of words in s and o components of

y. The function computing similarity between two unigrams favors exact matches to partial matches.

3.4 Example

Query string: *travel with backpack*
Commonsense triples to expand query:
 $t1$:(tourists, use, travel maps)
 $t2$:(tourists, carry, backpacks)
 $t3$:(backpack, is a type of, bag)

Say we have a document x with features:
 Textual - "A tourist reading a map by the road."
 Visual - person, bag, bottle, bus

The query will now successfully retrieve the above document, whereas it would have been missed by text-only systems.

4 Datasets

For the purpose of demonstration we choose a topical domain – *Tourism*. Our CSK knowledge base and image dataset obey this constraint.

CSK acquisition through OpenIE: We consider a slice of Wikipedia pertaining to the domain *tourism* as the text corpus to extract CSK from. Nouns from the Wikipedia article titled 'Tourism'(seed document) constitute our basic language model. We collect articles by traversing the Wiki Category hierarchy tree while pruning out those with substantial topic drift. The Jaccard Distance (Equation 6) of a document from the seed document is used as a metric for pruning.

$$JaccardDistance = 1 - WeightedJaccardSimilarity \tag{6}$$

where,

$$WeightedJaccardSimilarity =$$
$$\frac{\Sigma_n min[f(d_i, w_n), f(D, w_n)]}{\Sigma_n max[f(d_i, w_n), f(D, w_n)]} \tag{7}$$

In Equation 7, acquired Wikipedia articles d_i are compared to the seed document D; $f(d', w)$ is the frequency of occurrence of word w in document d'. For simplicity only articles with Jaccard distance of 1 from the seed document are pruned out. The corpus of domain-specific pages thus collected constitute ~5000 Wikipedia articles.

Table 1: Query Benchmark for evaluation

aircraft	international	diesel	transport
airport	vehicle	dog	park
backpack	travel	fish	market
ball	park	housing	town
bench	high	lamp	home
bicycle	road	old	clock
bicycle	trip	road	signal
bird	park	table	home
boat	tour	tourist	bus
bridge	road	van	road

The OpenIE tool ReVerb (Fader et al., 2011) run against our corpus produces around 1 million noisy SPO triples. After filtering with our basic language model we have ~22,000 moderately clean assertions.

Image Dataset: For the purpose of experiments we construct our own image dataset. ~50,000 images with descriptions are collected from the following datasets: Flickr30k (Young et al., 2014), Pascal Sentences (Rashtchian et al., 2010), SBU Captioned Photo Dataset (Ordonez et al., 2011), and MSCOCO (Lin et al., 2014). The images are collected by comparing their textual descriptions with our basic language model for *Tourism*. An existing object detection algorithm – LSDA (Hoffman et al., 2014) – is used for object detection in the images. The detected object classes are based on the 7000 leaf nodes of ImageNet (Deng et al., 2009). We also expand these classes by adding their super-classes or hypernyms with the same confidence score.

Query Benchmark: We construct a benchmark of 20 queries from co-occurring Flickr tags from the YFCC100M dataset (Thomee et al., 2015). This benchmark is shown in Table 1. Each query consists of two keywords that have appeared together with high frequency as user tags in Flickr images.

5   Experiments

Baseline Google search results on our image dataset form the baseline for the evaluation of *Know2Look*. We consider the results in two settings – search only on original image caption (Vanilla Google), and on image captions along with detected object classes (Extended Google). The later is done to aid

Table 2: Comparison of *Know2Look* with baselines

	Average Precision@10
Vanilla Google	0.47
Extended Google	0.64
Know2Look	0.85

Google in its search by providing additional visual cues. We exploit the domain restriction facility of Google search (*query string site:domain name*) to get Google search results explicitly on our dataset.

Know2Look In addition to the setup for Extended Google, *Know2Look* also performs query expansion with CSK. In most cases we win over the baseline since CSK captures additional concepts related to query terms enhancing latent information that may be present in the images. We consider the top 10 retrieval results of the two baselines and *Know2Look* for the 20 queries in our query benchmark[1]. We compare the three systems by Precision@10. Table 2 shows the values of Precision@10 averaged over 20 queries for each of the three systems – *Know2Look* performs better than the baselines.

6   Conclusion

In this paper we propose the incorporation of commonsense knowledge for image retrieval. Our architecture, *Know2Look*, expands queries by related commonsense knowledge and retrieves images based on their visual and textual contents. By utilizing the visual and commonsense modalities we make search results more appealing to the humans than traditional text-only approaches. We support our claim by comparing *Know2Look* to Google search on our image data set. The proposed concept can be easily extrapolated to document retrieval. Moreover, in addition to using noisy OpenIE triples as commonsense knowledge, we aim to leverage existing commonsense knowledge bases for future evaluations of *Know2Look*.

Acknowledgment: We would like to thank Anna Rohrbach for her assistance with visual object detection of our image data set using LSDA. We also thank Ali Shah for his help with visualization of the evaluation results.

[1]http://mpi-inf.mpg.de/~sreyasi/queries/evaluation.html

References

Michele Banko, Michael J Cafarella, Stephen Soderland, Matthew Broadhead, and Oren Etzioni. 2007. Open information extraction for the web. In *IJCAI*, volume 7, pages 2670–2676.

Xinlei Chen, Abhinav Shrivastava, and Abhinav Gupta. 2013. Neil: Extracting visual knowledge from web data. In *Proceedings of the IEEE International Conference on Computer Vision*, pages 1409–1416.

Ritendra Datta, Dhiraj Joshi, Jia Li, and James Z Wang. 2008. Image retrieval: Ideas, influences, and trends of the new age. *ACM Computing Surveys (CSUR)*, 40(2):5.

Jia Deng, Wei Dong, Richard Socher, Li-Jia Li, Kai Li, and Li Fei-Fei. 2009. Imagenet: A large-scale hierarchical image database. In *Computer Vision and Pattern Recognition, 2009. CVPR 2009. IEEE Conference on*, pages 248–255. IEEE.

Anthony Fader, Stephen Soderland, and Oren Etzioni. 2011. Identifying relations for open information extraction. In *Proceedings of the Conference on Empirical Methods in Natural Language Processing*, pages 1535–1545. Association for Computational Linguistics.

Ali Farhadi, Mohsen Hejrati, Mohammad Amin Sadeghi, Peter Young, Cyrus Rashtchian, Julia Hockenmaier, and David Forsyth. 2010. Every picture tells a story: Generating sentences from images. In *Computer Vision–ECCV 2010*, pages 15–29. Springer.

Judy Hoffman, Sergio Guadarrama, Eric S Tzeng, Ronghang Hu, Jeff Donahue, Ross Girshick, Trevor Darrell, and Kate Saenko. 2014. Lsda: Large scale detection through adaptation. In *Advances in Neural Information Processing Systems*, pages 3536–3544.

Yann LeCun, Yoshua Bengio, and Geoffrey Hinton. 2015. Deep learning. *Nature*, 521(7553):436–444.

Douglas B Lenat. 1995. Cyc: A large-scale investment in knowledge infrastructure. *Communications of the ACM*, 38(11):33–38.

Xiao Lin and Devi Parikh. 2015. Don't just listen, use your imagination: Leveraging visual common sense for non-visual tasks. In *Proceedings of the IEEE Conference on Computer Vision and Pattern Recognition*, pages 2984–2993.

Tsung-Yi Lin, Michael Maire, Serge Belongie, James Hays, Pietro Perona, Deva Ramanan, Piotr Dollár, and C Lawrence Zitnick. 2014. Microsoft coco: Common objects in context. In *Computer Vision–ECCV 2014*, pages 740–755. Springer.

Hugo Liu and Push Singh. 2004. Conceptneta practical commonsense reasoning tool-kit. *BT technology journal*, 22(4):211–226.

Ying Liu, Dengsheng Zhang, Guojun Lu, and Wei-Ying Ma. 2007. A survey of content-based image retrieval with high-level semantics. *Pattern Recognition*, 40(1):262–282.

Mateusz Malinowski and Mario Fritz. 2014. A multi-world approach to question answering about real-world scenes based on uncertain input. In *Advances in Neural Information Processing Systems*, pages 1682–1690.

George A Miller. 1995. Wordnet: a lexical database for english. *Communications of the ACM*, 38(11):39–41.

Margaret Mitchell, Xufeng Han, Jesse Dodge, Alyssa Mensch, Amit Goyal, Alex Berg, Kota Yamaguchi, Tamara Berg, Karl Stratos, and Hal Daumé III. 2012. Midge: Generating image descriptions from computer vision detections. In *Proceedings of the 13th Conference of the European Chapter of the Association for Computational Linguistics*, pages 747–756. Association for Computational Linguistics.

Alexander Mordvintsev, Christopher Olah, and Mike Tyka. 2015. Inceptionism: Going deeper into neural networks. *Google Research Blog. Retrieved June*.

Vicente Ordonez, Girish Kulkarni, and Tamara L. Berg. 2011. Im2text: Describing images using 1 million captioned photographs. In *Neural Information Processing Systems (NIPS)*.

Cyrus Rashtchian, Peter Young, Micah Hodosh, and Julia Hockenmaier. 2010. Collecting image annotations using amazon's mechanical turk. In *Proceedings of the NAACL HLT 2010 Workshop on Creating Speech and Language Data with Amazon's Mechanical Turk*, pages 139–147. Association for Computational Linguistics.

Fereshteh Sadeghi, Santosh K Divvala, and Ali Farhadi. 2015. Viske: Visual knowledge extraction and question answering by visual verification of relation phrases. In *Computer Vision and Pattern Recognition (CVPR), 2015 IEEE Conference on*, pages 1456–1464. IEEE.

Karen Simonyan and Andrew Zisserman. 2014. Very deep convolutional networks for large-scale image recognition. *arXiv preprint arXiv:1409.1556*.

Push Singh, Thomas Lin, Erik T Mueller, Grace Lim, Travell Perkins, and Wan Li Zhu. 2002. Open mind common sense: Knowledge acquisition from the general public. In *On the move to meaningful internet systems 2002: Coopis, doa, and odbase*, pages 1223–1237. Springer.

Niket Tandon, Gerard de Melo, Fabian Suchanek, and Gerhard Weikum. 2014. Webchild: Harvesting and organizing commonsense knowledge from the web. In *Proceedings of the 7th ACM international conference on Web search and data mining*, pages 523–532. ACM.

Niket Tandon, Gerard de Melo, Abir De, and Gerhard Weikum. 2015. Knowlywood: Mining activity knowledge from hollywood narratives. In *Proc. CIKM*.

Niket Tandon, Charles Hariman, Jacopo Urbani, Anna Rohrbach, Marcus Rohrbach, and Gerhard Weikum. 2016. Commonsense in parts: Mining part-whole relations from the web and image tags. *AAAI*.

Bart Thomee, David A. Shamma, Gerald Friedland, Benjamin Elizalde, Karl Ni, Douglas Poland, Damian Borth, and Li-Jia Li. 2015. The new data and new challenges in multimedia research. *arXiv preprint arXiv:1503.01817*.

Ramakrishna Vedantam, Xiao Lin, Tanmay Batra, C Lawrence Zitnick, and Devi Parikh. 2015. Learning common sense through visual abstraction. In *Proceedings of the IEEE International Conference on Computer Vision*, pages 2542–2550.

Oriol Vinyals, Alexander Toshev, Samy Bengio, and Dumitru Erhan. 2014. Show and tell: A neural image caption generator. *arXiv preprint arXiv:1411.4555*.

Josiah K Wang, Fei Yan, Ahmet Aker, and Robert Gaizauskas. 2014. A poodle or a dog? evaluating automatic image annotation using human descriptions at different levels of granularity. *V&L Net 2014*, page 38.

Peter Young, Alice Lai, Micah Hodosh, and Julia Hockenmaier. 2014. From image descriptions to visual denotations: New similarity metrics for semantic inference over event descriptions. *Transactions of the Association for Computational Linguistics*, 2:67–78.

ChengXiang Zhai. 2008. Statistical language models for information retrieval. *Synthesis Lectures on Human Language Technologies*, 1(1):1–141.

Row-less Universal Schema

Patrick Verga & Andrew McCallum
College of Information and Computer Sciences
University of Massachusetts Amherst
{pat, mccallum}@cs.umass.edu

Abstract

Universal schema jointly embeds knowledge bases and textual patterns to reason about entities and relations for automatic knowledge base construction and information extraction. In the past, entity pairs and relations were represented as learned vectors with compatibility determined by a scoring function, limiting generalization to unseen text patterns and entities. Recently, 'column-less' versions of Universal Schema have used compositional pattern encoders to generalize to all text patterns. In this work we take the next step and propose a 'row-less' model of universal schema, removing explicit entity pair representations. Instead of learning vector representations for each entity pair in our training set, we treat an entity pair as a function of its relation types. In experimental results on the FB15k-237 benchmark we demonstrate that we can match the performance of a comparable model with explicit entity pair representations using a model of attention over relation types. We further demonstrate that the model performs with nearly the same accuracy on entity pairs never seen during training.

1 Introduction

Automatic knowledge base construction (AKBC) is the task of building a structured knowledge base (KB) of facts using raw text evidence, and often an initial seed KB to be augmented (Carlson et al., 2010; Suchanek et al., 2007; Bollacker et al., 2008). Extracted facts about entities and their relations are useful for many downstream tasks such as question answering and query understanding. An effective approach to AKBC is Universal Schema, in which relation extraction is modeled as a matrix factorization problem wherein each row of the matrix is an entity pair and each column represents a relation between entities. Relations derived from a KB schema and from free text are thus embedded into a shared space allowing for a rich representation of KB relations, the union of all KB schemata.

This formulation is still limited in terms of its generalization, however. In its original form, Universal Schema can reason only about entity pairs and text relations explicitly seen at train time; it cannot predict relations between new entity pairs. In this work we present a 'rowless' extension of Universal Schema. Rather than representing each entity pair with an explicit dense vector, we encode entity pairs as aggregate functions over their relation types. This allows Universal Schema to form predictions for all entity pairs regardless of whether that pair was seen during training, and provides a direct connection between the prediction and its provenance.

Many models exist which address this issue by operating at the level of entities rather than entity pairs. A knowledge base is naturally described as a graph, in which entities are nodes and relations are labeled edges (Suchanek et al., 2007; Bollacker et al., 2008). In the case of *knowledge graph completion*, the task is akin to link prediction, assuming an initial set of (s, r, o) triples. See Nickel et al. (2015) for a review. No accompanying text data is necessary, since links can be predicted using properties of the graph, such as transitivity. In order to generalize well, prediction is often posed as low-rank matrix or tensor factorization. A variety of model variants have been suggested, where the probability of a given edge existing depends on a multi-linear form (Nickel et al., 2011; García-Durán et al., 2015; Yang et al., 2015; Bordes et al., 2013; Wang et al., 2014; Lin et al., 2015), or non-linear interactions between s, r, and o (Socher et al., 2013). These entity-based models have recall advantages over entity pairs. The model can predict relations between any two entity pairs in the absence of other information such as the pair's contextual occurrence in text.

However, entity models have been shown to be less precise than entity pair models when text is used to augment knowledge base facts. Both Toutanova et al. (2015) and Riedel et al. (2013) observe that the entity pair model outperforms entity models in cases where the entity pair was seen at training time. Since Universal

Proceedings of AKBC 2016, pages 63–68,
San Diego, California, June 12-17, 2016. ©2016 Association for Computational Linguistics

Schema leverages large amounts of unlabeled text we desire the benefits of entity pair modeling, and row-less Universal Schema facilitates learning entity pairs without the drawbacks of the traditional one-embedding-per-pair approach.

In this paper we investigate Universal Schema models without explicit entity pair representations. Instead, entity pairs are represented using an aggregation function over their relation types. This allows our model to naturally make predictions about any entity pair in new textual mentions, regardless of whether they were seen at train time additionally giving the model direct access to provenance. We show that an attention-based aggregation function outperforms several simpler functions and matches a model using explicit entity pairs. We then demonstrate that these 'row-less' models accurately predict on entity pairs unseen during training.

2 Background

2.1 Universal Schema

The Universal Schema (Riedel et al., 2013) approach to AKBC jointly embeds any number of KB and text corpora into a shared space to jointly reason over entities and their relations (Figure 1). The problem of relation extraction is posed as a matrix completion task where rows are entity pairs and columns are KB relations and textual patterns. The matrix is decomposed into two low-rank matrices resulting in embeddings for each entity pair, relation, and textual pattern. Reasoning is then performed directly on these embeddings.

Riedel et al. (2013) proposed several model variants operating on entities and entity pairs, and subsequently many other extensions have been proposed (Yao et al., 2013; Gardner et al., 2014; Neelakantan et al., 2015; Rocktaschel et al., 2015). Recently, Universal Schema has been extended to encode compositional representations of textual relations (Toutanova et al., 2015; Verga et al., 2016) allowing it to generalize to all textual patterns and reason over arbitrary text.

2.2 'Column-less' Universal Schema

The original Universal Schema approach has two main drawbacks: similar patterns do not share statistics, and the model is unable to make predictions about textual patterns not explicitly seen at train time.

Recently, 'column-less' versions of Universal Schema have been proposed to address these issues (Toutanova et al., 2015; Verga et al., 2016). These models learn compositional pattern encoders to parameterize the column matrix in place of directly embedding textual patterns. Compositional Universal Schema facilitates more compact sharing of statistics by composing similar patterns from the same sequence of word embeddings – the text

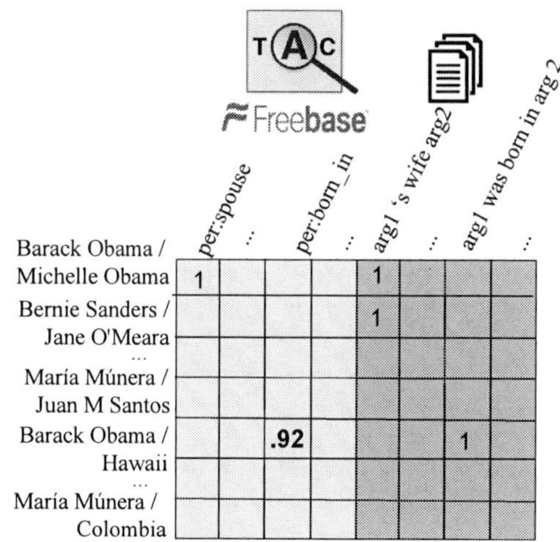

Figure 1: Universal schema represents relation types and entity pairs as a matrix. 1s denote observed training examples and the bolded .92 is predicted by the model.

patterns 'lives in the city' and 'lives in the city of' no longer exist as distinct atomic units. More importantly, Compositional Universal Schema can thus generalize to all possible textual patterns, facilitating reasoning over arbitrary text at test time.

3 Model

3.1 'Row-less' Universal Schema

While column-less Universal Schema addresses reasoning over arbitrary textual patterns, it is still limited to reasoning over entity pairs seen at training time. Verga et al. (2016) approach this problem by using Universal Schema as a sentence classifier – directly comparing a textual relation to a KB relation to perform relation extraction. However, this approach is unsatisfactory for two reasons. The first is that this creates an inconsistency between training and testing, as the model is trained to predict compatibility between entity pairs and relations and not relations directly. Second, it considers only a single piece of evidence in making its prediction.

We address both of these concerns in our 'row-less' Universal Schema. Rather than encoding each entity pair explicitly, we take the compositional approach of encoding entity pairs as an aggregation over their observed relation types (Figure 2). A learned entity pair embedding can be seen as a summarization of all relation types for which that entity pair was seen. Rather than learn this summarization as a single embedding, we reconstruct an entity pair representation from an aggregate of its relation types, essentially learning a mixture model rather than a single centroid.

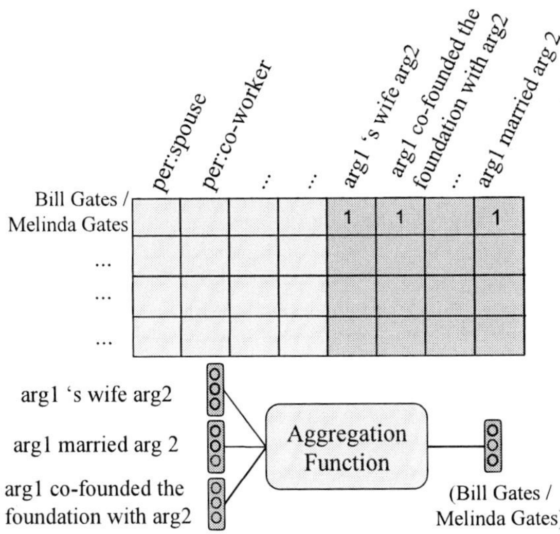

Figure 2: Row-less Universal Schema encodes an entity pair as an aggregation of its observed relation types.

3.2 Aggregation Functions

In this work we examine several aggregation functions. **Mean Pool** creates a single centroid for the entity pair by averaging all of its relation vectors. While this intuitively makes sense as an approximation for the explicit entity pair representation, averaging large numbers of embeddings can lead to a noisy signal. **Max Pool** also creates a single centroid for the entity pair by taking a dimension-wise max over the observed relation type vectors. Both mean pool and max pool are query-independent and form the same representation for the entity pair regardless of the query relation.

We also examine two query-specific aggregation functions. These models are more expressive than a single vector that is forced to to act as a centroid to all possible relation types an entity pair can take on. For example, the entity pair Bill and Melinda Gates could hold the relation 'per:spouse' or 'per:co-worker'. A query-specific aggregation mechanism can produce separate representations for this entity pair dependent on the query.

The **Max Relation** aggregation function represents the entity pair as its most similar relation to the query vector of interest. This model has the advantage of creating a query-specific entity pair representation but is more susceptible to noisy training data as a single incorrect piece of evidence could be used to form a prediction.

Finally, we look at an **Attention** aggregation function over relation types (Figure 3) which is similar to a single-layer memory network (Sukhbaatar et al., 2015) . In this model the query is scored with an input representation of each relation type followed by a softmax, giving a

weighting over each relation type. This output is then used to get a weighted sum over a set of output representations for each relation type resulting in a query-specific vector representation of the entity pair. The model pools relevant information over the entire set of relations and selects the most salient aspects to the query relation.

3.3 Training

Riedel et al. (2013) use Bayesian Personalized Ranking (BPR) (Rendle et al., 2009) to train their Universal Schema models. BPR ranks the probability of observed triples above unobserved triples rather than explicitly modeling unobserved edges as negative. Each training example is an entity pair/relation type triple observed in the training text corpora or KB. Rather than BPR, Toutanova et al. (2015) use a sampled softmax criterion where they use 200 negative samples [1] to approximate the negative log likelihood. Results shown were obtained using sampled softmax which outperformed BPR in our early experiments.

Our training procedure for relation-only Universal Schema model is similar to the original model. We first pool all of the observed triples in our training data creating entity pair-specific relation sets R^{Ep}. We remove entity pairs with only a single observed relation type. We then construct training examples for each observed relation type of an entity and an aggregation of all other relation types observed with that entity; for each observed relation type $r_i \in R^{Ep}$, we construct a positive training example $(r_i, \{R^{Ep} \setminus r_i\})$. We randomly sample a different relation to act as the negative sample.

All models were implemented in Torch[2] and were trained using Adam (Kingma and Ba, 2015). They each were trained with embedding dimension 25 and used 200 negative samples except for max pool which performed better with two negative samples. The entity pair model used a batch size 1024, $\ell_2 = 1e\text{-}8$, $\epsilon = 1e\text{-}4$, and learning rate .01. The aggregation models all used batch size 4096, $\ell_2 = 0$, $\epsilon = 1e\text{-}8$, and learning rate .01. The column vectors were initialized with the columns learned by the entity pair model. Randomly initializing the query encoders and tying the output and attention encoders performed better and all results use this method. Models were tuned to maximize mean reciprocal rank (MRR) on the validation set with early stopping.

---

[1]Many past papers restrict negative samples to be of the same type as the positive example. We simply sample uniformly from the entire set of entities that would form a valid entity pair.

[2]https://github.com/patverga/torch-relation-extraction

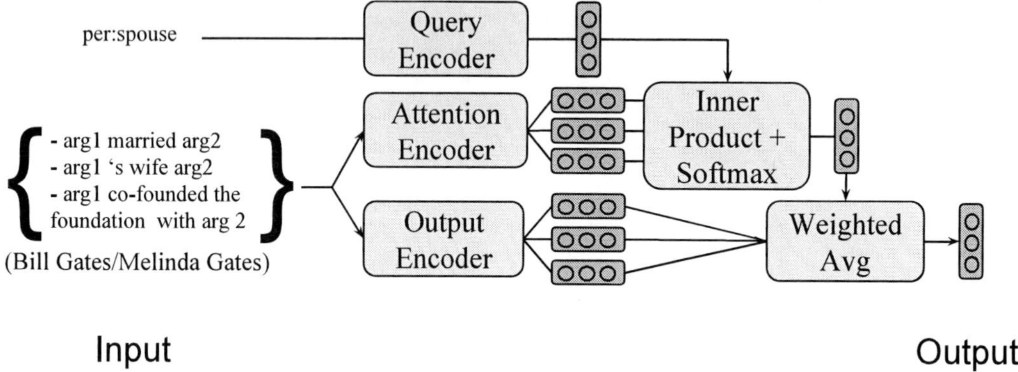

Figure 3: In the Attention model the query is dotted with an input representation of each relation type followed by a softmax, giving a weighting over each relation type. This output is then used to get a weighted sum over a set of output representations for each relation type. The result is a query-specific vector representation of the entity pair. The Max Relation model simply takes the max dot product rather than a softmax and weighted average.

4 Experimental Results

4.1 Data and Evaluation

We evaluate our models on the FB15k-237 dataset from Toutanova et al. (2015). The data is composed of a small set of 237 Freebase relations and approximately 4 million textual patterns from Clueweb with entities linked to Freebase (Gabrilovich et al., 2013). In past studies, for each (subject, relation, object) test triple, negative examples are generated by replacing the object with all other entities, filtering out triples that are positive in the data set. The positive triple is then be ranked among the negatives. In our experiments we limit the possible generated negatives to those entity pairs that have textual mentions in our training set. This way we can evaluate how well the model classifies textual mentions as Freebase relations. We also filter textual patterns with length greater than 35. We report the percentage of positive triples ranked in the top 10 amongst their negatives as well as the MRR scaled by 100.

4.2 Results

Our results are shown in Table 1. The model with explicit entity pair representations outperforms the 'rowless' variant by 2.9 MRR and 2.7% Hits@10. However, these results do show that relation aggregation is competitive with entity pair embeddings and it is possible to have a Universal Schema model without entity embeddings. With further experimentation we are confident that the 'row-less' model will perform on-par or better than the entity pair model.

The max model performs competitively with the attention model. This is not entirely surprising as it is a simpli-

fied version of the attention model. Further, the attention model reduces to the max relation model for entity pairs with only a single observed relation type. In our data, 64.8% of entity pairs have only a single observed relation type and 80.9% have 1 or 2 observed relation types.

We also explore the models' abilities to predict on unseen entity pairs (Table 2). We remove all training examples that contain a positive entity pair in either our validation or test set. We use the same validation and test set as in Table 1. The entity pair model predicts random relations as it is unable to make predictions on unseen entity pairs. The max pool and mean pool each suffer approximately 30% relative decrease in MRR and 20% decrease in Hits@10.

Both the max relation and attention models perform nearly as well whether the entity pairs were observed during training or not. The attention model performs slightly better than the max relation model in this scenario.

Model	MRR	Hits@10
Entity-pair Embeddings	31.85	51.72
Mean Pool	25.89	45.94
Max Pool	29.61	49.93
Max Relation	31.71	**51.94**
Attention	**31.92**	51.67

Table 1: The percentage of positive triples ranked in the top 10 amongst their negatives as well as the mean reciprocal rank (MRR) scaled by 100 on a subset of the FB15K-237 dataset. Negative examples were restricted to entity pairs that occurred in the KB or text portion of the training set.

Model	MRR	%dec	Hits@10	%dec
Entity-pair Embeddings	5.23	83.6	11.94	76.9
Mean Pool	18.10	30.1	35.76	22.2
Max Pool	20.80	29.8	40.25	19.4
Max Relation	28.46	10.3	48.15	7.3
Attention	**29.75**	**6.8**	**49.69**	**3.8**

Table 2: Predicting entity pairs that were not seen at train time. The percentage of positive triples ranked in the top 10 amongst their negatives as well as the mean reciprocal rank (MRR) scaled by 100 on a subset of the FB15K-237 dataset. Also shown is the percent relative decrease in MRR and Hits@10 between Table 1 (entity pairs seen during training) and this table (entity pairs unseen during training).

5 Conclusion

In this paper we explore a row-less extension of Universal Schema that forgoes explicit entity pair representations for an aggregation function over relation types. This extension allows prediction between all entity pairs in new textual mentions – whether seen at train time or not – and also provides a natural connection to the provenance supporting the prediction.

In this work we show that an aggregation function based on query-specific attention over relation types outperforms query independent aggregations. We show that aggregation models are able to predict on par with entity pair models for seen entity pairs and, in the case of attention, suffer very little loss for unseen entity pairs.

We also limited our pattern encoders to lookup-tables. In future work we will combine the column-less and row-less approach to make a fully compositional Universal Schema model. This will allow Universal Schema to generalize to all new textual patterns and entity pairs.

Acknowledgments

We thank Emma Strubell, David Belanger, Luke Vilnis, and Arvind Neelakantan for helpful discussions and edits. This work was supported in part by the Center for Intelligent Information Retrieval, in part by Defense Advanced Research Projects Agency (DARPA) under agreement #FA8750-13-2-0020 and contract #HR0011-15-2-0036, and in part by the National Science Foundation (NSF) grant numbers DMR-1534431, IIS-1514053 and CNS-0958392. The U.S. Government is authorized to reproduce and distribute reprints for Governmental purposes notwithstanding any copyright notation thereon, in part by DARPA via agreement #DFA8750-13-2-0020 and NSF grant #CNS-0958392. Any opinions, findings and conclusions or recommendations expressed in this material are those of the authors and do not necessarily reflect those of the sponsor.

References

[Bollacker et al.2008] Kurt Bollacker, Colin Evans, Praveen Paritosh, Tim Sturge, and Jamie Taylor. 2008. Freebase: a collaboratively created graph database for structuring human knowledge. In *Proceedings of the ACM SIGMOD International Conference on Management of Data.*

[Bordes et al.2013] Antoine Bordes, Nicolas Usunier, Alberto García-Durán, Jason Weston, and Oksana Yakhnenko. 2013. Translating embeddings for modeling multi-relational data. In *Advances in Neural Information Processing Systems.*

[Carlson et al.2010] Andrew Carlson, Justin Betteridge, Bryan Kisiel, Burr Settles, Estevam R. Hruschka, and A. 2010. Toward an architecture for never-ending language learning. In *In AAAI.*

[Gabrilovich et al.2013] Evgeniy Gabrilovich, Michael Ringgaard, and Amarnag Subramanya. 2013. Facc1: Freebase annotation of clueweb corpora, version 1 (release date 2013-06-26, format version 1, correction level 0). *Note: http://lemurproject. org/clueweb09/FACC1/Cited by*, 5.

[García-Durán et al.2015] Alberto García-Durán, Antoine Bordes, Nicolas Usunier, and Yves Grandvalet. 2015. Combining two and three-way embeddings models for link prediction in knowledge bases. *CoRR*, abs/1506.00999.

[Gardner et al.2014] Matt Gardner, Partha Talukdar, Jayant Krishnamurthy, and Tom Mitchell. 2014. Incorporating vector space similarity in random walk inference over knowledge bases. In *Empirical Methods in Natural Language Processing.*

[Kingma and Ba2015] Diederik Kingma and Jimmy Ba. 2015. Adam: A method for stochastic optimization. In *3rd International Conference for Learning Representations (ICLR).*

[Lin et al.2015] Yankai Lin, Zhiyuan Liu, Maosong Sun, Yang Liu, and Xuan Zhu. 2015. Learning entity and relation embeddings for knowledge graph completion. In *Proceedings of AAAI.*

[Neelakantan et al.2015] Arvind Neelakantan, Benjamin Roth, and Andrew McCallum. 2015. Compositional vector space models for knowledge base completion. *Proceedings of the 53rd Annual Meeting of the Association for Computational Linguistics.*

[Nickel et al.2011] Maximilian Nickel, Volker Tresp, and Hans-Peter Kriegel. 2011. A three-way model for collective learning on multi-relational data. In *International Conference on Machine Learning.*

[Nickel et al.2015] Maximilian Nickel, Kevin Murphy, Volker Tresp, and Evgeniy Gabrilovich. 2015. A review of relational machine learning for knowledge graphs: From multi-relational link prediction to automated knowledge graph construction. *arXiv preprint arXiv:1503.00759.*

[Rendle et al.2009] Steffen Rendle, Christoph Freudenthaler, Zeno Gantner, and Lars Schmidt-Thieme. 2009. Bpr: Bayesian personalized ranking from implicit feedback. In *Proceedings of the Twenty-Fifth Conference on Uncertainty in Artificial Intelligence*, pages 452–461. AUAI Press.

[Riedel et al.2013] Sebastian Riedel, Limin Yao, Andrew McCallum, and Benjamin M. Marlin. 2013. Relation extraction with matrix factorization and universal schemas. In *HLT-NAACL.*

[Rocktaschel et al.2015] Tim Rocktaschel, Sameer Singh, and Sebastian Riedel. 2015. Injecting logical background knowledge into embeddings for relation extraction. In *Annual Conference of the North American Chapter of the Association for Computational Linguistics (NAACL)*.

[Socher et al.2013] Richard Socher, Danqi Chen, Christopher D Manning, and Andrew Ng. 2013. Reasoning with neural tensor networks for knowledge base completion. In *Advances in Neural Information Processing Systems*.

[Suchanek et al.2007] Fabian M. Suchanek, Gjergji Kasneci, and Gerhard Weikum. 2007. Yago: A core of semantic knowledge. In *Proceedings of the 16th International Conference on World Wide Web*.

[Sukhbaatar et al.2015] Sainbayar Sukhbaatar, Jason Weston, Rob Fergus, et al. 2015. End-to-end memory networks. In *Advances in Neural Information Processing Systems*, pages 2431–2439.

[Toutanova et al.2015] Kristina Toutanova, Danqi Chen, Patrick Pantel, Hoifung Poon, Pallavi Choudhury, and Michael Gamon. 2015. Representing text for joint embedding of text and knowledge bases. In *Empirical Methods in Natural Language Processing (EMNLP)*.

[Verga et al.2016] Patrick Verga, David Belanger, Emma Strubell, Benjamin Roth, and Andrew McCallum. 2016. Multilingual relation extraction using compositional universal schema. *Annual Conference of the North American Chapter of the Association for Computational Linguistics (NAACL)*.

[Wang et al.2014] Zhen Wang, Jianwen Zhang, Jianlin Feng, and Zheng Chen. 2014. Knowledge graph embedding by translating on hyperplanes. In *Proceedings of the Twenty-Eighth AAAI Conference on Artificial Intelligence*, pages 1112–1119. Citeseer.

[Yang et al.2015] Bishan Yang, Wen-tau Yih, Xiaodong He, Jianfeng Gao, and Li Deng. 2015. Embedding entities and relations for learning and inference in knowledge bases. *International Conference on Learning Representations 2014*.

[Yao et al.2013] Limin Yao, Sebastian Riedel, and Andrew McCallum. 2013. Universal schema for entity type prediction. In *Proceedings of the 2013 workshop on Automated knowledge base construction*, pages 79–84. ACM.

An Attentive Neural Architecture for Fine-grained Entity Type Classification

Sonse Shimaoka[†*]   **Pontus Stenetorp**[‡]   **Kentaro Inui**[†]   **Sebastian Riedel**[‡]
{simaokasonse,inui}@ecei.tohoku.ac.jp
{p.stenetorp,s.riedel}@cs.ucl.ac.uk
[†]Graduate School of Information Sciences, Tohoku University
[‡]Department of Computer Science, University College London

Abstract

In this work we propose a novel attention-based neural network model for the task of fine-grained entity type classification that unlike previously proposed models recursively composes representations of entity mention contexts. Our model achieves state-of-the-art performance with 74.94% loose micro F1-score on the well-established FIGER dataset, a relative improvement of 2.59% . We also investigate the behavior of the attention mechanism of our model and observe that it can learn contextual linguistic expressions that indicate the fine-grained category memberships of an entity.

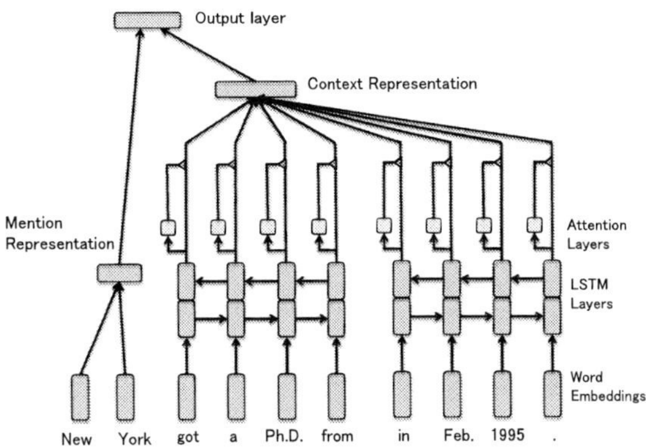

Figure 1: An illustration of our proposed model predicting fine-grained semantic types for the mention "New York" in the sentence "She got a Ph.D from New York in Feb. 1995.".

1 Introduction

Entity type classification is the task of assigning semantic types to mentions of entities in sentences. Identifying the types of entities is useful for various natural language processing tasks, such as relation extraction (Ling and Weld, 2012), question answering (Lee et al., 2006), and knowledge base population (Carlson et al., 2010). Unfortunately, most entity type classification systems use a relatively small number of types (e.g. `person`, `organization`, `location`, `time`, and `miscellaneous` (Grishman and Sundheim, 1996)) which may be too coarse-grained for some NLP applications (Sekine, 2008). To address this shortcoming, a series of recent work has investigated entity type classification with a large set of fine-grained types (Lee et al.,

2006; Ling and Weld, 2012; Yosef et al., 2012; Yogatama et al., 2015; Del Corro et al., 2015).

Existing fine-grained entity type classification systems have used approaches ranging from sparse binary features to dense vector representations of entities to model the entity mention and its context. However, no previously proposed system has attempted to learn to recursively compose representations of entity context. For example, one can see that a phrase "got a Ph.D. from" is indicative of the next words being an educational institution, something which would be helpful for fine-grained entity type classification.

In this work our main contributions are two-fold:

1. A first model for fine-grained entity type classification that learns to recursively compose representations for the context of each mention and attains state-of-the-art performance on a

---

[*]This work was conducted during a research visit to University College London.

69

Proceedings of AKBC 2016, pages 69–74,
San Diego, California, June 12-17, 2016. ©2016 Association for Computational Linguistics

well-established dataset.

2. The observation that by incorporating an attention mechanism into our model, we not only achieve better performance, but also are able to observe that the model learns contextual linguistic expressions that indicate fine-grained category memberships of an entity.

2 Related Work

To the best of our knowledge, Lee et al. (2006) were the first to address the task of fine-grained entity type classification. They defined 147 fine-grained entity types and evaluated a conditional random fields-based model on a manually annotated Korean dataset. Sekine (2008) advocated the necessity of a large set of types for entity type classification and defined 200 types which served as a basis for future work on fine-grained entity type classification.

Ling and Weld (2012) defined a set of 112 types based on Freebase and created a training dataset from Wikipedia using a distant supervision method inspired by Mintz et al. (2009). For evaluation, they created a small manually annotated dataset of newspaper articles and also demonstrated that their system, FIGER, could improve the performance of a relation extraction system by providing fine-grained entity type predictions as features. Yosef et al. (2012) organised 505 types in a hierarchical taxonomy, with several hundreds of types at different levels. Based on this taxonomy they developed a multi-label hierarchical classification system. In Yogatama et al. (2015) the authors proposed to use label embeddings to allow information sharing between related labels. This approach lead to improvements on the FIGER dataset, and they also demonstrated that fine-grained labels can be used as features to improve coarse-grained entity type classification performance. Del Corro et al. (2015) introduced the most fine-grained entity type classification system to-date, it operates on the the entire WordNet hierarchy with more than $16,000$ types.

While all previous models relied on hand-crafted features, Dong et al. (2015) defined 22 types and created a two-part neural classifier. They used a recurrent neural networks to recursively obtain a vector representation of each entity mention and used

a fixed-size window to capture the context of each mention. The key difference between our work and theirs lies in that we use recursive neural networks to compose context representations and that we employ an attention mechanism to allow our model to focus on relevant expressions.

3 Models

3.1 Task Formulation

We formulate the entity type classification problem as follows. Given an entity mention and its left and right context, our task is to predict its types. Formally, the input is $l_1, ..., l_C, m_1, ..., m_M, r_1, ..., r_C$, where C is the window size of the left and right context, l_i and r_i represents a word in those contexts, M is the window size of the mention, and m_i is a mention word. If a context or a mention extends beyond the sentence length, a padding symbol is used in-place of a word. Given this input we compute a probability $y_k \in \mathbb{R}$ for each of the K types.

At inference, the type k is predicted if y_k is greater than 0.5 or y_k is the maximum value $\forall k \in K$. The motivation of the former is that it acts as a cut-off, while the latter enforces the constraint that each mention is assigned at least one type.

3.2 General Model

While both mentions and contexts play important roles in determining the types, the complexity of learning to represent them are different. During initial experiments, we observed that our model could learn from mentions significantly easier than from the context, leading to poor model generalization. This motivated us to use different models for modeling mentions and contexts. Specifically, all of our models described below firstly compute a mention representation $v_m \in \mathbb{R}^{D_m \times 1}$ and context representation $v_c \in \mathbb{R}^{D_c \times 1}$ separately, and then concatenate them to be passed to the final logistic regression layer with weight matrix $W_y \in \mathbb{R}^{K \times (D_m + D_c)}$:

$$y = \frac{1}{1 + \exp\left(-W_y \begin{bmatrix} v_m \\ v_c \end{bmatrix}\right)} \tag{1}$$

Note that we did not include a bias term in the above formulation since the type distribution in the training and test corpus could potentially be significantly different due to domain differences. That is, in logistic regression, a bias fits to the empirical distribution of types in the training set, which would lead to bad performance on a test set that has a different type distribution.

The loss L for a prediction y when the true labels are encoded in a binary vector $t \in \{0,1\}^{K \times 1}$ is the following cross entropy loss function:

$$L(y,t) = \sum_{k=1}^{K} -t_k \log(y_k) - (1 - t_k) \log(1 - y_k) \tag{2}$$

3.3 Mention Representation

Mention representations are computed by averaging all the embeddings of the words in the mention. Let the vocabulary be V and the function $u : V \mapsto \mathbb{R}^{D_m \times 1}$ be a mapping from a word to its embedding. Formally, the mention representation v_m is obtained as follows.

$$v_m = \frac{1}{M} \sum_{i=1}^{M} u(m_i) \tag{3}$$

During our experiments we were surprised by the fact that unlike the observations made by Dong et al. (2015), complex neural models did not work well for learning mention representations compared to the simpler model described above. One possible explanation for this would be labeling discrepancies between the training and test set. For example, the label time is assigned to days of the week (e.g. "Friday", "Monday", and "Sunday") in the test set, but not in the training set, whereas explicit dates (e.g. "Feb. 24" and "June 4th") are assigned the time label in both the training and test set. This may be harmful for complex models due to their tendency to overfit on the training data.

3.4 Context Representation

We compare three methods for computing context representations.

3.4.1 Averaging Encoder

Applying the same averaging approach as for the mention representation for both the left and right context. Thus, the concatenation of those two vectors becomes the representation of the context:

$$v_c = \frac{1}{C} \sum_{i=1}^{C} \begin{bmatrix} u(l_i) \\ u(r_i) \end{bmatrix} \tag{4}$$

3.4.2 LSTM Encoder

The left and right context are encoded recursively using an LSTM cell (Hochreiter and Schmidhuber, 1997). Given an input embedding $u_i \in \mathbb{R}^{D_m \times 1}$, the previous output $h_{i-1} \in \mathbb{R}^{D_h \times 1}$, and the previous cell state $s_{i-1} \in \mathbb{R}^{D_h \times 1}$, the high-level formulation of the recursive computation by an LSTM cell is as follows:

$$h_i, s_i = lstm(u_i, h_{i-1}, s_{i-1}) \tag{5}$$

For the left context, the model reads sequences $l_1, ..., l_C$ from left to right to produce the outputs $\overrightarrow{h_1^l}, ..., \overrightarrow{h_C^l}$. For the right context, the model reads sequences $r_C, ..., r_1$ from right to left to produce the outputs $\overleftarrow{h_1^r}, ..., \overleftarrow{h_C^r}$. Then the representation v_c is obtained by concatenating $\overrightarrow{h_C^l}$ and $\overleftarrow{h_1^r}$:

$$v_c = \begin{bmatrix} \overrightarrow{h_C^l} \\ \overleftarrow{h_1^r} \end{bmatrix} \tag{6}$$

A more detailed formulation of the LSTM used in this work can be found in Sak et al. (2014).

3.4.3 Attentive Encoder

While an LSTM can encode sequential data, it still finds it difficult to learn long-term dependencies. Inspired by recent work using attention mechanisms for natural language processing (Hermann et al., 2015; Rocktäschel et al., 2015), we circumvent this problem by introducing a novel attention mechanism. We also hypothesize that by incorporating an attention mechanism the model can recognize informative expressions for the classification and make the model behavior more interpretable.

The computation of the attention mechanism is as follows. Firstly, for both the right and left context, we encode the sequences using bi-directional LSTMs (Graves, 2012). We denote the outputs as $\overrightarrow{h_1^l}, \overleftarrow{h_1^l}, ..., \overrightarrow{h_C^l}, \overleftarrow{h_C^l}$ and $\overrightarrow{h_1^r}, \overleftarrow{h_1^r}, ..., \overrightarrow{h_C^r}, \overleftarrow{h_C^r}$.

For each output layer of the bi-directional LSTMs, we compute a scalar value $\tilde{a}_i \in \mathbb{R}$ using a two-layer feed forward neural network $e_i \in \mathbb{R}^{D_a \times 1}$ and weight matrices $W_e \in \mathbb{R}^{D_a \times 2D_h}$ and $W_a \in \mathbb{R}^{1 \times D_a}$. We then normalize these scalar values such that they sum to 1. We refer to these normalized scalar values $a_i \in \mathbb{R}$ as attentions. Lastly, we take a weighted sum of the output layers of the bidirectional LSTMs as the representation of the context weighted by the attentions a_i:

$$e_i^l = \tanh\left(W_e \begin{bmatrix} \overrightarrow{h_i^l} \\ \overleftarrow{h_i^l} \end{bmatrix}\right) \tag{7}$$

$$\tilde{a}_i^l = \exp(W_a e_i^l) \tag{8}$$

$$a_i^l = \frac{\tilde{a}_i^l}{\sum_{i=1}^C \tilde{a}_i^l + \tilde{a}_i^r} \tag{9}$$

$$v_c = \sum_{i=1}^C a_i^l \begin{bmatrix} \overrightarrow{h_i^l} \\ \overleftarrow{h_i^l} \end{bmatrix} + a_i^r \begin{bmatrix} \overrightarrow{h_i^r} \\ \overleftarrow{h_i^r} \end{bmatrix} \tag{10}$$

The equations for computing e_i^r, $\tilde{a}_i^r$, and a_i^r were omitted for brevity and the overall picture of our proposed model is illustrated in Figure 1.

4   Experiment

4.1   Dataset

To train and evaluate our model we use the publicly available FIGER dataset with 112 fine-grained types from Ling and Weld (2012). The sizes of our datasets are $2,600,000$ for training, $90,000$ for development, and 563 for testing. Note that the train and development sets were created from Wikipedia, whereas the test set is a manually annotated dataset of newspaper articles.

4.2   Pre-trained Word Embeddings

The only features used by our model are pre-trained word embeddings that were not updated during training to help the model generalize for words not appearing in the training set. Specifically, we used the freely available 300 dimensional cased word embeddings trained on 840 billion tokens from the Common Crawl supplied by Pennington et al. (2014). As embeddings for out-of-vocabulary words, we used the embedding of the "unk" token from the pre-trained embeddings.

4.3   Evaluation Criteria

Following Ling and Weld (2012), we evaluate the model performances by strict, loose macro, and loose micro measures. For the i-th instance, let the set of the predicted types be $\hat{T}_i$, and the set of the true types be T_i. Then the precisions and recall for each measure are computed as follows.

- strict

$$Precision = Recall = \frac{1}{N} \sum_{i=1}^N \delta(\hat{T}_i = T_i) \tag{11}$$

- loose macro

$$Precision = \frac{1}{N} \sum_{i=1}^N \frac{|\hat{T}_i \cap T_i|}{|\hat{T}_i|} \tag{12}$$

$$Recall = \frac{1}{N} \sum_{i=1}^N \frac{|\hat{T}_i \cap T_i|}{|T_i|} \tag{13}$$

- loose micro

$$Precision = \frac{\sum_{i=1}^N |\hat{T}_i \cap T_i|}{\sum_{i=1}^N |\hat{T}_i|} \tag{14}$$

$$Recall = \frac{\sum_{i=1}^N |\hat{T}_i \cap T_i|}{\sum_{i=1}^N |T_i|} \tag{15}$$

Where N is the total number of instances.

4.4   Hyperparameter Settings

As hyperparameters, all three models used the same $D_m = 300$ dimensional word embeddings, the hidden-size of the LSTM was set to $D_h = 100$, and the hidden-layer size of the attention module was set to $D_a = 50$. We used Adam (Kingma and Ba, 2014) as our optimization method with a learning rate of 0.005 with a mini-batch size of $1,000$. As a regularizer we used dropout with probability 0.5 applied to the mention representation.

The context window size was set to $C = 15$ and mention window size was set to $M = 5$. It should be noted that our approach is not restricted to using fixed window sizes, rather this is an implementation detail arising from current limitations of the machine learning library used when handling dynamic-width recurrent neural networks. For each epoch we iterated over the training data set ten times and then evaluated the model performance on the development set. After training we picked up the best model

Sentence	Prediction
... ... The film is a remake of [Secrets (1924)] , a silent film starring Norma Talmadge	/film 0.986 /art 0.982
The film is a remake of Secrets (1924) , a silent film starring [Norma Talmadge]	/person 0.999 /actor 0.987
... ... The festival brought together the foremost filmmakers , including Francois Truffaut , [Roman Polanski] , Robert Enrico , and others	/person 1.00 /director 0.963 /author 0.958 /artist 0.950 /actor 0.871
... ... Jim Hodges , the Democratic nominee , handily defeated Republican Governor [David Beasley] to become the 114th governor of South Carolina	/person 1.00 /politician 0.983
She is best known for roles in various TV Dramas and tokusatsu shows such as [Ultraseven X] and Kamen Rider Kiva	/broadcats_program 0.892

Figure 2: Examples of our model attending over contexts for a given mention.

Models	P	R	F1
Ling and Weld (2012)	-	-	69.30
Yogatama et al. (2015)	**82.23**	64.55	72.35
Averaging Encoder	68.63	69.07	68.65
LSTM Encoder	72.32	70.36	71.34
Attentive Encoder	73.63	**76.29**	**74.94**

Table 1: Loose Micro Precision (P), Recall (R), and F1-score on the test set

Models	Strict	Loose Macro	Loose Micro
Ling and Weld (2012)	52.30	69.90	69.30
Yogatama et al. (2015)	-	-	72.25
Averaging Encoder	51.89	72.24	68.65
LSTM Encoder	55.60	73.95	71.34
Attentive Encoder	**58.97**	**77.96**	**74.94**

Table 2: Strict, Loose Macro and Loose Micro F1-scores

on the development set as our final model and report the performance on the test set. Our model implementation was done in Python using the TensorFlow (Abadi et al., 2015) machine learning library.

4.5 Results

The performance of the various models are summarized Tables 1 and 2. We see that the Averaging base line performs well in spite of its relative simplicity, the LSTM model shows some improvements, and the attention model performs better than any previously proposed method. In Figure 2, we visualize the attentions for several instances that were manually selected from the development set. It is clear that our proposed model is attending over expressions relevant for the entity types such as immediately adjacent to the mention such as "starring" and "Republican Governor", as well as more distant expressions such as "filmmakers".

5 Conclusion

In this paper, we proposed a novel state-of-the-art neural network architecture with an attention mechanism for the task of fine-grained entity type classification. We also demonstrated that the model can successfully learn to attend over expressions that are important for the classification of fine-grained types.

Acknowledgments

This work was supported by CREST-JST, JSPS KAKENHI Grant Number 15H01702, a Marie Curie Career Integration Award, and an Allen Distinguished Investigator Award. We would like to thank the anonymous reviewers and Koji Matsuda for their helpful comments and feedback.

References

Martín Abadi, Ashish Agarwal, Paul Barham, Eugene Brevdo, Zhifeng Chen, Craig Citro, Greg S. Corrado, Andy Davis, Jeffrey Dean, Matthieu Devin, Sanjay Ghemawat, Ian Goodfellow, Andrew Harp, Geoffrey Irving, Michael Isard, Yangqing Jia, Rafal Jozefowicz, Lukasz Kaiser, Manjunath Kudlur, Josh Levenberg, Dan Mané, Rajat Monga, Sherry Moore, Derek Murray, Chris Olah, Mike Schuster, Jonathon Shlens, Benoit Steiner, Ilya Sutskever, Kunal Talwar, Paul Tucker, Vincent Vanhoucke, Vijay Vasudevan, Fernanda Viégas, Oriol Vinyals, Pete Warden, Martin Wattenberg, Martin Wicke, Yuan Yu, and Xiaoqiang Zheng. 2015. TensorFlow: Large-scale machine learning on heterogeneous systems.

Andrew Carlson, Justin Betteridge, Richard C Wang, Estevam R Hruschka Jr, and Tom M Mitchell. 2010. Coupled semi-supervised learning for information extraction. In *Proceedings of the third ACM international conference on Web search and data mining*, pages 101–110. ACM.

Luciano Del Corro, Abdalghani Abujabal, Rainer Gemulla, and Gerhard Weikum. 2015. Finet: Context-aware fine-grained named entity typing. In *Conference on Empirical Methods in Natural Language Processing*, pages 868–878. ACL.

Li Dong, Furu Wei, Hong Sun, Ming Zhou, and Ke Xu. 2015. A hybrid neural model for type classification of entity mentions. In *Proceedings of the 24th International Conference on Artificial Intelligence*, pages 1243–1249. AAAI Press.

Alex Graves. 2012. *Supervised sequence labelling.* Springer.

Ralph Grishman and Beth Sundheim. 1996. Message understanding conference-6: A brief history. In *COLING*, volume 96, pages 466–471.

Karl Moritz Hermann, Tomas Kocisky, Edward Grefenstette, Lasse Espeholt, Will Kay, Mustafa Suleyman, and Phil Blunsom. 2015. Teaching machines to read and comprehend. In *Advances in Neural Information Processing Systems*, pages 1684–1692.

Sepp Hochreiter and Jürgen Schmidhuber. 1997. Long short-term memory. *Neural computation*, 9(8):1735–1780.

Diederik Kingma and Jimmy Ba. 2014. Adam: A method for stochastic optimization. *arXiv preprint arXiv:1412.6980*.

Changki Lee, Yi-Gyu Hwang, Hyo-Jung Oh, Soojong Lim, Jeong Heo, Chung-Hee Lee, Hyeon-Jin Kim, Ji-Hyun Wang, and Myung-Gil Jang. 2006. Fine-grained named entity recognition using conditional random fields for question answering. In *Information Retrieval Technology*, pages 581–587. Springer.

Xiao Ling and Daniel S Weld. 2012. Fine-grained entity recognition. In *In Proc. of the 26th AAAI Conference on Artificial Intelligence*. Citeseer.

Mike Mintz, Steven Bills, Rion Snow, and Dan Jurafsky. 2009. Distant supervision for relation extraction without labeled data. In *Proceedings of the Joint Conference of the 47th Annual Meeting of the ACL and the 4th International Joint Conference on Natural Language Processing of the AFNLP: Volume 2-Volume 2*, pages 1003–1011. Association for Computational Linguistics.

Jeffrey Pennington, Richard Socher, and Christopher D Manning. 2014. Glove: Global vectors for word representation. In *EMNLP*, volume 14, pages 1532–1543.

Tim Rocktäschel, Edward Grefenstette, Karl Moritz Hermann, Tomáš Kočiskỳ, and Phil Blunsom. 2015. Reasoning about entailment with neural attention. *arXiv preprint arXiv:1509.06664*.

Hasim Sak, Andrew W Senior, and Françoise Beaufays. 2014. Long short-term memory recurrent neural network architectures for large scale acoustic modeling. In *INTERSPEECH*, pages 338–342.

Satoshi Sekine. 2008. Extended named entity ontology with attribute information. In *LREC*, pages 52–57.

Dani Yogatama, Dan Gillick, and Nevena Lazic. 2015. Embedding methods for fine grained entity type classification. In *Proceedings of the 53rd Annual Meeting of the Association for Computational Linguistics and the 7th International Joint Conference on Natural Language Processing of the Asian Federation of Natural Language Processing, ACL*, pages 26–31.

Mohamed Amir Yosef, Sandro Bauer, Johannes Hoffart, Marc Spaniol, and Gerhard Weikum. 2012. Hyena: Hierarchical type classification for entity names. In *24th International Conference on Computational Linguistics*, pages 1361–1370. ACL.

Regularizing Relation Representations by First-order Implications

Thomas Demeester
Ghent University - iMinds
Ghent, Belgium
`tdmeeste@intec.ugent.be`

Tim Rocktäschel and **Sebastian Riedel**
University College London
London, UK
`{t.rocktaschel,s.riedel}@cs.ucl.ac.uk`

Abstract

Methods for automated knowledge base construction often rely on trained fixed-length vector representations of relations and entities to predict facts. Recent work showed that such representations can be regularized to inject first-order logic formulae. This enables to incorporate domain-knowledge for improved prediction of facts, especially for uncommon relations. However, current approaches rely on propositionalization of formulae and thus do not scale to large sets of formulae or knowledge bases with many facts. Here we propose a method that imposes first-order constraints directly on relation representations, avoiding costly grounding of formulae. We show that our approach works well for implications between pairs of relations on artificial datasets.

1 Introduction

Many methods for automated knowledge base (KB) construction rely on learned relation and entity vector representations (Nickel et al., 2015). Such representations are hard to learn for relations with only few supporting facts in KBs. Moreover, inference on KBs such as Freebase (Bollacker et al., 2008) could still benefit from common-sense knowledge contained in ontologies like WordNet (Miller, 1995) or PPDB (Ganitkevitch et al., 2013). It is thus desirable to be able to use various kinds of domain or ontological knowledge, for instance in the form of first-order logic formulae, to help knowledge base inference. Furthermore, such formulae make use of learned representations as well as help to learn better representations.

One way to incorporate logical formulae is to regularize relation and entity-pair representations (Rocktäschel et al., 2015). However, in their method first-order formulae need to be grounded for all entity pairs in the KB. As a result of this propositionalization, the method does not scale to large KBs or many formulae. Another recent method is based on imposing rules as constraints in an integer linear program (Wang et al., 2015). This approach suffers from a similar scalability problem, since every rule is imposed for all occurrences of facts in the training data.

To alleviate this computational bottleneck, we propose a method to incorporate first-order implications directly (and only) into relation representations. The idea is to map relation and entity-pair representations into a well-chosen subspace in which formulae can be expressed as direct regularizers of relation representations without imposing them on entity representations too. As such, the proposed method is suited for problems with large numbers of rules and facts.

Our approach is based on the concept of order-embeddings, introduced by Vendrov et al. (2016). Order-embeddings capture partial orderings, such as textual entailment, directly in vector representations. This idea can be extended towards relation representations in KBs. In particular, we show how to construct order-embeddings for capturing implications between relations, such that these implications hold for any possible entity-pair.

The model presented here is also related to Kruszewski et al. (2015). They demonstrate that textual entailment can be captured by mapping real-

Proceedings of AKBC 2016, pages 75–80,
San Diego, California, June 12-17, 2016. ©2016 Association for Computational Linguistics

valued vectors into (approximate) Boolean valued vectors. This is achieved by requiring that Boolean vector representations of more specific words or sentences are included in the representation of more general ones. Furthermore, these representations may be useful for modeling other types of logical relationships, such as negation or conjunction. It is our goal to extend the approach towards arbitrary first-order formulae between relations. Therefore, as a first step we investigate whether restricting the relation embedding space to approximate Boolean vectors still allows us to reconstruct training facts and imposed implications.

The rest of the paper is organized as follows. We first revisit matrix factorization for KB construction (§2), before introducing a factorization model that regularizes approximately Boolean relation representations to incorporate first-order implications (§3). Finally, we show empirical results on synthetic knowledge bases. We explore how enforcing restrictions on representations influences the ability to model the observed data, analyze the learned relation representations qualitatively, and investigate the impact of injecting implications (§4).

2 Model

Before introducing first-order regularization of relation representations, we revisit one possible model that uses relation (and entity-pair) representations to estimate the probability of a fact: the universal schema matrix factorization proposed by Riedel et al. (2013). Let $\mathcal{R}$ be a set of relations r and $\mathcal{P}$ a set of entity pairs (e_i, e_j) (which we will shortly write as e from now on). We can represent facts, $i.e.$, possible combinations of entity pairs and relations, as a binary matrix of size $|\mathcal{P}| \times |\mathcal{R}|$. The probability that a particular relation and entity pair combination is a valid fact can be modeled by the sigmoid of the dot product of the relation's vector representation $v(r)$ and the entity-pair's vector representation $v(e)$:

$$p\big(z = 1 | v(r), v(e)\big) = \sigma\big(v(r)^T v(e)\big), \quad (1)$$

with the binary target variable z indicating validity of the considered fact and $v(r), v(e) \in \mathbb{R}^k$. The representations $v(r)$ and $v(e)$ can be found by minimizing the negative log-likelihood of true given training facts (together with a set of negative facts) using stochastic gradient descent. The contribution to this loss from relation r and entity pair e takes the following form

$$\mathcal{L}_F(r, e) = -z \log(p) - (1 - z) \log(1 - p) \quad (2)$$

with p short-hand for the probability in eq. (1).

In this paper we propose various forms of $v(r)$ and $v(e)$. However, when the representations are chosen to be unrestricted real-valued vectors, i.e., $v(r) = \rho \in \mathbb{R}^k$ and $v(e) = e \in \mathbb{R}^k$ for some fixed embedding length k, we get the latent feature **Model F** by Riedel et al. (2013).

Note that often no explicit negative instances are available for training, in which case unobserved facts can be randomly sampled and assumed to be negative.

2.1 Non-Negative Embedding Space

With the model described above we do not have any control over the learned representations. However, the embeddings can gain useful properties once we restrict them in an appropriate way. We propose the following restrictions, motivated below: we require all components of $v(e)$ to be non-negative, and we confine relation representations $v(r)$ to lie within the unit hypercube $(0, 1)^k$.

We want to be able to model implications between relations by defining an order relation on their vector representations. An in-depth description of order-embeddings is given in Vendrov et al. (2016), but the main idea applied to relation representations is as follows. Consider a pair of relations r_p and r_q such that r_p implies r_q for any entity pair for which r_p holds (which we shortly write as '$r_p \Rightarrow r_q$'). For their vector representations we require that the component-wise inequality $v_i(r_p) \leq v_i(r_q)$ holds ($i = 1, \ldots, k$). Note that enforcing this locally for every relation pair will also lead to globally consistent relation representations (e.g. imposing $r_s \Rightarrow r_t$ and $r_t \Rightarrow r_u$ will satisfy $r_s \Rightarrow r_u$ by construction). Relations that hold true more often will have larger entries, whereas relation vectors with the overall lowest values will represent the most specific relations (such as leaf nodes in an ontology).

If $r_p \Rightarrow r_q$ holds, it needs to hold for any entity pair e. Thus, we require that $\forall e \in \mathcal{P}$:

$$p\big(z = 1 | v(r_p), v(e)\big) \leq p\big(z = 1 | v(r_q), v(e)\big).$$

If $v_i(r_p) \le v_i(r_q)$ $(i = 1, \ldots, k)$, and we restrict all components of $\boldsymbol{v}(e)$ to be non-negative, then by construction $\boldsymbol{v}(r_p)^T \boldsymbol{v}(e) \le \boldsymbol{v}(r_q)^T \boldsymbol{v}(e)$, and with eq. (1), the above requirement is satisfied.

Besides the ability to capture pairwise implications, we also want to incorporate more complex first-order formulae and need to be able to express these as a function of the relation and entity-pair representations. Approximate Boolean vectors discussed in Kruszewski et al. (2015) provide an attractive direction, but studying how they can be adapted to suit the relation extraction use case is out of scope of the current work. To pave the way for future work on incorporating arbitrary first-order constraints, we will however investigate whether constraining relation representations to the unit hypercube $\boldsymbol{v}(r) \in (0, 1)^k$ still allows us to reliably encode observed facts and impose implications.

2.2 Training Restricted Representations

There are different ways to impose the discussed restrictions on vector representations. In this work, we choose $\boldsymbol{v}(r) = \sigma(\boldsymbol{\rho})$, and $\boldsymbol{v}(e) = \text{ReLU}(e)$ or $\exp(e)$, where $\text{ReLU}(e) = \log(1 + \exp e)$ is the component-wise smooth approximation of the rectified linear unit, and with again $\boldsymbol{\rho} \in \mathbb{R}^k$ and $e \in \mathbb{R}^k$. The imposed restrictions constrain the set of usable loss functions for training. Indeed, the lowest value of $\sigma\big(\boldsymbol{v}(r)^T \boldsymbol{v}(e)\big)$ is 0.5, which makes training with the loss function in eq. (2) no longer practical. The problem can be avoided if the dot product $\boldsymbol{v}(r)^T \boldsymbol{v}(e)$ is first mapped from the positive real axis to entire $\mathbb{R}$. Among various options, we choose the logarithm because

$$\sigma\left(\log \big(\boldsymbol{v}(r)^T \boldsymbol{v}(e) \big) \right) = \frac{\boldsymbol{v}(r)^T \boldsymbol{v}(e)}{1 + \boldsymbol{v}(r)^T \boldsymbol{v}(e)}, \quad (3)$$

such that the loss from eq. (2) simplifies to

$$\begin{aligned}
\mathcal{L}_F(r, e) = &- z \log \big(\boldsymbol{v}(r)^T \boldsymbol{v}(e) \big) \\
&+ \log \big(1 + \boldsymbol{v}(r)^T \boldsymbol{v}(e) \big). \quad (4)
\end{aligned}$$

The expression on the right-hand side of eq. (3) represents an alternative form of the probability in eq. (1) for training and predicting the validity of facts using non-negative embeddings. Note that since log and exp are inverse functions, choosing $\boldsymbol{v}(e) = \exp(e)$ leads to values of $\log\big(\boldsymbol{v}(r)^T \boldsymbol{v}(e)\big)$ with the same order of magnitude as e, unlike the

choice $\boldsymbol{v}(e) = \text{ReLU}(e)$. This may be the reason why the former seems to work better in practice (see § 3). Yet another option would be to construct an approximate Boolean factorization for both, entity pairs and relations, whereby $\boldsymbol{v}(r) = \sigma(\boldsymbol{\rho})$ and $\boldsymbol{v}(e) = \sigma(e)$. Finding a suitable loss function is less straightforward, but we tested the quadratic loss on $\boldsymbol{v}(r)^T \boldsymbol{v}(e)$. As shown in the following section, this additional restriction reduces the ability of the model to reconstruct facts.

2.3 Implication Regularization

We will refer to the loss term $\mathcal{L}_F$ introduced above as the *fact loss*, as it measures how well training facts are recovered with low-dimensional representations. To impose logical constraints, we add an additional loss term per rule which we will call the *implication loss* $\mathcal{L}_I$. As already described, the required order relation between two relations can be expressed by their representations as $\bigwedge_{i=1}^{k} v_i(r_p) \le v_i(r_q)$. We thus propose the following loss term for every implication $r_p \Rightarrow r_q$,

$$\mathcal{L}_I^{r_p \Rightarrow r_q} = \sum_{i=1}^{k} \log\big(1 + \text{ReLU}(\rho_{p,i} - \rho_{q,i})\big). \quad (5)$$

As before, other choices are possible. It is however essential to ensure that only positive values of $\rho_{p,i} - \rho_{q,i}$ are penalized, which is obtained by applying the ReLU function (see § 2.2). The difficulty in choosing an appropriate loss function is that its behavior needs to be compatible with the fact loss. For instance, the simple loss $\text{ReLU}(\rho_{p,i} - \rho_{q,i})$ seems not to work in practice as balancing both losses during optimization becomes difficult. The particular form of $\mathcal{L}_I$ in eq. (5) was obtained in a similar way to eq. (4), and originates from simplifying

$$-\sum_{i=1}^{k} \log\left(1 - \sigma\big(\log \text{ReLU}(\rho_{p,i} - \rho_{q,i})\big)\right).$$

We empirically found that this loss works well in practice and behaves in an intuitive way. For example, injecting the formulae $r_p \Rightarrow r_q$ and $r_q \Rightarrow r_p$ leads to roughly identical representations for both relations.

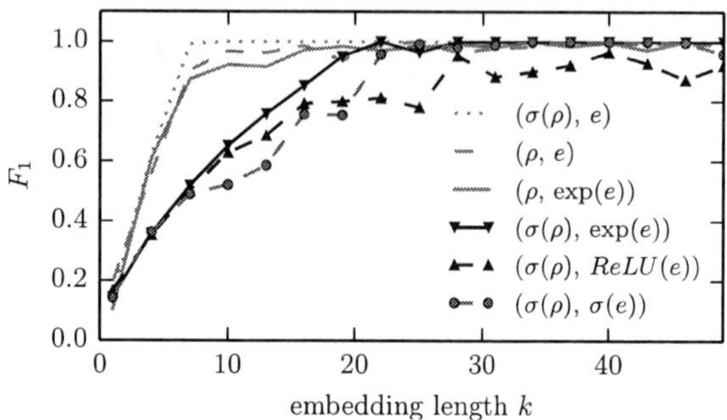

Figure 1: Ability of various methods $\big(v(r), v(e)\big)$ to reconstruct binary matrices, on a sampled KB with 50 entities (249 observed entity pairs) and 20 relations.

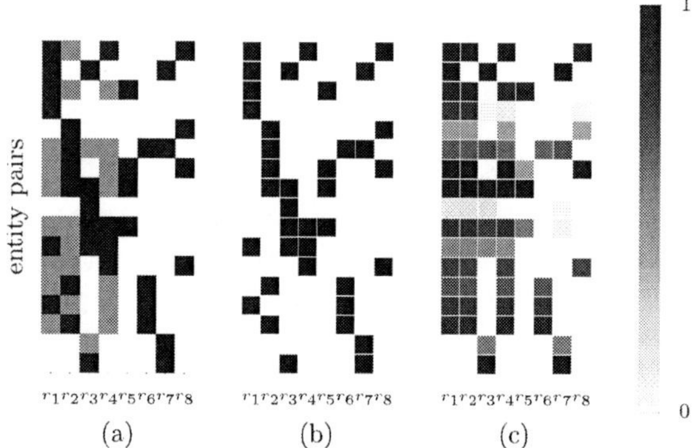

Figure 2: Toy example with 8 relations, 17 observed entity pairs, and 5 implication rules $(r_4 \Rightarrow r_1)$, $(r_7 \Rightarrow r_3)$, $(r_4 \Rightarrow r_2)$, $(r_6 \Rightarrow r_4)$, and $(r_5 \Rightarrow r_4)$. (a) Original knowledge base (dark blue: known facts; white: unknown facts; light blue: inferred facts from rules); (b) reconstructed with embedding size 15 with $\mathcal{L} = \mathcal{L}_F$, and (c) with $\mathcal{L} = \mathcal{L}_F + \mathcal{L}_I$.

3 Experiments

To gain insights into the proposed models, we investigate their behavior on small-scale artificial KB inference datasets that we can adapt to different possible scenarios. Concretely, we sample facts for a predefined number of entities and relations. Then, we generate implications for sampled pairs of relations and add a fraction of implied facts to the training data and the rest to a test set. This gives us control over how much an implication is visible for training representations of facts in the KB.

Fact Reconstruction in Non-Negative Space We first investigate whether restricting embedding spaces still allows to reconstruct observed facts. To this end, we consider a dataset with 20 relations and

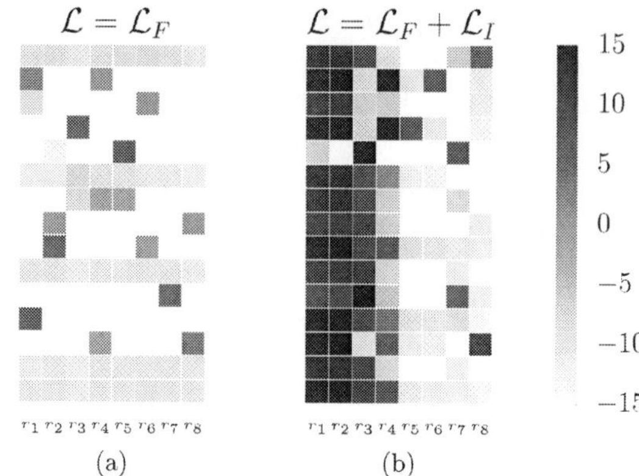

Figure 3: The columns are the 15-dimensional representations ρ_1 to ρ_8 for the relations r_1 to r_8 in the toy example of Fig. 2. (a) Only fact loss $\mathcal{L}_F$ applied; (b) including implication loss $\mathcal{L}_I$.

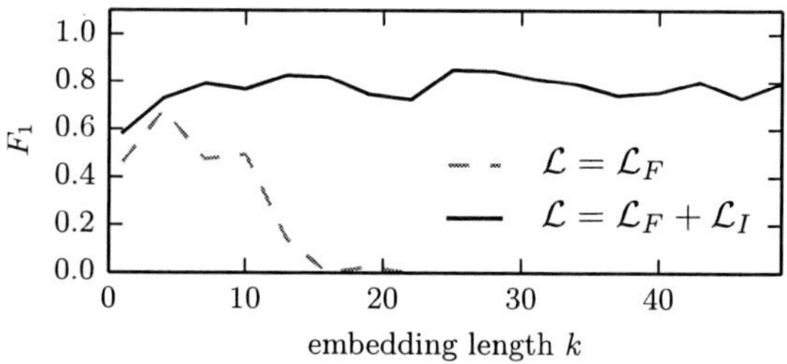

Figure 4: Ability of correctly predicting unseen facts implied by observed facts on a dataset with 20 relations, 249 observed entity pairs, and 10 pairwise implications with 50% evidence for the observed facts, with the model $\big(\sigma(\rho), \exp(e)\big)$.

50 entities, leading to observations for 249 entity pairs. We calculate the F_1 score for reconstructing all training facts, assuming that all unobserved facts are negative. Fig. 1 shows the result for different combinations of restricting the relation and entity pair embedding spaces. Every model maps a relation r and entity-pair e into vector space, denoted by $\big(v(r), v(e)\big)$ where ρ and e represent the learned real-valued (i.e., non-restricted) representations before mapping into a non-negative subspace. The results are shown as a function of the embedding size k. We found that from the two models that satisfy both the relation and the entity pair restriction, the one with $v(e) = \exp(e)$ seems to work best and will be used in the remainder of the experiments. As expected, imposing restrictions leads to a reduced ability to fit the data exactly and hence requires higher-dimensional vector representations of relations and entity-pairs.

Implication Regularization To visualize what happens when regularizing relation representations based on given implications, we sample a small KB with 8 relations, 17 entity pair observations and the following five implications: $r_4 \Rightarrow r_1$, $r_7 \Rightarrow r_3$, $r_4 \Rightarrow r_2$, $r_6 \Rightarrow r_4$ and $r_5 \Rightarrow r_4$. We add 20% of the facts that can be inferred from these rules as training data and use the rest as test data.

Fig. 2(a) shows observed facts (dark blue), as well as test facts (light blue). With an embedding size of 15, $\mathcal{L}_F$ is able to perfectly reconstruct the training data, as shown in Fig. 2(b), but therefore overfits. In contrast, when imposing implications we can reconstruct training facts and predict test facts that could be inferred by these implications (Fig. 2(c)). Note that in Fig. 2(b) the predictions are made with high confidence, whereas in Fig. 2(c) the reconstruction is not perfect, with the predictions distributed between 0 and 1. This is due to the fact that during training the loss related to some of the facts is influenced both by the implication loss and by a conflicting contribution from the fact loss (due to the random sampling of negative examples among the unobserved ones). Although this effect is an artifact of the small scale of the example (where non-observed facts are sampled more often than in a large and sparse situations), it underlines the importance of properly weighting both loss terms, for which further research on large-scale data is needed.

The learned relation embeddings are visualized in Fig. 3. We can see that regularizing relation embeddings by implications leads to representations that satisfy the order imposed by the implications (see Fig. 3(b)).

For the final experiment, we again consider the dataset used for Fig. 1, but this time we inject 10 pairwise implications and add half of the additional facts that can be inferred from them to the training set. The others are added to the test set, together with as many sampled negative test facts. The F_1 value on the test facts for different embedding sizes is shown in Fig. 4. We found that the implication loss successfully acts as a regularizer, yielding F_1 scores of around 80% for predicting unobserved valid facts even with large embedding sizes where a model without this regularization drastically overfits.

4 Conclusion and Future Work

We have presented a scalable method to incorporate first-order implications into relation representations for knowledge base inference. It alleviates the need for propositionalization of such formulae and we plan to use it to improve large-scale knowledge base inference with many formulae extracted from ontologies. We discussed and illustrated the method in a matrix factorization setting, but it can be applied to any model that produces relation and entity (or entity-pair) representations that can be mapped into non-negative space. In future work, we will investigate ways to efficiently incorporate more complex formulae as well, involving conjunctions, disjunctions, and negations.

Acknowledgments

We thank Sameer Singh and Dirk Weissenborn for fruitful discussions, and the reviewers as well as Johannes Welbl for comments on drafts of this paper. This work was supported by the Research Foundation - Flanders (FWO), Ghent University - iMinds, Microsoft Research through its PhD Scholarship Programme, an Allen Distinguished Investigator Award, and a Marie Curie Career Integration Award.

References

[Bollacker et al.2008] Kurt Bollacker, Colin Evans, Praveen Paritosh, Tim Sturge, and Jamie Taylor. 2008. Freebase: a collaboratively created graph database for structuring human knowledge. In *Proceedings of the 2008 ACM SIGMOD international conference on Management of data*, pages 1247–1250. ACM.

[Ganitkevitch et al.2013] Juri Ganitkevitch, Benjamin Van Durme, and Chris Callison-Burch. 2013. Ppdb: The paraphrase database. In *HLT-NAACL*, pages 758–764.

[Kruszewski et al.2015] German Kruszewski, Denis Paperno, and Marco Baroni. 2015. Deriving boolean structures from distributional vectors. *Transactions of the Association for Computational Linguistics*, 3:375–388.

[Miller1995] George A Miller. 1995. Wordnet: a lexical database for english. *Communications of the ACM*, 38(11):39–41.

[Nickel et al.2015] Maximilian Nickel, Kevin Murphy, Volker Tresp, and Evgeniy Gabrilovich. 2015. A review of relational machine learning for knowledge graphs: From multi-relational link prediction to automated knowledge graph construction. *arXiv preprint arXiv:1503.00759.*

[Riedel et al.2013] Sebastian Riedel, Limin Yao, Andrew McCallum, and Benjamin M Marlin. 2013. Relation extraction with matrix factorization and universal schemas.

[Rocktäschel et al.2015] Tim Rocktäschel, Sameer Singh, and Sebastian Riedel. 2015. Injecting Logical Background Knowledge into Embeddings for Relation Extraction. In *Annual Conference of the North American Chapter of the Association for Computational Linguistics (NAACL).*

[Vendrov et al.2016] Ivan Vendrov, Ryan Kiros, Sanja Fidler, and Raquel Urtasun. 2016. Order-embeddings of images and language. *arXiv preprint*, abs/1511.06361.

[Wang et al.2015] Quan Wang, Bin Wang, and Li Guo. 2015. Knowledge base completion using embeddings and rules. In *Proceedings of the 24th International Conference on Artificial Intelligence*, IJCAI'15, pages 1859–1865. AAAI Press.

Applying Universal Schemas for Domain Specific Ontology Expansion

Paul Groth, Sujit Pal, Darin McBeath, Brad Allen and **Ron Daniel**
{p.groth, sujit.pal, d.mcbeath, b.allen, r.daniel}@elsevier.com
Elsevier Labs
1600 John F. Kennedy Boulevard, Suite 1800,
Philadelphia, PA

Abstract

Manually created large scale ontologies are useful for organizing, searching, and repurposing content ranging from scientific papers and medical guidelines to images. However, maintenance of such ontologies is expensive. In this paper, we investigate the use of universal schemas (Riedel et al., 2013) as a mechanism for ontology maintenance. We apply this approach on top of two unique data sources: 14 million full-text scientific articles and chapters, plus a 1 million concept hand-curated medical ontology. We show that using a straightforward matrix factorization algorithm one can achieve 0.7 F1 measure on a link prediction task in this environment. Link prediction results can be used to suggest new relation types and relation type synonyms coming from the literature as well as predict specific new relation instances in the ontology.

1 Introduction

Scholarly information has been a key domain of interest for the automated knowledge base construction (AKBC) community (Ororbia II et al., 2014). A range of techniques have been applied to wide variety of tasks including: the construction of pathway databases (Friedman et al., 2001), genomic knowledge extraction (Poon et al., 2014); scientific question answering (Clark et al., 2016), and scientific entity search (Sinha et al., 2015).

In this work, we focus on augmenting an existing rich domain specific ontology with additional information. We show that existing well-known unsupervised approaches can generate interesting input for domain experts in their ontology maintenance task. We apply these approaches to two unique resources:

- The full text of all 14 million documents (journal papers and book chapters) within Elsevier's ScienceDirect database. This covers over 24 major disciplines and over 2500 journals.
- The Elsevier Merged Medical Taxonomy (EMMeT) - a manually curated ontology containing nearly one million concepts, three million synonyms, more than 30 relation types, and more than three million instances of relations between those concepts.

EMMeT is used within a number of Elsevier's search engines to provide structured search results. For example, within Clinical Key (a literature search engine for clinicians), a user may search for "breast cancer" but wants to know specific treatment procedures for a particular sub type of the cancer (e.g. Malignant Neoplasm of the breast outer quadrant). EMMeT allows for the traversal from superclass to subclass to procedure to be made. However, the maintenance of EMMeT is a time consuming process requiring domain experts (e.g. trained doctors) to read the literature, update, and curate the ontology. This includes not only the addition of new relations but also revising existing relations, adding new synonyms and finding additional evidence for statements within the ontology. We also aim to show that automated approaches can provide a quick and relatively high quality entry point that can augment curated knowledge bases. This work is an initial step in applying automated knowledge base techniques in this setting.

Proceedings of AKBC 2016, pages 81–85,
San Diego, California, June 12-17, 2016. ©2016 Association for Computational Linguistics

An important aspect of this work is that it shows that a rather straightforward implementation of the universal schema approach (Riedel et al., 2013) to relation extraction can be effective in a domain specific setting. Prior work has used universal schemas for more general encyclopedic knowledge bases such as Freebase or TAC KBP datasets. Here, we apply it to the medical domain. Our implementation is built in the Spark distributed computing framework (Zaharia et al., 2010). For a discussion and comparison of universal schemas to other AKBC methods, we refer the reader to Section 2 of (Verga et al., 2015), which provides an excellent overview.

The contributions of this paper are as follows:

- a confirmation that the universal schema approach can be effective in a domain specific settings; and

- an exemplar of how straightforward AKBC methods can be applied using widely available compute platforms.

We begin with a description of our system followed by an set of initial experiments and then conclude.

2 System Description

Our CAT3-KB system consists of seven steps depicted in Figure 1: open information extraction, ontology ingestion, concept resolution, matrix construction, matrix factorization, matrix completion, and curation. We now describe these steps in turn.

Open IE ScienceDirect content consists of XML representations of articles. From this XML, we extract the plain text of articles. These articles are fed through a Spark-based reimplementation of Re-Verb (Fader et al., 2011). At a high level, ReVerb identifies relation phrases by looking for text spans starting with a verb and ending with a preposition (e.g. "is the leading cause of"). Noun phrases before and after the span are used as the arguments of the subsequent relation instance (i.e. fact). We lemmatize all relations, and only keep relation types that have more than 5 distinct argument pairs and that occur more than 25 times. These parameters are adjustable. From the original 14 million articles (representing approximately 1 TB of text), 475 million facts are returned. This amount of data is an example of why it is helpful to employ a distributed computing framework such as Spark.

Ontology Ingestion To combine the lemmatized surface form relations from the prior step with an imported ontology, we first ingest the ontology into an annotation engine. We have developed the Solr Dictionary Annotator (SoDA)[1], a high performance dictionary based annotation engine for Spark. SoDA is specifically designed to support large dictionaries such as EMMeT. Because of the diversity of scientific content and the availability of large ontologies, performing concept recognition type tasks using a dictionary approach is often effective. Importantly, this approach allows us to adjust our knowledge base to different domains by ingesting different ontologies.

Concept Resolution In this stage, we run SoDA against the noun phrase arguments of the lemmatized surface form relation instances. It matches the arguments to concepts within the ingested ontology. This process includes fuzzy string matching against all the synonyms of the various concepts. The output of this step is a knowledge graph consisting of known concepts linked by both surface form relation instances as well as by relations from the ontology.

The concept resolution step reduces the 475 million Open IE facts to 46 million where both surface form arguments match EMMeT concepts. We add in the three million facts from EMMeT, giving us a medical knowledge base of 49 million facts.

Matrix Construction Following (Riedel et al., 2013), we construct a matrix from those 49 million facts. The rows are the pairs of arguments in each fact, and the columns are the lemmatized relations (or the known relations from EMMeT). The cells have binary values; one where the two arguments are linked by that relation, zero where not. As described later, our initial experiments use subsets of this matrix.

Matrix Factorization (Riedel et al., 2013) presents a number of models based on the universal schema representation. A key insight of that work was that these models could take advantage of techniques from collaborative filtering. We apply this insight directly and build a model using alternating

---

[1] https://databricks.com/blog/2016/02/10/how-elsevier-labs-implemented-dictionary-annotation-at-scale-with-apache-spark-on-databricks.html

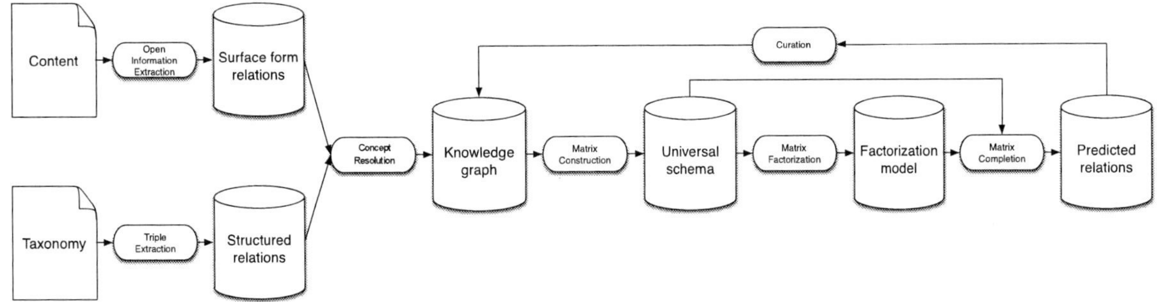

Figure 1: The Architecture of CAT3-KB

least squares (ALS) to approximate the given universal schema as the product of two lower rank matrices. Each relation is approximated by one factor and each concept-concept pair is approximated by another. In our setting, we use Spark's existing parallel implementation of an implicit feedback version of ALS with regularization. The number of iterations, regularization, and implicit feedback baseline confidence parameters are all set empirically. Those settings are given later in the experimental section.

From our initial observations, results appear to be robust to differing parameter settings but we have yet to perform a full sensitivity analysis. The output of this step are an Nxk and an Mxk factor matrices, where N is the number of concept-concept pairs and M is the number of lemmatized and EMMeT relations. The results described here are for k = 30.

Matrix Completion To generate a set of predicted relation instances, we approximate the original matrix by multiplying the two matrix factors. The resulting matrix is no longer binary; it has values between 0. and 1.0, inclusive. Therefore, we need to determine a threshold where a score generated by the model should be considered to constitute a relation instance.

To determine the threshold, we first perform ten-fold cross validation on the input matrix. For each fold we factorize and complete the matrix, then report precision, recall and F1 measure between the original and completed matrix. This comparison is done for 11 different threshold values. Based on these results, we select the threshold that maximizes the F1 measure. After determining a threshold using the cross validation described above, we run matrix factorization across the entire input matrix and select those facts that score above the threshold.

An important point to make is that we are predicting new relations that do no explicitly appear in the literature or in the input ontology. To clarify, while just looking at the Open IE facts or input knowledge graph relations is of interest, our goal here is to predict new links not within that knowledge graph.

Curation The final step is to provide the set of predicted facts to experts for analysis and use in their application. These may be used to refine the input taxonomy through the addition of relations or inserted back into the input knowledge graph.

3   Initial Experiments

We have conducted an initial set of tests with small subsets of the input matrix so that we can easily examine the outputs manually and quickly iterate. Two subsets were created, based on concepts that appear frequently within in the Clinical Key search logs. The two concepts were "glaucoma" and "rheumatoid arthritis". For each concept, we create a small subset of the input graph by selecting the rows which have the concept in the arg1 position, and all columns that have any values in those rows. For glaucoma, this results in a matrix with 173 rows and 83 columns. The matrix is sparse[2] containing 356 existing relation instances. The columns for the EMMeT relations are relatively dense, the columns for the surface form relations are relatively sparse. We run 10 fold cross-validation on the input matrix and try 11 different threshold values in each fold. Results were averaged over the 10 folds and plotted in Figure 2. We achieve a maximum F1 measure of .71 at a threshold of 0.3, although F1 is not especially sensitive to the threshold. In our initial exper-

---

[2]The sparsity ratio is 1.

83

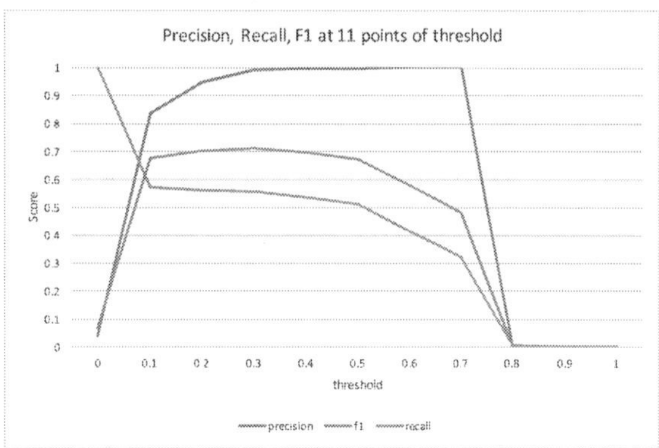

Figure 2: Performance in the glaucoma experiment

iments, we wanted to increase recall, so a threshold of 0.08 was chosen.

The complete glaucoma subset was factorized, completed, and thresholded. We found 22 relation instances that were not in the input knowledge graph. Figure 3 depicts several interesting examples.[3] We see synonymous surface forms (e.g. develop following) as well as relations between glaucoma and class concepts (e.g. age over 40). Note, that in Figure 3 we replace the concept ids with their preferred term from the EMMeT ontology.

For rheumatoid arthritis, the subset matrix had 258 rows by 70 columns and contained 465 known relation instances. The best performing threshold for F1 was slightly different than for the glaucoma example - a threshold of 0.2 gave the maximum F1 of 0.75. Here too we found a number of interesting and new relation instances. One that stood out in the result set was the ability to predict a new relation instance that used an ontology relation, namely (rheumatoid arthritis, emmet:isRiskFactor , amyloidosis). In the input set of relations, the link between arthritis and amyloidosis was that of causation and a potential complication.

4   Conclusion

This work presents CAT3-KB - a system for automated knowledge based construction based on universal schemas and implemented using the Spark

---

[3]It is important not to take the results too literally. Glaucoma is (probably) not the second leading cause of functional visual field loss, although it is the second leading cause of blindness in the US. This points out the need for human curation of the results before they are included in an ontology like EMMeT.

distributed computing framework. A key attribute of our system is that it is primarily unsupervised. Using straightforward AKBC techniques (open information extraction, dictionary matching, and universal schemas), we were able to generate a 49 million fact knowledge graph which combined knowledge from medical text and from a large medical taxonomy. We were then able to perform link prediction with subsets of that graph allowing us to produce suggestions for ontology expansion.

We see the importance of this initial system, not in advancing new algorithms, but in showing the applicability and reusability of state-of-the-art AKBC methods over real world datasets.

There are a number of avenues for future work. From a use case perspective, we have presented this initial system to Elsevier's in-house ontology team. They were encouraged by the system and presented several use cases that we think are of interest to the AKBC community:

1. Querying over the ontology. This is a semantic search problem in which the aim is to find existing relations for a given query. Given an existing relation like "emmet:hasCause", the knowledge base can provide many surface forms that are synonymous. This will help ontology browsing and also adding synonyms to the ontology.

2. Provide evidence to confirm existing ontology relations. Medicine is particularly concerned with being based in evidence. Being able to link a particular fact with textual passages that support it is valuable for credibility.

3. Provide evidence for new relation instances not yet in an ontology. Being able to suggest that two concepts should be linked by one of the ontology's semantic types, and being able to back that up with paragraph level text passages, is a tremendous savings in the effort for ensuring the ontology is grounded in the literature.

From a system's perspective, our first step is to perform larger experiments representing the entire knowledge graph as a universal schema. We also intend to implement more sophisticated models based on the universal schema representation. Likewise, a

ARG1	REL	ARG2
glaucoma	developed many years after	chronic inflammation of uveal tract
glaucoma	develop following	chronic inflammation of uveal tract
glaucoma	can appear soon in	family history of glaucoma
glaucoma	can appear soon in	age over 40
glaucoma	is considered the second leading cause of	functional visual field loss
glaucoma	remains the second leading cause of	functional visual field loss

Figure 3: Examples of new relation instances for glaucoma

comparison to other distant suppression mechanisms would be informative. Additionally, we need to perform sensitivity analysis on our various parameter settings. We also would like to explore the applicability to other ontologies or combinations there of. In the longer term, a key question we have is ranking facts to be shown to experts.

In closing, we believe that AKBC methods have matured to the extent where they can be a key asset for ontologist in the maintenance and creation of large scale domain-specific ontologies.

Acknowledgements

We thank the reviewers for their important suggestions and guidance on directions for future work.

References

Peter Clark, Oren Etzioni, Tushar Khot, Ashish Sabharwal, Oyvind Tafjord, Peter Turney, and Daniel Khashabi. 2016. Combining retrieval, statistics, and inference to answer elementary science questions.

Anthony Fader, Stephen Soderland, and Oren Etzioni. 2011. Identifying relations for open information extraction. In *Proceedings of the Conference on Empirical Methods in Natural Language Processing*, pages 1535–1545. Association for Computational Linguistics.

Carol Friedman, Pauline Kra, Hong Yu, Michael Krauthammer, and Andrey Rzhetsky. 2001. Genies: a natural-language processing system for the extraction of molecular pathways from journal articles. *Bioinformatics*, 17(suppl 1):S74–S82.

Alexander G. Ororbia II, Jian Wu, and Lee C. Giles. 2014. Citeseerx: Intelligent information extraction and knowledge creation from web-based data. In *The 4th Workshop on AutomatedKnowledge Base Construction*, May.

Hoifung Poon, Chris Quirk, Charlie DeZiel, and David Heckerman. 2014. Literome: Pubmed-scale genomic knowledge base in the cloud. *Bioinformatics*.

Sebastian Riedel, Limin Yao, Benjamin M. Marlin, and Andrew McCallum. 2013. Relation extraction with matrix factorization and universal schemas. In *Joint Human Language Technology Conference/Annual Meeting of the North American Chapter of the Association for Computational Linguistics (HLT-NAACL '13)*, June.

Arnab Sinha, Zhihong Shen, Yang Song, Hao Ma, Darrin Eide, Bo-June (Paul) Hsu, and Kuansan Wang. 2015. An overview of microsoft academic service (mas) and applications. In *Proceedings of the 24th International Conference on World Wide Web*, WWW '15 Companion, pages 243–246, New York, NY, USA. ACM.

Patrick Verga, David Belanger, Emma Strubell, Benjamin Roth, and Andrew McCallum. 2015. Multilingual relation extraction using compositional universal schema. *arXiv preprint arXiv:1511.06396*.

Matei Zaharia, Mosharaf Chowdhury, Michael J. Franklin, Scott Shenker, and Ion Stoica. 2010. Spark: Cluster computing with working sets. In *Proceedings of the 2Nd USENIX Conference on Hot Topics in Cloud Computing*, HotCloud'10, pages 10–10, Berkeley, CA, USA. USENIX Association.

Design of Word Association Games using Dialog Systems for Acquisition of Word Association Knowledge

Yuichiro Machida[†,1] **Daisuke Kawahara**[†] **Sadao Kurohashi**[†] **Manabu Sassano**[‡]

[†]Graduate School of Informatics, Kyoto University
[‡]Yahoo Japan Corporation

`machida@nlp.ist.i.kyoto-u.ac.jp`, `{dk, kuro}@i.kyoto-u.ac.jp`, `msassano@yahoo-corp.jp`

Abstract

We present a design for acquiring word association knowledge of high quality on the basis of a game with a purpose (GWAP). We evaluate automatically acquired word associations using a word association game as a GWAP. In the word association game, a player is given a set of associated words as a hint and is asked to answer a word that can be associated with the hint. If many players can answer the correct keyword, we judge the set of associated words to be of high quality. This word association game was implemented in a smartphone-based dialog system, which has been installed into more than one million smartphones. Our analysis of numerous game logs demonstrated that our framework can effectively select word associations of high quality.

1 Introduction

In recent years, semantic analysis has received attention as an active research area in natural language processing (NLP). It is indispensable to build language resources for accurate semantic analysis. One such resource is word associations, e.g., "glass" has an association with "fragile," "cup," and "reflect." Compiling large-scale word association knowledge of high quality is important to capture the semantic relations among words in texts, enabling deep and accurate discourse analyses. Hereafter, we designate the target word as **keyword**[2]. Words with which the

keyword has an association are designated as **associated words**.

There are manually crafted resources of word associations, such as thesauri and ontologies, which have been compiled by lexicographers and which have contributed to many studies in NLP. However, it takes long times and high costs to create a large thesaurus. Furthermore, it is difficult to update it continuously to adapt to neologisms and the changing use of a word.

To reduce the creation cost, methods for automatically acquiring word associations from a large corpus have been studied (e.g., (Lin, 1998; Mikolov et al., 2013)). Although such methods can acquire large-scale resources of word associations, they tend to have lower precision than manually created ones, which would harm the performance of subsequent NLP applications.

To cope with potential difficulties existing both in manual methods and automatic ones, it is necessary to combine the two methods, taking their respective benefits. This paper presents a method for compiling large-scale word association knowledge of high quality by evaluating automatically acquired word associations manually, not by linguistic experts but by the wisdom of crowds.

To make use of the wisdom of crowds, crowdsourcing has been employed widely (e.g., (Snow et al., 2008; Kawahara et al., 2014)). Crowdsourcing is a low-cost service that enlists numerous human workers to make judgments that are difficult for computers.[3] However, costs are still high when we

---

[1]The first author is now affiliated with Recruit Lifestyle Co., Ltd.

[2]A keyword can be a word or a phrase, but we call both "keywords."

[3]In this paper, we refer to microtask crowdsourcing as "crowdsourcing."

86

Proceedings of AKBC 2016, pages 86–91,
San Diego, California, June 12-17, 2016. ©2016 Association for Computational Linguistics

conduct a very large-scale task by aggregating many small-cost microtasks. We employ a game with a purpose (GWAP) (von Ahn, 2006) to use the wisdom of crowds. GWAP dispatches tasks as a game, and thus it is the process by which a game play implicitly corresponds to the execution of another task. Since game players do not want money but instead want fun, the use of GWAP engenders greater cost reductions than crowdsourcing.

We perform a **word association game** using a dialog system on smartphones as GWAP. We evaluate the quality of automatically acquired Japanese word associations based on logs obtained from game players. For example, if players correctly answer the keyword "glass" for the given associated words "fragile," "cup," and "reflect," these associated words can be regarded as high quality for the keyword. We use such a game to evaluate automatically acquired word associations at no cost.

2 Related Work

In recent years, crowdsourcing has been used for data construction and evaluation in NLP (e.g., (Snow et al., 2008; Hill et al., 2015; Schnabel et al., 2015)). Snow et al. (2008) demonstrated that annotations by crowdworkers have almost identical quality with those by experts in various NLP tasks. The motivation of crowdworkers in crowdsourcing is monetary.

Another type of wisdom of crowds is GWAP, for which a player's motivation differs from that of crowdsourcing. Their motivation is "enjoying the game." Therefore, we need not pay for the players, and can reduce the number of low-quality or dishonest workers. Many approaches using GWAP have been proposed in the field of NLP, such as anaphora resolution (Hladká et al., 2009), paraphrasing (Poesio et al., 2013), constructing semantic network (Lafourcade, 2007), and word sense disambiguation (Venhuizen et al., 2013). However, they are designed in a text-based style. Text-based games are probably less enjoyable for players.

Some studies have specifically examined nontext-based games, i.e., video games (Vannella et al., 2014; Jurgens and Navigli, 2014). Video games are familiar for ordinary people and are much more enjoyable than text-based games. For example, Vannella et al. (2014) developed a video game to validate the associations between images and senses. They reported that the annotation quality using the video game is better than crowdsourcing. The enjoyable game design improves the quality of annotations by crowds. However, because playing a video game requires a certain amount of time, it is a bit difficult to play it in one's spare-time. Furthermore, developing an attractive video game would be a time-consuming task.

Our word association game works on a dialog system to encourage player motivation. The game progresses interactively, so that many players can play easily. Moreover, we need not spend much time to develop it because the game system is simple.

3 Automatic Acquisition of Word Associations

We first explain our model for acquiring word associations. Then, we describe a method for clustering the acquired word associations to efficiently make questions for the word association game.

3.1 Definition and Collection of Word Associations

In general, many relations exist among words, such as hypernym-hyponym relations and part-whole relations. However, we do not care about the kind of relation but the strength between words. Matsuo et al. (2006) used pointwise mutual information (PMI) and chi-square as the strength measures of relations, and acquired associated words using graph clustering. Our method is based on this method, but uses word frequencies and PMI as the strength measures as proposed by Shin and Kurohashi (2014). We used a Japanese Web corpus of 4.2 million sentences and Japanese Wikipedia to acquire associated words for nouns, verbs, and adjectives.

3.2 Clustering Word Associations

Next, we cluster the acquired associated words according to their basic meanings. By clustering associated words, we can not only structure associated word knowledge, but also efficiently produce questions for the word association game to evaluate the acquired associated words. Presume that there is a fruit cluster like {fruit, banana, orange, · · ·} among associated words of "apple." We can evaluate the quality not from all words in the fruit cluster but only from a few words in the cluster. We can reduce the number of questions for a keyword using clustering. We perform clustering based on the Girvan-Newman algorithm (Girvan and Newman, 2002).

4 Design of Word Association Game

To evaluate the quality of a set of automatically acquired word associations, we designed a word association game.

Our key idea is that humans can associate a given set of associated words with a keyword or its similar words if these associated words are of high quality. For example, if players answer the keyword "glass" or its similar word "window" for the given associated words "fragile," "cup" and "reflect," these associated words can be regarded as high quality for the keyword. Based on this idea, we conduct a word association game in which a player is given a set of automatically acquired associated words as a hint and is asked to answer a word that can be associated with the hint. We compare the answers of players with the keyword, and judge that the acquired associated words are of high quality if many answers are the keyword or similar words.

In this way, we do not evaluate the quality of each associated word for a keyword. We instead acquire large-scale word association knowledge of high quality verified as a whole. By using this strategy, we do not require a large number of annotations, i.e., game plays, for the quality judgment of a keyword. For keywords that are judged to be of low quality using our method, it is possible to conduct another stage of crowdsourcing to evaluate each associated word.

The word association game operates on a dialog system on a smartphone application as shown in Figure 1. We adopted a dialog system as a platform because enjoyment of conversations can promote game plays and vice versa. We developed a word association game as a dialog chatting function in Yahoo! Onsei Assist (Yahoo Japan's Voice Assistant, hereinafter YOA),[4] which is a spoken dialog smartphone application provided by Yahoo Japan.

---

[4]http://v-assist.yahoo.co.jp/

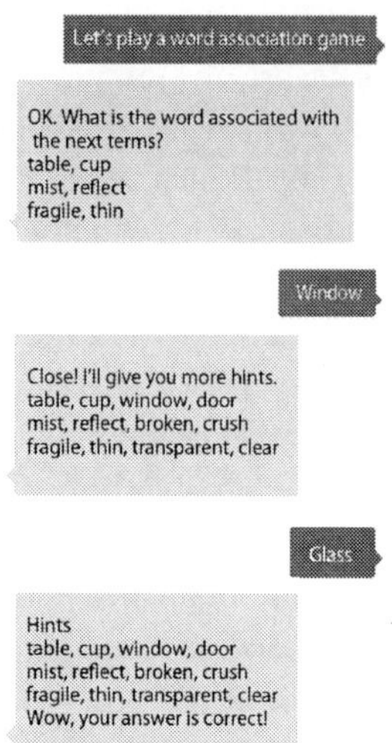

Figure 1: Word association game. Blue balloons show utterances of the player. All utterances of the player and the system are translated into English.

4.1 Method for Making Word Association Game

The word association game is executed as follows.

1. If a player utters a sentence such as "連想ゲームしよう" (Let's play a word association game) in the mode of normal dialog processing, the word association game is booted up.[5]

2. A keyword is selected randomly from a pool of keywords.

3. One noun cluster, verb cluster, and adjective cluster of associated words are randomly selected.

4. A question is created using two words as a hint in order of the degree of association in each selected cluster (six words in total).

5. A player utters an answer to the question.

6. The answer is judged. If it corresponds to the keyword, the game ends and YOA returns to the mode of normal dialog processing; otherwise steps 3 and 4 are called again to add more hints to the question.

7. The player utters an answer to the revised question.

8. The answer is judged. In any case, the game ends and YOA returns to the mode of normal dialog processing.

---

[5]It was announced to YOA users that they can play a word association game.

For our experiment, we selected 100 keywords ranked between 3,000 and 10,000 in order of word frequency on the Web. Of these, we manually judged that 85 keywords have a high-quality set of associated words; 15 keywords do not.[6] These manual labels are used as a gold standard set in Section 5.2. Since high enjoyment for a game requires a somewhat high ratio of keywords with high-quality associated words, we set this ratio as high in our first-phase experiment for evaluation purposes. To practically operate the game, we would be able to lower the ratio to around half using keywords evaluated to be of high quality at the moment and keywords without evaluation.

4.2 Answer Judgment

At steps 6 and 8 in the procedure described above, the player answer is judged automatically as one of the following three classes: "Exact," "Near" and "Bad." When the answer of the player is the same as the keyword, the judgment is "Exact." When the answer is similar to the keyword, the judgment is "Near." Similarity between words is calculated based on distributional/distributed similarity (Lin, 1998; Mikolov et al., 2013). The answer of a player is judged as "Near" if its similarity to the keyword is greater than a threshold.

5 Evaluating Word Associations with the Word Association Game

We evaluated word associations by analyzing game logs of our word association game. The word association game has been operating since the middle of December 2014. To date, 87 keywords out of 100 have been used for the game. We analyzed game logs of approximately a month and a half.

From the game logs of our word association game, we can obtain the utterance time, player ID, and utterance contents of each player. Table 1 lists statistics of game logs for a month and a half.

5.1 Method for Aggregating Answers

To evaluate a set of associated words for a keyword, we adopted five answers that are highly ranked in

---

[6]In the experiment, 87 keywords out of these 100 were actually used for the word association game because of the specifications of YOA.

Player IDs	9,997
Plays	19,438
Exact	6,930
Near	4,470
Bad	10,895
Mode response interval	20.0s
Average plays per player	1.9
Max plays per player	59

Table 1: Statistics of game logs of a month and a half.

		human annotation	
		appropriate	inappropriate
Game log	appropriate	70	6
	inappropriate	6	5

Table 2: Comparison with human annotations.

order of frequency in the answers for the keyword. The purpose of this is to exclude unintentional utterances and errors of speech recognition caused by spoken dialog. We calculated precision for a keyword using its five answers as follows:

$$\text{precision} = \frac{|Exact| + |Near|}{|Exact| + |Near| + |Bad|},$$

where $|Exact|$ denotes the frequency of answers judged as "Exact." $|Near|$ and $|Bad|$ are defined in the same way.

We evaluated the quality of word associations in terms of the precision defined above. We judged the associated words of a keyword to be of high quality if its precision is higher than 0.3, and vice versa. This threshold was set empirically by considering the remaining noises of speech recognition and similar words that failed to be recognized.

5.2 Acquired Evaluations of Word Associations

We obtained automatic judgments for the target 87 keywords by aggregating answers. We compared these automatic judgments with the gold standard labels described in Section 4.1. Table 2 reports this comparison. We achieved a precision of 0.92, a recall of 0.92, and an F-score of 0.92. From these results, we can see that the quality of automatically acquired word associations can be evaluated precisely using our word association game.

5.3 Analysis of Word Associations with High Precision

High precision basically means high quality of associated words for a keyword. Table 3 shows play-

keyword	question examples	players' answers	prec
event	site, live, information, various inform, festival, boost special, big, official, latest memorial, plan, information, various enjoy, fun, festival, boost one-man, great, safety memorial, plan, information, various inform, festival, boost special, big, official, latest	**event**:41 party:19 concert:16 festival:12 sports festival:9	0.907
ice cream	chocolate, cake, ice, milk taste, smell, serve with, bake delicious, sweet, fresh, plenty milk, fresh cream, dessert, yogurt mix, melt, eat, make dense, smooth, cold, hot chocolate, cake, milk, fresh cream taste, smell, mix, melt delicious, sweet, dense, smooth	**ice cream**:55 cake:33 ice:32 pudding:19 soft ice cream:17	0.891

Table 3: Examples of players' answers with high precision. All keywords, question examples, and players' answers are translated into English. Bolded words and underlined words are judged as "Exact" and "Near," respectively.

keyword	question examples	players' answers	prec
line	distance, horse, curve, leg reach, loop, get away from, go past vertical, zigzag, long, fast count, length, distance, horse face, run, reach, loop simple, round, vertical, zigzag count, length, curve, leg face, run, get away from, go past simple, round, long, fast	horse race:101 leg:7 horse:7 race track:6 marathon:5	0.0
theme	lecture, this, work, exhibition along, mistake, summarize, drill down forever, important, familiar, main lecture, this, common, discussion along, mistake, tackle, learn forever, important, various, wide range of research, paper, lecture, this decide, draw, along, mistake ambitious, deep, forever, important	university,29 space,10 STAP cell,10 ocean,7 chemical,6	0.0

Table 4: Examples of players' answers with low precision. All keywords, question examples, and players' answers are translated into English.

ers' answers for some keywords that have high precision. Players' answers for the keyword "アイスクリーム" (ice cream) include similar words to the keyword, such as "ケーキ" (cake), "アイス" (ice), and "プリン" (pudding). Since the set of associated words includes appropriate associated words, the high precision actually indicates the quality of associated words. Although "ソフトクリーム" (soft ice cream) included in the players' answers is a similar word to the keyword, it cannot be identified as "Near." It is necessary to increase the coverage of similar word identification in future studies.

Furthermore, it is possible to acquire new associated words from players' answers with high precision. In Table 3, players' answers for the keyword "イベント" (event) include "パーティー" (party), "コンサート" (concert) and "運動会" (sports festival) in addition to the keyword itself. Although "パーティー" (party) and "コンサート" (concert) were automatically acquired as associated words, "運動会" (sports festival) was not acquired but an appropriate associated word. In this way, we can acquire novel associated words from the word association game.

5.4 Analysis of Word Associations with Low Precision

Table 4 shows players' answers for some keywords that have precision lower than 0.3. We can see that the low precision means low quality of associated words for a keyword. For example, the keyword "直線" (line) has low precision. Its players' answers were not similar to the keyword but were words that are related to horse racing. Actually, the associated words for this keyword, such as "距離" (distance) and "コーナー" (curve), can be readily associated with horse racing. Therefore, they are unsuitable for associated words for "直線" (line).

Furthermore, players' answers with low precision help not only find associated words of low quality but also analyze errors in the method for acquiring associated words. The above associated words were associated with horse racing because the domain of the Web corpus was biased to horse racing. In this way, we can speculate about the contexts of the acquired associated words, which correspond to error analysis of the acquisition method.

6 Conclusion

We have presented a method for compiling large-scale word association knowledge of high quality. We first automatically acquire and cluster word associations. Then we evaluate these by taking advantage of GWAP. The framework used for evaluating word associations is implemented as a word association game operating on a smartphone-based dialog system. Our analysis of a large volume of game logs has indicated that our framework can extract word associations of high quality effectively.

References

Michelle Girvan and Mark E. J. Newman. 2002. Community structure in social and biological networks. *Proc. of National Academy of Sciences*, 99(12):7821–7826.

Felix Hill, Roi Reichart, and Anna Korhonen. 2015. SimLex-999: Evaluating semantic models with (genuine) similarity estimation. *Computational Linguistics*, 41(4):665–695.

Barbora Hladká, Jiří Mírovský, and Pavel Schlesinger. 2009. Play the language: Play coreference. In *Proc. of ACL-IJCNLP 2009*, pages 209–212.

David Jurgens and Roberto Navigli. 2014. It's all fun and games until someone annotates: Video games with a purpose for linguistic annotation. *Transactions of the Association for Computational Linguistics*, 2:449–464.

Daisuke Kawahara, Yuichiro Machida, Tomohide Shibata, Sadao Kurohashi, Hayato Kobayashi, and Manabu Sassano. 2014. Rapid development of a corpus with discourse annotations using two-stage crowdsourcing. In *Proc. of COLING2014*, pages 269–278.

Mathieu Lafourcade. 2007. Making people play for Lexical Acquisition with the JeuxDeMots prototype. In *SNLP'07: 7th International Symposium on Natural Language Processing*, page 7, Pattaya, Chonburi, Thailand.

Dekang Lin. 1998. Automatic retrieval and clustering of similar words. In *Proc. of COLING-ACL98*, pages 768–774.

Yutaka Matsuo, Takeshi Sakaki, Kôki Uchiyama, and Mitsuru Ishizuka. 2006. Graph-based word clustering using a web search engine. In *Proc. of EMNLP2006*, pages 542–550.

Tomas Mikolov, Ilya Sutskever, Kai Chen, Gregory S. Corrado, and Jeffrey Dean. 2013. Distributed representations of words and phrases and their compositionality. In *Proc. of Advances in Neural Information Processing Systems 26*, pages 3111–3119.

Massimo Poesio, Jon Chamberlain, Udo Kruschwitz, Livio Robaldo, and Luca Ducceschi. 2013. Phrase detectives: Utilizing collective intelligence for internet-scale language resource creation. *ACM Trans. Interact. Intell. Syst.*, 3(1):3:1–3:44.

Tobias Schnabel, Igor Labutov, David Mimno, and Thorsten Joachims. 2015. Evaluation methods for unsupervised word embeddings. In *Proc. of EMNLP2015*, pages 298–307.

Yoshiharu Shin and Sadao Kurohashi. 2014. Graph-based representation of documents based on nominal related words knowledge and its applications. In *Proc. of NLP2014 (in Japanese)*, pages 1007–1010.

Rion Snow, Brendan O'Connor, Daniel Jurafsky, and Andrew Y. Ng. 2008. Cheap and fast—but is it good?: Evaluating non-expert annotations for natural language tasks. In *Proc. of EMNLP2008*, pages 254–263.

Daniele Vannella, David Jurgens, Daniele Scarfini, Domenico Toscani, and Roberto Navigli. 2014. Validating and extending semantic knowledge bases using video games with a purpose. In *Proc. of ACL2014*, pages 1294–1304.

Noortje J. Venhuizen, Valerio Basile, Kilian Evang, and Johan Bos. 2013. Gamification for word sense labeling. In *Proc. of 10th International Conference on Computational Semantics (IWCS 2013)*, pages 397–403.

Luis von Ahn. 2006. Games with a purpose. *IEEE Computer*, 39(6):92–94.

Call for Discussion:
Building a New Standard Dataset for Relation Extraction Tasks

Teresa Martin and **Fiete Botschen** and **Ajay Nagesh** and **Andrew McCallum**
University of Massachusetts
140 Governors Drive
Amherst, MA 01003, USA
`tmartin, fbotschen, ajaynagesh, mccallum@cs.umass.edu`

Abstract

This paper is an attempt to raise pertinent questions and act as platform to generate fruitful discussions within the AKBC community about the need for a large scale dataset for relation extraction. For proper training and evaluation of relation extraction tasks, the weaknesses of datasets used so far need to be tackled: mainly the size (too small) and the amount of data that is actually labelled (unlabelled data leading to recall problems). We have the vision of building a new large and fully labelled dataset for entity pairs connected via binary relations from both Freebase as well as other datasets, such as Clueweb. Concerning the process of building, we present pioneering work on a roadmap which will serve as the foundation for the intended discussion within the community. Points to discuss arise within the following steps: first, the source data has to be preprocessed in order to ensure that the set of relations consists of valid relations only; second, we suggest a method to find the most relevant relations for an entity pair; and third, we outline approaches on how to actually label the data. It is necessary to discuss several key issues in the process of generating this dataset. This will enable us to thoroughly create a dataset that will have the potential to serve as a standard to the community.

1 Motivation

A challenging problem for artificial intelligence is Information Extraction (IE) - extracting structured facts from raw unstructured text. A particularly

	rel_1	rel_2	...	rel_x
(ent_1, ent_2)	1	0	...	0
(ent_1, ent_2)	0	1	...	0
...	...	...	...	...
(ent_m, ent_n)	0	0	...	0

Table 1: Labelling structure of Freebase for binary RE tasks. Rows: all entity pairs. Columns: all relations. A cell is labelled with 1 as 'true' if its connection of entity pair and relation is contained in FB. The label 0 means that this combination of relation and entity pair is not contained in FB - which can be either that it is actually 'false' or that it is actually 'true' but not contained because no one added it.

important instance of this is Relation Extraction (RE), the detection of mentions of semantic relationships between entities in text. A typical RE task is classifying relations as 'true' or 'false' when looking at pairs of entities: e.g., for the entity pair (ent_1, ent_2) = ('Barack Obama', 'Michelle Obama'), decide whether the relation rel = 'marriedTo' is 'true' or 'false'. Two of the most widely used datasets for this task are the NYTimes dataset (Riedel et al., 2013) and FB15k (Bordes et al., 2013) (and its extension, FB15k-237 (Toutanova et al., 2015)). The latter is based on Freebase (FB) (Bollacker et al., 2008), a manually constructed knowledge base (KB) of entity pairs linked via relations. Table 1 clarifies how the labelling structure of FB is used for binary RE tasks.

The first problem is the small size of FB. Statistics on the incompleteness of FB can be found in (Min et al., 2013). For instance, 78% of person entities do not have nationalities. Also, when training on FB15k it might happen that there is only one single

Proceedings of AKBC 2016, pages 92–96,
San Diego, California, June 12-17, 2016. ©2016 Association for Computational Linguistics

	FB and NYTimes	FB and Toutanova CW
documents	1.8m	800m
entities	n.a.	14.5k
entity pairs	418k	2m
relation types	4k	2.7m
relation types from FB	1.5k	237
relation types from text	4k	2.7m

Table 2: Statistics over the data used in different works. Rows: the statistics. Columns: the different works.

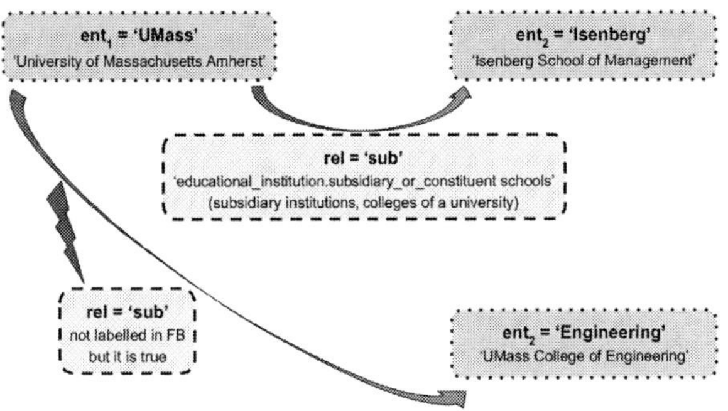

Figure 1: Situation leading to recall problem. The entities $ent_1 =$ 'UMass' and $ent_2 =$ 'Isenberg' are connected via the relation $rel =$ 'sub'. UMass Amherst has several other subsidiary colleges which do exist in FB e.g., $ent_2 =$ 'Engineering' but this relation does not exist for this entity pair in FB. Evaluation is misleading if non-existence is interpreted as 'false'.

case of a relation. If this case is in the test set it cannot be learned at all. Thus, evaluation is restricted to relation types within the FB schema. To extend and broaden the coverage of FB many approaches include unlabelled data from text corpora. However the choice of the unlabelled text varies between different contributions, see table 2 for a comparison of dataset statistics between two commonly used datasets. For RE and Universal Schemas (Riedel et al., 2013), data is used from the NYTimes corpus (Sandhaus, 2008) and FB. In comparison to other unlabelled corpora, the NYTimes corpus is quite small. To represent text, data could be used from FB and a (subset of) already existing datasets. For example, FB15k-237 (Toutanova et al., 2015) is a combination of Clueweb(CW) and FB data. CW is a webcrawl that comes annotated with FB entities (Gabrilovich et al., 2013). In the work with FB15k-237, relations are expressed as parse paths but not as entire text and in addition the majority of test entity pairs have no textual or other KB evidence. In terms of increasing quality of FB, we suggest to increase the number of relations by adding data from other datasets. As mentioned above, this could be CW or other already available datasets. By that, more relations should be covered as well as evaluating against entities which are not included in FB is possible.

The second problem is the so called 'recall problem' in FB with misleading results concerning recall when evaluating RE tasks. As illustrated in figure 1, the measure of recall is misleading when non-existent relations for entity pairs in FB are assumed to be 'false' just because they do not appear so far. This assumption is dangerous as non-existent rela-

tions in FB could indeed be 'true'. The recall problem occurs in the evaluation of a lot of work on RE due to incomplete labelling, e.g., in (Riedel et al., 2013) evaluating on (1.5k) FB relation types and in (Toutanova et al., 2015) evaluating on 237 FB relation types.

In order to avoid the recall problem, a fully labelled version is needed, where for each entity pair all relations should be labelled as 'true' or 'false'. Another source evoking the recall problem are entity mentions not being identified, or being attached to wrong types and hence recall is decreased. The recall problem is also claimed and tackled in the context of work on logical background knowledge (Rocktäschel et al., 2015). There, it is approached with a method avoiding manual labelling: simple logic formulae over patterns and relations are used to incorporate additional domain knowledge. The authors mention manual incorporation of such additional knowledge as an avenue for further research. Our effort is similar in spirit to TAC KBP tasks [1]. The number of documents given as input in KBP tasks are fairly small (around 50,000 articles) since the evaluation set is created by human annotators by labelling the responses from all participating teams. The KBP tasks are aimed at benchmarking various approaches and not to create a benchmark dataset

---

[1] `http://www.nist.gov/tac/2015/KBP/ColdStart/guidelines/TAC_KBP_2015_ColdStartTaskDescription_1.1.pdf`

that can be used for training. A filtering approach as proposed by us is not adopted in KBP. Our filtering approach becomes essential due to the sheer size of CW corpus. Our proposal is similar to the FACC1 annotation on CW (Gabrilovich et al., 2013). The difference is that FACC1 annotations are aimed at entity linking where as our approach is aimed at relation extraction. We want to discuss a roadmap for a labelling procedure involving human labelling.

2 Roadmap for Creation of the Dataset

2.1 First: Preprocessing of Source Data

Working with a crawl of web data (e.g., CW) yields one preprocessing problem: how can one extract usable relations from this kind of source data? A usable relation is a word sequence that actually is a relation for at least one entity pair. Filtering usable relations out of crawled data can be approached in several ways: for example, the word sequence between the entity pair can be considered as the relation. This is the approach taken in (Verga et al., 2015) and in many other work on open-domain IE. But this presents another hurdle: not all such word sequences are valid relations. To give an example, the sequence *'as well as'* may occur between two entities in a sentence like *'Max as well as Peter are happy.'* however this sequence is not an interesting candidate for any binary relation in IE. As a solution to this, patterns which do not make sense can be excluded by a fixed set of rules, e.g. 'must contain a verb', 'must not contain personal pronouns', 'must contain at least n words' etc. A commonly used approach related to fixed rules is to detect appositives as in (Yao et al., 2013). Coming up with a fixed rule set is problematic though as there is always the risk of excluding patterns that are actually usable. As an alternative to fixed rule sets one can come up with learned models to select usable relations. Another approach is to use dependency parsers such as (Chen and Manning, 2014) or openIE style RE (Verga et al., 2015). However, dependency parsers often focus on the syntax of text which is not ideal given the need of propositional information. Hence, important information might get lost. Others use dependency trees (Stanovsky et al., 2016) in order to explore propositional structure of text. This in return might help to decide whether a certain fraction of the text is actually a usable relation. Data from web crawlers is not only noisy, but also there are a lot of relation candidates which are just too seldom to be learned. It would be an option to follow (Riedel et al., 2013) by excluding entity pairs and relations that occur less than 10 times in the corpus. To sum it up, selecting usable relations when working with big data plays an important role. More unusable relations lead to worse results inevitably. Also, openIE patterns are too noisy to be worthwhile for downstream processing tasks which require RE. Hence, finding good ways to filter unstructured texts is an integral part of constructing the proposed dataset.

2.2 Second: Reduction to Relevant Relations

The number of relations to label for each entity pair is immense: possibly more than a million, depending on how much of the non-valid relation are filtered out during preprocessing. This number is so high as it expresses the number of unique relation instances instead of classes of relations e.g., not the class 'marriedTo' but all mentions like 'married', 'married to', 'happily married', etc. are counted as relations. It is not feasible to label all relations for each entity pair manually. Therefore, other approaches to obtain a full labelling need to be discussed. It is easy to observe that the most of these relations do not make sense at all regarding a specific entity pair. Those would be labelled as 'false' anyway and therefore do not require manual checking. This is why the following question arises: can we find a reasonable way to automatically select the most relevant relations for an entity pair? This would reduce the effort of labelling drastically. To achieve this reduction, we suggest to discuss the following: once there is a representation of entity pairs as well as relations in a common space, the relations closest to an entity pair can be determined. The Universal Schema model as presented in (Riedel et al., 2013) and developed further in (Verga et al., 2015) seems to fit to this need of representation learning. By training the baseline Universal Schema model on the combination of FB and CW data, embeddings are learned jointly for the entity pairs and for the relations. To find the most relevant relations for a given entity pair of interest, the cosine distance between the vector embedding of this entity pair and the vector embeddings of all the relations can be calculated, respectively. The result is a relevance ranking over all the relations specific to this entity pair. From this point, a fixed number of most relevant relations can be selected for manual labelling.

2.3 Third: Labelling Procedure

Table 3 sketches how the data to label could be structured. Labelling of relations has to be done entity pairwise because both the observed relations as well as the ranking over relevance of non-observed relations is specific to an entity pair. Looking at one specific entity pair, some relations might exist in FB already and we suggest to label them 'true'; some relations might be observed in CW and we suggest to accept them as 'true' but probably still consider a checking. Most importantly, all the remaining relations (ranked by relevance for this pair) are not observed and therefore labelled with 'false' by default. All of these default false relations need to be checked and turned to 'true' accordingly. In order to obtain a first fully labelled subset to experiment with, we suggest the following: for $c = 3$ different chosen entities, take all their entity pairs and label their first $r = 300$ most relevant relations. It is difficult to estimate the time required to label even one entity pair's $r = 300$ most relevant relations because this depends on two factors: (a) the quality of the relations; e.g., if relations are not filtered cautiously and even non-valid relations are listed it is quick to tag those relations as 'false' (b) the depths to which the person who labels is familiar with the entity pair; e.g., someone who knows a lot about an entity pair has to do less research in order to decide whether a relation is 'true' or 'false'.

3 Topics for Discussion

First of all, feedback on the need of the proposed dataset is important in order to shape the procedure of building it to the actual needs of the community.

Furthermore, many points of discussion arise along the suggested roadmap for creating the dataset. Concerning the preprocessing, section 2.1:

- Which way to go to get potential relations out of the raw sentences from CW containing entity pairs?
- How to deal with entities annotated with confidence scores in CW and thus how to identify entity mentions reliable?
- Possibilities to map CW relations to corresponding FB relations?

Concerning the reduction to relevant relations, section 2.2:

- Weighing the danger of relying on ONE model trained on the dataset we want to improve (Universal Schema model) in order to learn the embeddings?
- Which measure to determine the closest relations for an entity pair?
- Possibilities of selecting valid relations from CW and reducing to most relevant relations in an end-to-end way?

Concerning the labelling, section 2.3:

- Is it sustainable to just label the non-observed relations even for CW?
- How to minimize influence of the labeller?
- Use crowd sourcing?

Finally, it will be difficult to compare the results on the new dataset with results on previous datasets. For comparison, the datasets should be the same with the only difference that the new one has some more relations labelled as 'true'.

4 Conclusion

Following the need for a large and fully labelled dataset for training and evaluating RE tasks, we presented pioneering explorations on how to build such a dataset out of FB and CW. The purpose of this paper is to provide a platform to facilitate discussions within the community to gather ideas, needs, opinions and feedback all of which will help in the further development of the suggested dataset.

References

Kurt Bollacker, Colin Evans, Praveen Paritosh, Tim Sturge, and Jamie Taylor. 2008. Freebase: a collaboratively created graph database for structuring human knowledge. In *Proceedings of the 2008 ACM SIGMOD international conference on Management of data*, pages 1247–1250. ACM.

specific entity pair (e_1, e_2)	observed in FB (any number)	observed in CW (any number)		not observed in FB and CW (all remaining, most relevant)	
	rel_{F1} $|(e_1, e_2)$	rel_{C1} $|(e_1, e_2)$	rel_{C2} $|(e_1, e_2)$	rel_{not1} $|(e_1, e_2)$	rel_{rnot2} $|(e_1, e_2)$
('UMass', 'Isenberg')	'subsidiary school'	','	-	'educational institution'	'released a documentary on'
('UMass', 'Boston')	-	'is located just 90 miles from'	'at'	'initially came to'	'is located on the slopes of'

Table 3: Sketch of the necessary labelling. Rows: entity pairs (e_1, e_2). Blocks of columns listing relations for the row's entity pair that exist in FB (first), in CW (second) or do not occur in neither of them (third). Regarding labelling, the first block (FB) is already 'true', the second block (CW) is 'true' but should be checked and the third block is where a labelling procedure is needed.

Antoine Bordes, Nicolas Usunier, Alberto Garcia-Duran, Jason Weston, and Oksana Yakhnenko. 2013. Translating embeddings for modeling multi-relational data. In C. J. C. Burges, L. Bottou, M. Welling, Z. Ghahramani, and K. Q. Weinberger, editors, *Advances in Neural Information Processing Systems 26*, pages 2787–2795. Curran Associates, Inc.

Danqi Chen and Christopher D Manning. 2014. A fast and accurate dependency parser using neural networks. In *EMNLP*, pages 740–750.

Evgeniy Gabrilovich, Michael Ringgaard, and Amarnag Subramanya. 2013. Facc1: Freebase annotation of clueweb corpora, version 1 (release date 2013-06-26, format version 1, correction level 0). *Note: http://lemurproject. org/clueweb09/FACC1/Cited by,* 5.

Bonan Min, Ralph Grishman, Li Wan, Chang Wang, and David Gondek. 2013. Distant supervision for relation extraction with an incomplete knowledge base. In *HLT-NAACL*, pages 777–782.

Sebastian Riedel, Limin Yao, Benjamin M. Marlin, and Andrew McCallum. 2013. Relation extraction with matrix factorization and universal schemas. In *Joint Human Language Technology Conference/Annual Meeting of the North American Chapter of the Association for Computational Linguistics (HLT-NAACL '13)*, June.

Tim Rocktäschel, Sameer Singh, and Sebastian Riedel. 2015. Injecting logical background knowledge into embeddings for relation extraction. In *Proceedings of the 2015 Human Language Technology Conference of the North American Chapter of the Association of Computational Linguistics*.

Evan Sandhaus. 2008. The new york times annotated corpus. *Linguistic Data Consortium, Philadelphia*, 6(12):e26752.

Gabriel Stanovsky, Jessica Ficler, Ido Dagan, and Yoav Goldberg. 2016. Getting more out of syntax with props.

Kristina Toutanova, Danqi Chen, Patrick Pantel, Pallavi Choudhury, and Michael Gamon. 2015. Representing text for joint embedding of text and knowledge bases. *ACL Association for Computational Linguistics*.

Patrick Verga, David Belanger, Emma Strubell, Benjamin Roth, and Andrew McCallum. 2015. Multilingual relation extraction using compositional universal schema. *arXiv preprint arXiv:1511.06396*.

Limin Yao, Sebastian Riedel, and Andrew McCallum. 2013. Universal schema for entity type prediction. In *Proceedings of the 2013 workshop on Automated knowledge base construction*, pages 79–84. ACM.

A Comparison of Weak Supervision methods for Knowledge Base Construction

Ameet Soni
Department of Computer Science
Swarthmore College
soni@cs.swarthmore.edu

Dileep Viswanathan
School of Informatics and Computing
Indiana University
diviswan@indiana.edu

Niranjan Pachaiyappan
School of Informatics and Computing
Indiana University
nirapach@indiana.edu

Sriraam Natarajan
School of Informatics and Computing
Indiana University
natarasr@indiana.edu

Abstract

We present a comparison of *weak* and *distant* supervision methods for producing proxy examples for supervised relation extraction. We find that knowledge-based weak supervision tends to outperform popular distance supervision techniques, providing a higher yield of positive examples and more accurate models.

1 Introduction

In performing *relation extraction* in knowledge base population (KBP), the need for human-annotated examples (i.e., *gold-standard*) examples, is prohibitively expensive. One solution is to generate a set of so-called *silver-standard* examples from *weak* or *distant supervision* methods.

While several papers have demonstrated the benefits of using these approaches (Mintz et al., 2009; Riedel et al., 2010; Takamatsu et al., 2012), we are not familiar with any work that compares methods for generating weak labels for KBP. In this work, we seek to address the question of which weak supervision techniques provide the best basis for learning accurate models and scale appropriately with the KBP task. We address two approaches:

- Distant supervision (DS) – this popular technique entails referencing external knowledge bases, such as Freebase, as a source of seed facts. These facts are then linked to a corpus to identify positive training examples. We consider two variations for a corpus – extracting positive sentences from the actual training/testing corpus (CDS) (i.e., newswire doc-

uments) versus using sentences from external data sources (EDS) (e.g., Wikipedia articles).

- Knowledge-based weak supervision (KWS) – Natarajan et al. (2014) showed that we can encode the "world knowledge" of domain experts, who have some inherent rules for identifying positive training examples during manual annotation (e.g., "home teams are more likely to win a game" for a sports corpus). Using these rules, we can automatically generate new positive examples that simulate the human expert's annotations in a training corpus.

In this paper, we present our approaches for generating examples in further detail. We evaluate all three approaches on the TAC KBP corpus. We will also describe our pipeline, which utilizes relational dependency networks (RDNs) (Neville and Jensen, 2007; Natarajan et al., 2010). We note that the central focus of this paper is not to showcase RDNs for this task – that has been done in previous work – but rather to investigate weak supervision techniques.

Our results show that knowledge-based weak supervision is the preferred choice for producing training examples when good rules are available, approaching the accuracy of gold-standard data sets. This method produces examples at a higher rate than DS with fewer mislabels and is flexible to adapt to a diverse set of relations. Distant supervision techniques scale quicker and excel when domain knowledge is difficult to encode. However, they tend to yield fewer results and are not applicable when a relevant database does not already exist.

97

Proceedings of AKBC 2016, pages 97–102,
San Diego, California, June 12-17, 2016. ©2016 Association for Computational Linguistics

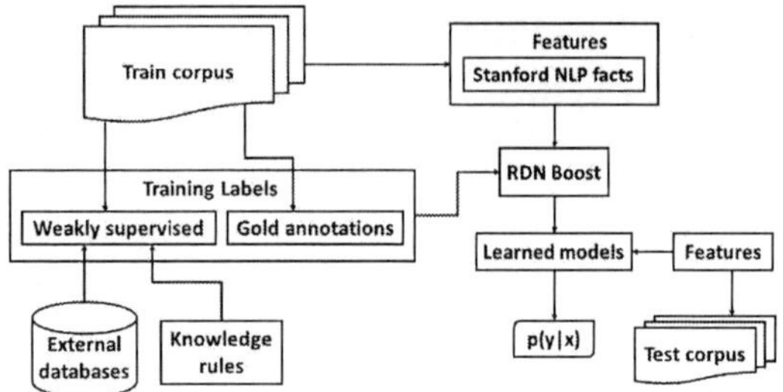

Figure 1: Full RDN relation extraction pipeline

2 The Relational Dependency Network Framework

In this work, we consider a framework for performing learning and inference from stochastic, noisy, relational data called Relational Dependency Networks (RDNs) (Neville and Jensen, 2007; Natarajan et al., 2010). RDNs extend dependency networks (DN) (Heckerman et al., 2001) to the relational setting. The key idea in a DN is to approximate the joint distribution over a set of random variables as a product of their marginal distributions, i.e., $P(y_1, ..., y_n | \mathbf{X}) \approx \prod_i P(y_i | \mathbf{X})$. It has been shown that employing Gibbs sampling in the presence of a large amount of data allows this approximation to be particularly effective. Note that, one does not have to explicitly check for acyclicity making these DNs particularly easy to be learned.

In an RDN, typically, each distribution is represented by a relational probability tree (RPT) (Neville et al., 2003). However, following previous work (Natarajan et al., 2010), we replace the RPT of each distribution with a set of relational regression trees (Blockeel and Raedt, 1998) built in a sequential manner i.e., replace a single tree with a set of gradient boosted trees. This approach has been shown to have state-of-the-art results in learning RDNs and we adapted boosting to learn for relation extraction. Since this method requires negative examples, we created negative examples by considering all possible combinations of entities that are not present in positive example set and sampled twice as many negatives as positive examples. We encourage the reader to refer to our previous work for in-depth details on the RDN algorithm (Neville et al., 2003; Natarajan et al., 2010).

The entire algorithmic pipeline is summarized in

Feature	Description
wordString	word with word id
wordPosition	location of the word
caselessWordString	word string in lower case
wordLemma	canonical form of word
isNEWord	whether word is NE
nextWords	two succeeding words
prevWords	two preceding words
nextPOS	POS for the succeeding words
prevPOS	POS for the preceding words
nextLemmas	canonical form of successors
prevLemmas	canonical form of predecessors
nextNE	succeeding NE phrases
prevNE	preceding NE phrases
lemmaBetween	canonical form of word occurring between two NEs
neBetween	word b/w two NEs is an NE
posBetween	POS of word b/w two NEs
Dependency Path	
rootChildLemma	canonical form of child of DPR
rootChildNER	child of DPR is NE
rootChildPOS	POS of child of DPR
rootLemma	lemma of DPR
rootNER	DPR is NER
rootPOS	POS of DPR

Table 1: Features derived from the training corpus used by our learning system. POS - part of speech. NE - Named Entity. DPR - root of dependency path tree.

Figure 1. Given a training corpus of raw text documents, our learning algorithm first converts these documents into a set of facts (i.e., features) that are encoded in first order logic (FOL). Raw text is processed using the Stanford CoreNLP Toolkit[1] (Manning et al., 2014) to extract parts-of-speech, word lemmas, etc. as well as generate parse trees, dependency graphs and named-entity recognition information. The full set of extracted features is available in Table 1. These features are used to train our RDN model. For some (unlabeled) test corpus, the RDN model is utilized to perform inference and identify positive entities.

3 Weak Supervision Frameworks

We analyze two general types of weak supervision that have been successfully applied in other natural language tasks – distant supervision and knowledge-based weak supervision.

---

[1] http://stanfordnlp.github.io/CoreNLP/

3.1 Distant supervision

Distant supervision entails the use of external knowledge (e.g., a database) to heuristically label examples. Following standard procedure, we use three data sources – Never Ending Language Learner (NELL) (Carlson et al., 2010), Wikipedia Infoboxes and Freebase. For a given target relation, we identify relevant database(s), where the entries in the database form *entity pairs* (e.g., an entry of $(Barack\ Obama, Malia\ Obama)$ for a parent database) that will serve as a seed for positive training examples. These pairs must then be mapped to *mentions* in our corpus – that is, we must find sentences in our corpus that contain both entities together (Zhang et al., 2012). This process is done heuristically and is fraught with potential errors and noise (Riedel et al., 2010).

We identify two methods for mapping entities to mentions to create positive training examples. The first maps entity pairs to sentences in a training corpus native to our test domain (e.g., TAC KBP 2014). We refer to this as Corpus Distant Supervision, or **CDS**. This has the advantage of providing examples that are similar to the problem at hand and closer to the test queries. However, this can potentially omit thousands of example mentions that occur in a different context than the training corpus (e.g., a corpus of business articles will not contain matches to actors or sports players). As a result, most entity pairs in a database will fail to map to a corpus (while others may have several mappings).

To overcome this limitation, we alternatively map entity pairs to mentions in their corresponding Wikipedia article(s). By scraping these articles for relevant sentences, we hypothesize that we can detect a higher hit rate for each database entry. Any sentence containing the relevant entity pair is processed as a positive training example for our learning algorithm. We will refer to this technique as **EDS** for external-text distant supervision.

3.2 Knowledge-based weak supervision

While the literature supports distant supervision as a viable alternative, the quality of the generated labels is crucially dependent on the heuristic that is being used to map the relations to the knowledge base. As noted by Riedel et al. (2010), the distant supervision assumption can be too strong, particularly when the source used for labeling the examples is external to the learning task at hand.

Natarajan et al. (2014) proposed work based on the following insight: labels are typically created by "domain experts" who annotate the labels carefully, and who typically employ some inherent rules in their mind to create examples. For instance, consider identifying a person's family relationship from news articles. We may have an *inductive bias* towards believing two persons in a sentence with the same last name are related, or that the words "son" or "daughter" are strong indicators of a parent relation. We call this *world knowledge* as it describes the domain (or the world) of the target relation. We aim to use such knowledge to create examples for learning from text.

To this effect, we encode the domain expert's knowledge in the form of first-order logic rules with accompanying weights to indicate the expert's confidence. We use the probabilistic logic formalism *Markov Logic Networks* (Domingos and Lowd, 2009) to perform inference on unlabeled text (e.g., the TAC KBP corpus). Potential entity pairs from the corpus are queried to the MLN, yielding (weakly-supervised) positive examples. We choose MLNs as they permit domain experts to easily write rules while providing a probabilistic framework that can handle noise, uncertainty, and preferences while simultaneously ranking positive examples.

In our experiments, we found that the difference between multiple weight settings do not affect the results as long as the ordering between the rules is maintained – only the *scale* of the probabilities varies. We use the Tuffy system (Niu et al., 2011) to perform inference. The inference algorithm implemented inside Tuffy appears to be robust and scales well to millions of documents[2].

For the KBP task, some rules that we used are shown in Table 2. For example, the first rule identifies any number following a person's name and separated by a comma is likely to be the person's age (e.g., "Sharon, 42"). The third and fourth rule provide examples of rules that utilize more textual features; these rules state the appearance of the lemma

---

[2] As the structure and weights are pre-defined by the expert, learning is not needed for our MLN

Weight	MLN Clause
1.0	entityType(a, "PER"), entityType(b, "NUM"), nextWord(a, c), word(c, ","), nextWord(c, b) → age(a, b)
0.6	entityType(a, "PER"), entityType(b, "NUM"), prevLemma(b, "age") → age(a, b)
0.8	entityType(a, "PER"), entityType(b, "PER"), nextLemma(a, "mother") → parents(a, b)
0.8	entityType(a, "PER"), entityType(b, "PER"), nextLemma(a, "father") → parents(a, b)
0.6	entityType(a, "PER"), entityType(b, "PER"), lemmaBetween(a, b, "husband") → spouse(a, b)
1.0	entityType(a, "ORG"), entityType(b, "PER"), prevPrevLemma(b, "found"), prevLemma(b, "by") → foundedBy(a, b)

Table 2: A sample of knowledge-based rules for weak supervision. The first value defines a weight, or confidence in the accuracy of the rule. The target relation appears at the end of each clause. "PER", "ORG", "NUM" represent entities that are persons, organizations, and numbers, respectively.

"mother" or "father" between two persons is indicative of a parent relationship (e.g.,"Malia's father, Barack, introduced her...").

4 Experiments and Results

We consider five TAC KBP relations from two categories, *person* and *organization*, chosen based on prior work for TAC KBP 2015. The relations are listed in the middle of Table 3 along with the counts of number of positives retrieved by each method (left). The TAC KBP 2014 corpus is used for training (or Wikipedia articles as is the case for EDS) while TAC KBP 2015 is used for testing. Another relation, age, is omitted from the results since a corresponding database is not available for distant supervision.

In our experiments, Freebase yields entity pairs for three out of the five relations ($siblings$, $spouse$, and $foundedBy$) while Wikipedia Infoboxes provides entity pairs for the $parents$ and $countryOfHeadquarters$ ($countryHQ$ for short) relations. NELL is utilized to supplement mentions for $siblings$. For KWS, a range of 4 to 8 rules are derived for each relation; only 5% of the training corpus was queried to generate KWS examples due – this proved sufficient for most relations although the number could easily be expanded as part of future work. Additionally, only the first 500 examples are actually utilized from Table 3. Performing larger runs is part of work in progress.

The results are obtained from averaging 5 different runs for each condition/relation. Across the runs, the test set is constant but the training set is subsampled with 75% membership to create more ro-

bust estimates of performance. The results are presented in right table of Table 3. We consider two standard metrics - area under the ROC curve and F1 score[3]. Table 3 also includes results after supplementing each weak/distant supervision with a small set (20) of gold-standard examples.

5 Discussion and Conclusions

Our experiments indicate strengths and weaknesses for each approach. The KWS framework, in general, outperforms the other methods in both metrics for the person relations, while being comparable for $countryHQ$. The tables do not even include age, the top performer for KWS. In fact, for several of the relations, the AUROC and F1 score approach or improve upon results when using a large, gold-standard training set (with the exception of $foundedBy$). For person relations, it produces more examples than either DS method, despite using only a fraction of the corpus. KWS struggles with creating good positive examples in our two organization relations, although it performed fairly similarly for headquarters despite limited examples. This was largely due to our inability to write discriminating rules that both achieves high recall and few false positives, demonstrating one drawback to the approach – the need for good (and formalisable) world knowledge.

Distant supervision did well where databases were easy to map – particularly, the organization relations and $parents$. There is no discernible difference between CDS and EDS, meaning that we can-

---

[3] Other metrics (e.g., accuracy, recall, AUPR) agree with the general conclusions presented here and are thus omitted

Positive Examples				AUROC			F1 score		
KWS	CDS	EDS	Relation	KWS	CDS	EDS	KWS	CDS	EDS
413	128	782	*parents*	**.68**(**.70**)	.62(.70)	.49(.67)	**.40**(**.40**)	.11(.19)	.08(.17)
1533	346	403	*spouse*	**.81**(**.83**)	.46(.49)	.53(.54)	**.24**(**.26**)	.04(.12)	.05(.08)
773	43	325	*siblings*	**.69**(**.73**)	.52(.64)	.58(.64)	**.26**(**.26**)	.10(.12)	.10(.21)
148	239	2207	*foundedBy*	.60(.65)	**.72**(**.74**)	.63(.67)	.21(.20)	**.26**(**.33**)	.26(.28)
21	168	1715	*countryHQ*	.58(.79)	.69(.72)	**.69**(**.80**)	.03(.57)	.06(.20)	.26(.43)

Table 3: LEFT Number of positive examples produced by each method per relation. The first three relations are person relations (*per*) while the last two describe organizations (*org*). **RIGHT** Area under the ROC curve (AUROC) and F1 measures for knowledge-based weak supervision (KWS), corpus distant supervision (CDS) and external source distant supervision (EDS). Numbers in parentheses are the results with 20 gold-standard examples. Emphasis indicates best performance for that relation.

not verify our hypothesis one way or the other (although the native corpus does slightly better in F1). This does give evidence that EDS is potentially useful when a large native corpus is not available for a task. If a large database exists with simple mapping heuristics, it can yield a large number of examples and perform well. Distant supervision is computationally faster and can easily scan an entire corpus, but MLNs yield a higher rate of positives and require less overhead.

Current efforts aim to expand upon these initial results by analyzing more relations (e.g., all 31 from TAC KBP) as well as by extending to other KB tasks such as medical abstract analysis. Furthermore, we were limited to only utilizing 5% of the corpus for KWS; an interesting question is whether there is a cap on the number of positives needed for good performance. Lastly, an interesting avenue of future work is whether the various weak supervision techniques can be combined together to achieve a more heterogeneous set of training examples. We hypothesize the data-centric approach of distant supervision would combine well with the knowledge-centric approach of KWS to achieve accuracies superior to even a large gold-standard set.

References

[Blockeel and Raedt1998] H. Blockeel and L. De Raedt. 1998. Top-down induction of first-order logical decision trees. *Artificial intelligence*, 101(1):285–297.

[Carlson et al.2010] A. Carlson, J. Betteridge, B. Kisiel, B. Settles, E. Hruschka Jr., and T.Mitchell. 2010. Toward an architecture for never-ending language learning. In *Proceedings of the Twenty-Fourth Conference on Artificial Intelligence (AAAI)*.

[Domingos and Lowd2009] P. Domingos and D. Lowd. 2009. *Markov Logic: An Interface Layer for AI*. Morgan & Claypool, San Rafael, CA.

[Heckerman et al.2001] D. Heckerman, D. Chickering, C. Meek, R. Rounthwaite, and C. Kadie. 2001. Dependency networks for inference, collaborative filtering, and data visualization. *Journal of Machine Learning Research*, pages 49–75.

[Manning et al.2014] C. Manning, M. Surdeanu, J. Bauer, J. Finkel, S. Bethard, and D. McClosky. 2014. The Stanford CoreNLP natural language processing toolkit. In *Proceedings of 52nd Annual Meeting of the Association for Computational Linguistics: System Demonstrations*, pages 55–60.

[Mintz et al.2009] M. Mintz, S. Bills, R. Snow, and D. Jurafsky. 2009. Distant supervision for relation extraction without labeled data. In *Proceedings of the Joint Conference of the 47th Annual Meeting of the ACL and the 4th International Joint Conference on Natural Language Processing of the AFNLP: Volume 2 - Volume 2*.

[Natarajan et al.2010] S. Natarajan, T. Khot, K. Kersting, B. Gutmann, and J. Shavlik. 2010. Boosting relational dependency networks. In *Proceedings of the International Conference on Inductive Logic Programming (ILP)*.

[Natarajan et al.2014] S. Natarajan, J. Picado, T. Khot, K. Kersting, C. Re, and J. Shavlik. 2014. Effectively creating weakly labeled training examples via approximate domain knowledge. In *International Conference on Inductive Logic Programming*.

[Neville and Jensen2007] J. Neville and D. Jensen. 2007. Relational dependency networks. In *Introduction to Statistical Relational Learning*. MIT Press.

[Neville et al.2003] J. Neville, D. Jensen, L. Friedland, and M. Hay. 2003. Learning relational probability trees. In *Proceedings of the ACM International Conference on Knowledge Discovery and Data Mining (SIGKDD)*, pages 625–630.

[Niu et al.2011] F. Niu, C. Ré, A. Doan, and J. W. Shavlik. 2011. Tuffy: Scaling up statistical inference in Markov logic networks using an RDBMS. *Proceedings of Very Large Data Bases (PVLDB)*, 4(6):373–384.

[Riedel et al.2010] S. Riedel, L. Yao, and A. McCallum. 2010. Modeling relations and their mentions without labeled text. In *Proceedings of the 2010 European conference on Machine learning and knowledge discovery in databases (ECML KDD)*.

[Takamatsu et al.2012] S. Takamatsu, I. Sato, and H. Nakagawa. 2012. Reducing wrong labels in distant supervision for relation extraction. In *Proceedings of the Association for Computational Linguistics (ACL)*.

[Zhang et al.2012] C. Zhang, F. Niu, C. Ré, and J. Shavlik. 2012. Big data versus the crowd: Looking for relationships in all the right places. In *Proceedings of the 50th Annual Meeting of the Association for Computational Linguistics: Long Papers - Volume 1*, pages 825–834.

A Factorization Machine Framework for Testing Bigram Embeddings in Knowledgebase Completion

Johannes Welbl, Guillaume Bouchard and **Sebastian Riedel**
University College London
London, UK
{j.welbl, g.bouchard, s.riedel}@cs.ucl.ac.uk

Abstract

Embedding-based Knowledge Base Completion models have so far mostly combined distributed representations of *individual* entities or relations to compute truth scores of missing links. Facts can however also be represented using pairwise embeddings, i.e. embeddings for *pairs* of entities and relations. In this paper we explore such bigram embeddings with a flexible Factorization Machine model and several ablations from it. We investigate the relevance of various bigram types on the `fb15k237` dataset and find relative improvements compared to a compositional model.

1 Introduction

Present day Knowledge Bases (KBs) such as YAGO (Suchanek et al., 2007), Freebase (Bollacker et al., 2008) or the Google Knowledge Vault (Dong et al., 2014) provide immense collections of structured knowledge. Relationships in these KBs often exhibit regularities and models that capture these can be used to predict missing KB entries. A common approach to KB completion is via tensor factorization, where a collection of fact triplets is represented as a sparse mode-3 tensor which is decomposed into several low-rank sub-components. Textual relations, i.e. relations between entity pairs extracted from text, can aid the imputation of missing KB facts by modelling them together with the KB relations (Riedel et al., 2013).

The general merit of factorization methods for KB completion has been demonstrated by a variety of models, such as RESCAL (Nickel et al., 2011), TransE (Bordes et al., 2013) and DistMult (Yang et al., 2014). These models learn distributed representations for entities and relations (be it as vector or as matrix) and infer the truth value of a fact by combining embeddings for these constituents in an appropriate composition function.

Most of these factorization models however operate on the level of embeddings for single entities and relations. The implicit assumption here is that facts are *compositional*, i.e. that the subject, relation and object of a fact are its atomic constituents. Semantic aspects relevant for imputing its truth can directly be recovered from its constituents when composing their respective embeddings in a score.

For further notation let E and R be sets of entities and relations, respectively. We denote a fact f stating a relation $r \in R$ between subject $s \in E$ and object $o \in E$ as $f = (s, r, o)$. Our goal is to learn embeddings for larger sub-constituents of f than just $s, r,$ and o: we want to learn embeddings also for the entity pair bigram (s, o) as well as the relation-entity bigrams (s, r) and (r, o). As an example, consider Freebase facts with relation `eating/practicer_of_diet/diet` and object `Veganism`. Overall only two objects are observed for this relation and it thus makes sense to learn a joint embedding for bigrams (r, o) together, instead of distinct embeddings for each atom alone and then having to learn their compatibility.

While Riedel et al. (2013) have trained embeddings only for entity pairs, we will in this paper explore the role of general bigram embeddings for KB completion, i.e. also the embeddings for

Proceedings of AKBC 2016, pages 103–107,
San Diego, California, June 12-17, 2016. ©2016 Association for Computational Linguistics

other possible pairs of entities and relations. This is achieved using a Factorization Machine (FM) framework (Rendle, 2010) that is modular in its feature components, allowing us to selectively add or discard certain bigram embeddings and compare their relative importance. All models are empirically compared and evaluated on the `fb15k237` dataset from Toutanova et al. (2015).

In summary, our main contributions are: i) Adressing the question of generic bigram embeddings in a KB completion model for the first time; ii) The adaption of Factorization Machines for this matter; iii) Experimental findings for comparing different bigram embedding models on `fb15k237`.

2 Related Work

In the Universal Schema model (model F), Riedel et al. (2013) factorize KB entries together with relations of entity pairs extracted from text, embedding textual relations in the same vector space as KB relations. Singh et al. (2015) extend this model to include a variety of other interactions between entities and relations, using different relation vectors to interact with subject, object or both. Jenatton et al. (2012) also recognize the need to integrate rich higher-order interaction information into the score. Like Nickel et al. (2011) however, their model specifies relationships as relation-specific bilinear forms of entity embeddings. Other embedding methods for KB completion include DistMult (Yang et al., 2014) with a trilinear score, and TransE (Bordes et al., 2013) which offers an intriguing geometrical intuition. Among the aforementioned methods, embeddings are mostly learned for individual subjects, relations or objects; merely model F (Riedel et al., 2013) constitutes the exception.

Some methods rely on more expressive composition functions to deal with non-compositionality or interaction effects, such as the Neural Tensor Networks (Socher et al., 2013) or the recently introduced Holographic Embeddings (Nickel et al., 2015). In comparison to the otherwise used (generalized) dot products, the composition functions of these models enable richer interactions between unit constituent embeddings. However, this comes with the potential disadvantage of presenting less well-behaved optimisation problems and being slower to

train. Factorization Machines have already been applied in a similar setting to ours by Petroni et al. (2015) who use them with contextual features for an Open Relation Extraction task, but without bigrams.

3 Model

3.1 Brief Recall of Factorization Machines

A Factorization Machine (FM) is a quadratic regression model with low-rank constraint on the quadratic interaction terms.[1] Given a sparse input feature vector $\phi = (\phi_1, \ldots, \phi_n)^T \in \mathbb{R}^n$, the FM output prediction $X \in \mathbb{R}$ is

$$X = \langle \mathbf{v}, \phi \rangle + \sum_{i,j=1}^{n} \langle \mathbf{w}_i, \mathbf{w}_j \rangle \cdot \phi_i \phi_j \qquad (1)$$

where $\mathbf{v} \in \mathbb{R}^n$, and $\forall i, j = 1, \ldots n : \mathbf{w}_i, \mathbf{w}_j \in \mathbb{R}^k$ are model parameters with $k \ll n$ and $\langle \cdot, \cdot \rangle$ denotes the dot product. Instead of allowing for an individual quadratic interaction coefficient per pair (i, j), the FM assumes that the matrix of quadratic interaction coefficients has low rank k; thus the interaction coefficient for feature pair (i, j) is represented by an inner product of k-dimensional vectors $\mathbf{w}_i$ and $\mathbf{w}_j$. The low rank constraint (i) provides a strong form of regularisation to this otherwise over-parameterized model, (ii) pools statistical strength for estimating similarly profiled interaction coefficients and (iii) retains a total number of parameters linear in n. In summary, with a FM one can efficiently harness a large set of sparse features and interactions between them while retaining linear memory complexity.

3.2 Feature Representation for Facts

For the KB completion task we will use a FM with unit and bigram indicator features to learn low-rank embeddings for both. To formalize this, we will refer to the elements of the set $\mathsf{U}_f = \{s, r, o\}$ as *units* of fact f, and to the elements of $\mathsf{B}_f = \{(s, r), (r, o), (o, s)\}$ as *bigrams* of fact f. Let $\iota_u \in \mathbb{R}^{|\mathsf{E}|+|\mathsf{R}|}$ be the one-hot indicator vector that encodes a particular unit[2] $u \in (\mathsf{E} \cup \mathsf{R})$. Furthermore we define $\iota_{(s,r)} \in \mathbb{R}^{|\mathsf{E}||\mathsf{R}|}$, $\iota_{(r,o)} \in \mathbb{R}^{|\mathsf{R}||\mathsf{E}|}$ and $\iota_{(o,s)} \in \mathbb{R}^{|\mathsf{E}|^2}$

---

[1]We disregard the more general extension to higher-order interactions that is described in the original FM paper and only consider the quadratic case. Also, we omit the global model bias as we found that it was not helpful for our task empirically.

[2]For subject and object the same entity embedding is used.

to be the one-hot indicator vectors encoding particular bigrams. Our feature vector $\phi(f)$ for fact $f = (s, r, o)$ then consists of simply the concatenation of indicator vectors for all its units and bigrams:

$$\phi(f) = \text{concat}(\iota_s, \iota_r, \iota_o, \iota_{(s,r)}, \iota_{(r,o)}, \iota_{(o,s)}) \quad (2)$$

This sparse set of features provides a rich representation of a fact with indicators for subject, relation and object, as well as any pair thereof.

3.3 Scoring a Fact

Harnessing the expressive benefits of a sigmoid link function for relation modelling (Bouchard et al., 2015), we define the truth score of a fact as $g(f) = \sigma(X_f)$ where σ is the sigmoid function and X_f is given as output of the FM model (1) with unit and bigram features $\phi(f)$ as defined in (2):

$$X_f = \langle \phi(f), \mathbf{v} \rangle + \sum_{i,j=1}^{n} \langle \mathbf{w}_i, \mathbf{w}_j \rangle \cdot \phi_i(f)\phi_j(f) \quad (3)$$

Since our feature vector $\phi(f)$ is sparse with only six active entries, we can re-express (3) in terms of the activated embeddings which we directly index by their respective units and bigrams:

$$X_f = \sum_{c \in (U_f \cup B_f)} v_c + \sum_{c_1, c_2 \in (U_f \cup B_f)} \langle \mathbf{w}_{c_1}, \mathbf{w}_{c_2} \rangle \quad (4)$$

This score comprises all possible interactions between any of the units and bigrams of f.

3.4 Model Ablations for Investigating Particular Bigram Embeddings

The score (4) can easily be modified and individual summands removed from it. In particular, when discarding all but one summand, model F is recovered, i.e. with $c_1 = (s, o)$; $c_2 = r$. On the other hand, alternatives to model F with other bigrams than entity pairs can be tested by removing all summands but the one of a single bigram $b \in B_f$ vs. the remaining complementary unit $u \in U_f$:

$$X_f^{u,b} = \mathbf{v}_u + \mathbf{v}_b + \langle \mathbf{w}_u, \mathbf{w}_b \rangle \quad (5)$$

This general formulation offers us a method for investigating the relative impact of all combinations of bigram vs. unit embeddings besides model F, namely the models with $u = s$; $b = (r, o)$ and with $u = o$; $b = (s, r)$.

3.5 Training Objective

Given sets of true training facts Ω^+ and sampled negative facts Ω^-, we minimize the following loss:

$$-\sum_{f \in \Omega^+} \log(1 + e^{X_f}) + \frac{1}{\eta} \sum_{f \in \Omega^-} \log(1 + e^{X_f}) \quad (6)$$

where the parametrization of X_f is learned. We use the hyperparameter $\eta \in \mathbb{R}^+$ for denoting the ratio of negative facts that are sampled per positive fact so that the contributions of true and false facts are balanced even if there are more negative facts than positives. The loss differs from a standard negative log-likelihood objective with logistic link, but we found that it performs better in practice. The intuition comes from the fact that instead of penalizing badly classified positive facts, we put more emphasis (i.e. negative loss) on positive facts that are correctly classified. Since we used an L_2 regularization and the loss is asymptotically linear, the resulting objective is continuous and bounded from below, guaranteeing a well defined local minimum.

4 Experiments

The bigram embedding models are tested on `fb15k237` (Toutanova et al., 2015), a dataset comprising both Freebase facts and lexicalized dependency path relationships between entities.

Training Details and Evaluation We optimized the loss using AdaM (Kingma and Ba, 2015) with minibatches of size 1024, using initial learning rate 1.0 and initialize model parameters from $\mathcal{N}(0, 1)$. Furthermore, a hyperparameter $\tau < 1$ like in (Toutanova et al., 2015) is introduced to discount the importance of textual mentions in the loss. When sampling a negative fact we alter the object of a given training fact (s, r, o) at random to $o' \in E$, and repeat this η times, sampling negative facts every epoch anew. There is a small implied risk of sampling positive facts as negative, but this is rare and the discounted loss weight of negative samples mitigates the issue further. Hyperparameters (L_2-regularisation, η, τ, latent dimension k) are selected in a grid search for minimising Mean Reciprocal Rank (*MRR*) on a fixed random subsample of size 1000 of the validation set. All reported results are for the test set. We use the competitive unit model

Model	τ	overall $HITS@$			MRR		
		1	3	10	overall	no TM	with TM
DistMult	0.0	18.2	27.0	37.9	24.8	28.0	16.2
full FM	0.0	20.1	28.7	38.9	26.4	29.3	18.3
(*) (s, o) vs. r	1.0	2.1	3.8	6.5	3.5	0.0	13.1
(**) (r, o) vs. s	0.1	24.9	34.8	45.8	32.0	34.7	24.8
(***) (s, r) vs. o	0.0	9.0	17.3	29.9	15.6	17.3	10.9
(*) + (**) + (***)	0.1	**25.9**	**36.2**	**47.4**	**33.2**	**35.0**	**28.3**

Table 1: Test set metrics for different models and varying unit and bigram embeddings on `fb15k237`, all performance numbers in % and best result in bold. The optimal value for τ is indicated as well.

DistMult as baseline and employ the same ranking evaluation scheme as in (Toutanova et al., 2015) and (Toutanova and Chen, 2015), computing filtered *MRR* and *HITS* scores whilst ranking true test facts among candidate facts with altered object. Particular bigrams that have not been observed during training have no learned embedding; a 0-embedding is used for these. This nullifies their impact on the score and models the back-off to using nonzero embeddings.

Results Table 1 gives an overview of the general results for the different models. Clearly, some of the bigram models can obtain an improvement over the unit DistMult model. In a more fine-grained analysis of model performances, characterized by whether entity pairs of test facts had textual mentions available in training (*with TM*) or not (*without TM*), the results exhibit a similar pattern like in (Toutanova et al., 2015): most models perform worse on test facts with TM, only model F, which can learn very little without relations has a reversed behavior. A side observation is that several models achieved highest overall MRR with $\tau = 0$, i.e. when not using TM.

The sum of the three more light-weight bigram models performs better than the full FM, even though the same types of embeddings are used. A possible explanation is that applying the same embedding in several interactions with other embeddings (as in the full FM) instead of only one interaction (like in (*)+(**)+(***)) makes it harder to learn since its multiple functionalities are competing.

Another interesting finding is that some bigram types achieve much better results than others, in particular model (**). A possible explanation becomes apparent with closer inspection of the test set: a given test fact f usually contains at least one bigram $b \in B_f$ which has never been observed yet. In these cases the bigram embedding is 0 by design and only

the offset values are used. The proportions of test facts for which this happens are 73%, 10% and 24% respectively for the bigrams (s, o), (r, o), and (s, r). Thus models (**) and (***) already have a definite advantage over model (*) that originates purely from the nature of the data. A trivial but somehow important lesson we can learn from this is that if we know about the relative prevalence of different bigrams (or more generally: sub-tuples) in our dataset, we can incorporate and exploit this in the sub-tuples we choose.

Finally, for the initial example with relation `eating/practicer_of_diet/diet` and object `Veganism`, we indeed find that in all instances model (**) with its (r, o) embedding gives the correct fact in the top 2 predictions, while the purely compositional DistMult model ranks it far outside the top 10. More generally, cases in which only a single object co-appeared with a test fact relation during training had $95, 3\%$ *HITS@1* with model (**) while only $52, 6\%$ for DistMult. This supports the intuition that bigram embeddings of (r, o) are in fact better suited for cases in which very few objects are possible for a relation.

5 Conclusion

We have demonstrated that FM provide an approach to KB completion that can incorporate embeddings for bigrams naturally. The FM offers a compact unified framework in which various tensor factorization models can be expressed, including model F.

Extensive experiments have demonstrated that bigram models can improve prediction performances substantially over more straightforward unigram models. A surprising but important result is that bigrams other than entity pairs are particularly appealing.

The bigger question behind our work is about

compositionality vs. non-compositionality in a broader class of knowledge bases involving higher order information such as time, origin or context in the tuples. Deciding which modes should be merged into a high order embedding without having to rely on heavy cross-validation is an open question.

Acknowledgments

We thank Théo Trouillon, Tim Rocktäschel, Pontus Stenetorp and Thomas Demeester for discussions and hints, as well as the reviewers for comments. This work was supported by an EPSRC studentship, an Allen Distinguished Investigator Award and a Marie Curie Career Integration Award.

References

Kurt Bollacker, Colin Evans, Praveen Paritosh, Tim Sturge, and Jamie Taylor. 2008. Freebase: a collaboratively created graph database for structuring human knowledge. In *SIGMOD 08 Proceedings of the 2008 ACM SIGMOD international conference on Management of data*, pages 1247–1250.

Antoine Bordes, Nicolas Usunier, Alberto Garcia-Durán, Jason Weston, and Oksana Yakhnenko. 2013. Translating embeddings for modeling multi-relational data. In *NIPS 26*.

Guillaume Bouchard, Sameer Singh, and Theo Trouillon. 2015. On approximate reasoning capabilities of low-rank vector spaces. In *AAAI Spring Syposium on Knowledge Representation and Reasoning (KRR): Integrating Symbolic and Neural Approaches*.

Xin Dong, Evgeniy Gabrilovich, Geremy Heitz, Wilko Horn, Ni Lao, Kevin Murphy, Thomas Strohmann, Shaohua Sun, and Wei Zhang. 2014. Knowledge vault: A web-scale approach to probabilistic knowledge fusion. In *Proceedings of the 20th ACM SIGKDD International Conference on Knowledge Discovery and Data Mining*, KDD '14, pages 601–610, New York, NY, USA. ACM.

Rodolphe Jenatton, Nicolas L. Roux, Antoine Bordes, and Guillaume R Obozinski. 2012. A latent factor model for highly multi-relational data. In *NIPS 25*, pages 3167–3175. Curran Associates, Inc.

Diederik P. Kingma and Jimmy Ba. 2015. Adam: A method for stochastic optimization. *The International Conference on Learning Representations (ICLR)*.

Maximilian Nickel, Volker Tresp, and Hans peter Kriegel. 2011. A three-way model for collective learning on multi-relational data. In Lise Getoor and Tobias Scheffer, editors, *Proceedings of the 28th International Conference on Machine Learning (ICML-11)*, pages 809–816, New York, NY, USA. ACM.

Maximilian Nickel, Lorenzo Rosasco, and Tomaso Poggio. 2015. Holographic Embeddings of Knowledge Graphs. Technical report, arXiv, October.

Fabio Petroni, Luciano Del Corro, and Rainer Gemulla. 2015. Core: Context-aware open relation extraction with factorization machines. In Llus Mrquez, Chris Callison-Burch, Jian Su, Daniele Pighin, and Yuval Marton, editors, *EMNLP*, pages 1763–1773. The Association for Computational Linguistics.

Steffen Rendle. 2010. Factorization machines. In *Data Mining (ICDM), 2010 IEEE 10th International Conference on*, pages 995–1000. IEEE.

Sebastian Riedel, Limin Yao, Benjamin M. Marlin, and Andrew McCallum. 2013. Relation extraction with matrix factorization and universal schemas. In *Joint Human Language Technology Conference/Annual Meeting of the North American Chapter of the Association for Computational Linguistics (HLT-NAACL '13)*, June.

Sameer Singh, Tim Rocktaschel, and Sebastian Riedel. 2015. Towards combined matrix and tensor factorization for universal schema relation extraction. In *NAACL Workshop on Vector Space Modeling for NLP*.

Richard Socher, Danqi Chen, Christopher D Manning, and Andrew Ng. 2013. Reasoning with neural tensor networks for knowledge base completion. In *NIPS 26*.

Fabian M. Suchanek, Gjergji Kasneci, and Gerhard Weikum. 2007. YAGO: a core of semantic knowledge unifying WordNet and Wikipedia. In *WWW '07: Proceedings of the 16th International World Wide Web Conference, Banff, Canada*, pages 697–706.

Kristina Toutanova and Danqi Chen. 2015. Observed versus latent features for knowledge base and text inference. In *Workshop on Continuous Vector Space Models and Their Compositionality (CVSC)*.

Kristina Toutanova, Danqi Chen, Patrick Pantel, Hoifung Poon, Pallavi Choudhury, and Michael Gamon. 2015. Representing text for joint embedding of text and knowledge bases. In *Empirical Methods in Natural Language Processing (EMNLP)*. ACL Association for Computational Linguistics, September.

Bishan Yang, Wen-tau Yih, Xiaodong He, Jianfeng Gao, and Li Deng. 2014. Embedding entities and relations for learning and inference in knowledge bases. *CoRR*, abs/1412.6575.

Association for Computational Linguistics
209 N. Eighth Street
Stroudsburg, Pennsylvania 18360

ISBN 978-1-5108-2517-8